GREAT YACHT RACES

Stewart, Tabori & Chang, Publishers
New York

GREAT YACHT RACES

Bob Fisher

Front Jacket

Dark and stormy skies in Christchurch Bay as Brian and Pam Saffery Cooper's Dragon *douses her spinnaker prior to rounding the leeward mark of the third inshore race of 1983 Admiral's Cup.*

Back Jacket

The Alan Gurney-designed 73-foot Windward Passage *running in the brisk Hawaiian breezes of the 1980 Pan-Am Clipper Cup.*

Title Page

Hitchhiker, *Peter Briggs' world champion Two-Tonner at the 1983 Admiral's Cup.*

End Papers

The Admiral's Cup in 1983.

Designed by Brian Trodd and Tony Taylor

Text Editor Peter Arnold

© 1984 by Cynthia Parzych Publishing, Inc., New York

All rights reserved. No part of the contents of this book may be reproduced by any means without the written permission of the publisher.

Produced by Cynthia Parzych Publishing, Inc.

Published in 1984 by Stewart, Tabori & Chang, Inc., New York

Distributed by Workman Publishing Company, Inc.
1 West 39th Street, New York, New York 10018

Printed and bound in Hong Kong
by Mandarin Publishers Ltd

Library of Congress Cataloging in Publication Data

Fisher, Bob, yachting correspondent.
    Great yacht races.

    Bibliography
    Includes index.
    1. Yacht racing — History.   I. Title.
GV826.5.F494   1984   797.1'4   84-234
ISBN 0-941434-57-5

For Dee, with love

ACKNOWLEDGMENTS

My thanks are primarily due to those people who sailed with and against me during three decades in some of the great races around the world. I enjoyed myself. Enjoyment is my prerequisite for racing sailing boats, as I hope it is for everybody. It has naturally been greater when we have won, and there is no doubt that success, or the prospect of it, is what keeps many people racing.

This book would never have been completed without the co-operation of many, principal among them John Gildersleeve, who loaned me an office where I could work away from the constant pressure of the telephone on my own. Without John's help the deadline would never have been met. Neither would it without the help of Fraser Associates of Buckingham. Harry and his staff not only sold me the word processor and its associated microprocessors, they answered all my queries and put me to rights when I went wrong using it. Bless 'em all.

I must thank too my fellow members of SINS (the Society of International Nautical Scribes) for the stimulation they have provided over the years. Some stimulation is always necessary, but I dare say that we overindulge. I will not single out anyone; they know who they are, and are all included.

Most especially I thank Brian and Cindy for having the confidence to go ahead with the project, and most particularly for their faith in me.

Contents

America's Cup

above: *The 134 ounces of sterling silver crafted by Garrards in 1848 which became the symbol of United States world yachting superiority – the America's Cup.*

right: America, *the schooner that started it all when she came to Britain in the year of the Great Exhibition and trounced the best of the yachting fleet in a race around the Isle of Wight.*

previous page: *The America's Cup is the head-to-head battle of two yachts – in 1983 it was* Liberty *for the United States and* Australia II.

When Garrards crafted 134 ounces of sterling silver into a baroque ewer back in 1848, its silversmiths cannot have imagined how much money, time, and effort would go into the sporting contests associated with it. On the twenty-fifth Challenge and Defense of the America's Cup alone, it is generally estimated that more than $50 million were expended, making it the most expensive sporting event in history. When the ewer changed hands on September 26, 1983, its 132 years' tenure by the New York Yacht Club was the longest running of any sporting trophy in international competition. A new era of its history began the next day as the Commodore of the New York Yacht Club, Robert Stone, presented it to Peter Dalziell, the Commodore of the Royal Perth Yacht Club, whose challenger, *Australia II,* had defeated the defender, *Liberty,* by four races to three at Newport, Rhode Island. *Australia II* crossed the finish line in that final race, the one dubbed "The Race of the Century," 41 seconds ahead of *Liberty* – 41 seconds that were to change the face of yachting history.

It all began very differently. In 1851, the year of the Great Exhibition, the international gathering of developments under the cover of Sir Joseph Paxton's Crystal Palace at the height of the Industrial Revolution, John Cox Stevens decided to build a yacht to display American shipbuilding to the Old World. It seemed to him

that the invitation to the world at large to take part in the Great Exhibition stretched thus far, and there would be an opportunity perhaps for him to increase his huge wealth in a wager with an English yacht owner or two on the performance of his craft. Stevens, just for once, hedged his bets and took five partners into the syndicate that commissioned the yacht.

To build it, they approached William H. Brown, mainly because he had the services of George Steers, who had designed some of the fastest pilot boats in New York. Stevens struck a deal with Brown that he would pay him $30,000 to build "in the best manner" a yacht which was "faster than any vessel in the United States brought to compete with her." Brown agreed to accept the boat back if she failed. It was an almost one-way bargain, and even then, Stevens, when he had accepted the boat, partially reneged on the deal. He claimed that his new yacht, called *America,* had beat a trialist, *Maria,* only because the latter had suffered from inferior handling and damage, and that being the case deducted $10,000 from the sum he paid Brown!

America crossed the Atlantic, and after an encounter with the British cutter *Laverock* on her run in to Cowes, in which the visitor showed a remarkable turn of speed, there were no takers for match races for sizable purses, even though Stevens had offered to sail *America* against any Royal Yacht Squadron vessel over a 20- to 70-

10

Galatea *racing* Wender *on the Clyde. The 102-foot 7-inch* Galatea *of Lieutenant Commander Henn RN was the Royal Northern Yacht Club's challenge in 1886. She spread a sail area of 7,505 square feet and displaced 158 tons.*

Thistle, *the 1887 challenger from the Royal Clyde Yacht Club, owned by a syndicate headed by James Bell.* Thistle *was designed by G.L. Watson and was 108 feet 6 inches overall with 8,968 square feet of sail.*

Vigilant, *C. Oliver Iselin's 124-foot defender of the Cup in 1893, racing againt the King's Britannia. Note how the crew are lying flat on the deck to save windage. Vigilant set 11,272 square feet of sail.*

mile course for a side stake of £10,000, then $50,000, and worth ten times that in today's value. There was definite cold shouldering of the yacht; one club, the Royal Victoria Yacht Club, refused her entry into its annual regatta because she was owned by a syndicate and not by a single gentleman. Popular opinion and the press were against the British yachtsmen for their churlish behavior, suggesting that they were like "a flock of pigeons paralysed by fear at the sight of a hawk." The RYS, in the face of all this criticism, demurred to the pressure and invited Stevens and his syndicate to join a race

around the Isle of Wight with the Garrards-crafted cup as the prize. The race was to take place on August 22, 1851.

America was last away from anchor when the starting gun fired for the race, running eastward in the Solent towards the Nab. There was confusion about the exact course; there were two sets of sailing instructions, one saying that the Nab Light Vessel must be left to starboard and the other omitting it altogether. *America's* instructions omitted it, and while the bulk of the fleet sailed out to round it, *America* went her own way to take the lead. At St.

The steel-hulled Vigilant *in dry dock. The long keel housed a centerboard which increased the draft from 13 feet 6 inches to 26 feet 3 inches. One gets the impression that it would have been unfavorable to meet her crew on a dark night in a back alley.*

Many times since, there are those who have wished that that is what had happened.

Stevens resigned as Commodore of the NYYC in 1855 and died two years later. Four weeks after Stevens' death, the Cup was handed over to the Club with a letter containing a deed of gift which was at least five years old — the original syndicate had long before made up its mind what it wanted to do with the Cup. The deed of gift stated that it should be for a match between yacht clubs, over the course used for the defending club's annual regatta, and that the challenging club should give six months' notice of its intent together with details of the challenging yacht — in order, presumably, that the defender could make a close match.

At the time, however, the American Civil War restricted the pleasure activities of rich New Yorkers, and it was not until that conflict was over, in 1865, that there was any real thought of the One Hundred Guineas Cup being raced for, despite friendly communications having been reestablished between the American and British yachting authorities. It was another five years before a challenge was made, by the social-climbing James Ashbury.

Ashbury's schooner *Cambria* had defeated an American yacht, *Sappho,* in a race around the Isle of Wight, and that win had encouraged Ashbury to challenge. The challenge was issued by the Royal Thames Yacht Club and defended by the fleet of the New York Yacht Club's schooners, including *America* and the 84-foot *Magic,* some 20 feet shorter than *Cambria,* a centerboarder. The Club's interpretation of a "match" left something to be desired, but Ashbury took it in good grace. His sportsmanship was prevailed upon considerably on that early

Catherine's Point, she was 2½ miles ahead, and in 2 hours of beating stretched her lead to 7 miles. On the run up the west Solent, the smallest of the fifteen British boats, *Aurora,* closed rapidly on *America* in the dying breeze, but this late run of *Aurora*'s was too late; *America* was already home, the prize-winner.

Stevens and his cronies took the Cup back home with them after selling the yacht, for a modest profit, and debated whether to melt it down and strike commemorative medals from it to record their victory for the grandchildren of the syndicate.

above: *The Earl of Dunraven, whose outspoken attacks on the American yacht* Defender *in 1895 led to his withdrawal from the final race and his expulsion from the New York Yacht Club.*

right: *Dunraven's problems were heightened by the spectator fleet which got in the way of his* Valkyrie III *during the Cup races.*

August day of 1870 when the match took place off New York. Many of his opponents had no idea of the racing rules, and several times *Cambria* was forced, when on starboard tack, to give way to others on port; a collision caused damage to the rigging of *Cambria*, which resulted in her foretopmast breaking. There was no protest from the gallant Ashbury even when *Cambria* finished tenth, 39 minutes, 17 seconds behind *Magic,* with *America* in fourth place.

Ashbury did dispute the Club's interpretation of match and gained some satisfaction, with the support of the only member of the original *America* syndicate, George Schuyler. He persuaded the NYYC to agree that the races should be between two yachts. The Club reserved the right to select its defender on the morning of the race. It gave the holders the advantage of choosing the right boat for the weather conditions each time, while the

Valkyrie III *leads* Defender *thirty minutes after the start of their first race.*

Sir Thomas Lipton's Shamrock *with gaff problems during her trial races in 1901, with Lipton's second challenger* Shamrock II.

challenger had to sail in all conditions.

As Commodore of the Royal Harwich Yacht Club, Ashbury issued his challenge for 1871 through its offices, but also added challenges through eleven other yacht clubs, one race for each with the result to be the best seven of twelve, and he proposed that the races be held off Newport, Rhode Island, in the open ocean. The NYYC did not respond to this until Ashbury arrived with the schooner *Livonia,* and a wordy battle began. Eventually a best-of-seven series was agreed upon, but Ashbury's scoring and that of the NYYC diverged even then. The 108-foot *Columbia* beat the 127-foot *Livonia* in the first race by 27 minutes. In the second, there was a dispute as to which way the outer mark should be rounded. *Columbia* won by 10½ minutes, but Ashbury claimed the race because *Columbia* had rounded the Sandy Hook lightship a different way from *Livonia.* The NYYC let the result stand

below: *The last race in 1901;* Columbia *crosses the finishing line 41 seconds ahead of* Shamrock II *to retain the Cup (*Australia II *beat* Liberty *by the same margin in the final race eighty-two years later).*

despite the protest. *Columbia* was disabled in the next race, and *Livonia* scored a win. Then *Sappho* took over the defender's role and twice defeated *Livonia* by big margins. The Cup was, or should have been, over. Ashbury, however, raced *Livonia* against the Commodore's *Dauntless* the next day and beat her, and when she did not appear on the following day for another race, Ashbury claimed that race and

rather than a warship or a grand ideal) in a best-of-three race battle of schooners.

The second Canadian challenge came five years later. Cuthbert was certain that he had designed a winner – the syndrome is common in Cup history. He challenged with his own 70-foot cutter *Atalanta* through the Bay of Quinte Yacht Club. The NYYC defended with the 69-foot cutter *Mischief* and handed Cuthbert an even

opposite page: Shamrock VI, *the ugliest of the British challengers but the one with which Sir Thomas Lipton came closest to winning the Cup.*

maintained that the scoreline now stood at 4 to 3 in his favor and demanded the Cup. Suffice it to say, he did not get it but went home and wrote a long letter accusing the Club of "unfair and unsportsmanlike proceedings."

The next two challenges came from Canada, the first in 1876, the year of the Centennial. It was a one-way affair in which the 107-foot *Countess of Dufferin,* designed by Alexander Cuthbert, was soundly trounced by the defender, the 106-foot *Madeleine* (the only defender in history to be named after a woman

bigger hiding, the margins in the two races being 28½ and 39 minutes.

In 1885, the challenge came from the Royal Yacht Squadron; it began as a paired challenge from *Genesta* and *Galatea,* both cutters designed by J. Beavor-Webb, the latter representing the Royal Northern Yacht Club in Scotland, hoping to race two weeks after *Genesta* if the Squadron's boat was unsuccessful. The NYYC rejected this idea and suggested that *Galatea's* challenge be put off until the following year, which indeed it was. Both challenges were

right: Reliance, *designed by Nat Herreshoff – the Wizard of Bristol – the longest boat, at 143 feet 8 inches overall, ever to sail in the America's Cup. She spread more than 16,000 square feet of canvas. Forty people are visible on deck – to say nothing of those working down below. She won three straight races in 1903.*

opposite page: Enterprise – *the first of the J-Class defenders designed by Starling Burgess and built at Bristol RI by Herreshoff.*

The lines of Enterprise, *drawn by Starling Burgess. The skeleton of these lines is shown below superimposed on those of* Britannia, *which appeared thirty-seven years later, to show the similarity. Engineering refinements made* Enterprise *much the faster.*

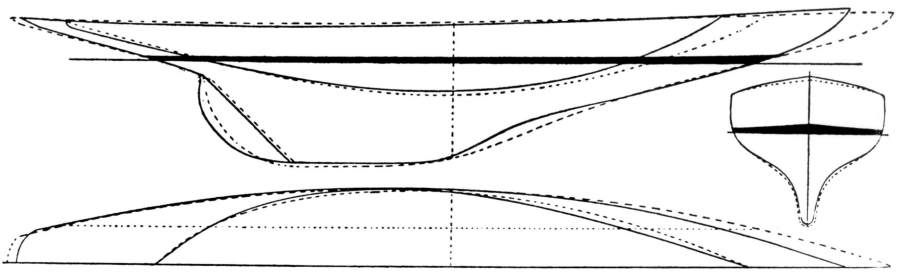

unsuccessful, the 94-foot Edward Burgess-designed *Puritan* twice beating the 96-foot *Genesta,* and the 100-foot Burgess creation *Mayflower* doing the same to *Galatea.*

In 1887, the challenge came from the Royal Clyde Yacht Club. The 109-foot George Watson-designed cutter was built in secret and launched behind a shroud to hide her underwater shape. When she was measured in New York, her waterline was 1½ feet longer than had been declared, and there was another Cup hoo-ha, which was only settled by the now seventy-six-year-old George Schuyler. *Thistle* was soundly defeated by the 107-foot *Volunteer,* another of Edward Burgess' designs, by 19 and 12 minutes. *Thistle* was sold to Kaiser Wilhelm II of Germany, who had her rerigged as a schooner.

The New York Yacht Club, at this time, decided that it was necessary for the rules and regulations concerning the Cup to be clarified and had a new deed of gift drafted to be signed by Schuyler. It was a wordy lawyer's document, but it did ensure that the races would be held on the open ocean on alternating triangular and windward/leeward 30-mile courses. The length of time between the challenge and the first race was increased from six to ten months, and the details of the challenger which had to be supplied had to include not just the waterline length, but also the draft, waterline, and extreme beam so that the designers of the defender would know what they were up against. It meant a six-year gap between Cup races because of antagonism toward the new deed of gift, which was interpreted as requiring the challenger's designer to give away the shape of the boat.

The challenge came through the Royal Yacht Squadron from the Earl of Dunraven, an Irish peer, for 1893. His 117-foot Watson-designed *Valkyrie II* met the Nathaniel Herreshoff-designed 124-foot *Vigilant,* a yacht which was "managed" by C. Oliver Iselin. *Vigilant* cost over $100,000 to build and had a crew of seventy. She won the first two races

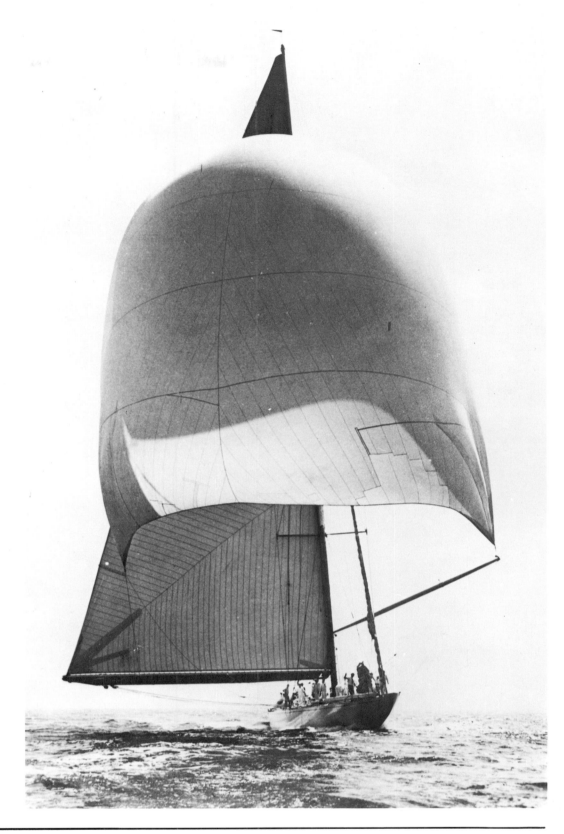

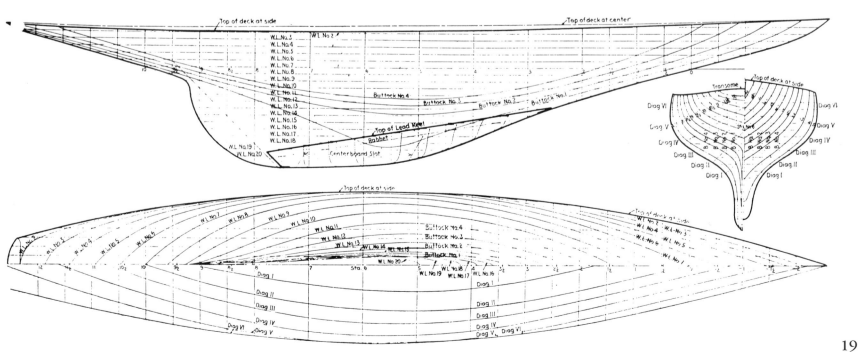

19

Rainbow, *the second successful combination of skipper Harold "Mike" Vanderbilt, was designed by Starling Burgess and built by Herreshoff. She beat* Endeavour, *the faster boat, by four races to two in 1934.*

easily but then was 2 minutes behind the challenger at the end of a 15-mile beat in 25-knot winds. Iselin and Herreshoff ordered the reef to be shaken out — a man was hoisted on a halyard and sent out along the 90-foot boom to cut the reef pennants — and the heavy-weather topsail to be replaced by a bigger one. That done, they set a spinnaker and a balloon jib and powered after *Valkyrie II,* beating her by just 40 seconds after the challenger had twice blown out spinnakers.

Dunraven went back to Britain full of hopes for a second challenge.

It came two years later and was to prove the most acrimonious. *Valkyrie III* was 129 feet long and designed by Watson. The same team produced *Defender,* 123 feet long and the first boat since *America* to sail for the Cup for the NYYC without a centerboard. *Defender* won the first race in a light breeze by 9 minutes. Dunraven asked that *Defender* be remeasured, as

he felt she was lower in the water and thus longer on the waterline – she was not – and then was involved in a start-line foul caused by a spectator boat. *Valkyrie III* won the race (*Defender* was damaged) by 47 seconds but was disqualified for the prestart foul. Dunraven was incensed. He wrote to the club and threatened not to sail if the spectator boats were on the course again. He also was convinced that it was *Valkyrie III,* not *Defender,* which had been fouled. Soon after the

start of the third race, Dunraven pulled *Valkyrie III* out and returned home to complain vociferously about his treatment. He alleged that *Defender's* crew had taken on ballast overnight and increased her waterline by 1 foot. The NYYC set up an investigative committee which proved, beyond doubt, that this had not occurred. Iselin and Herreshoff were cleared. It led the NYYC to expel Dunraven from their membership the following year.

top: Endeavour, *Sir Thomas Sopwith's first and most successful challenger.*

above: Endeavour II *rigged as a ketch for her passage to Newport from Cowes in 1937.*

21

Columbia, *the first 12-Metre to defend the Cup for America, trounced the British* Sceptre *in 1958.*

The 1958 races were really no contest. Britain's Sceptre *was never in touch with* Columbia.

Something had to be done to heal this wound. In England, there was a great deal of support for Dunraven, and a challenge from the Royal Victoria Yacht Club was withdrawn. The solution lay in a challenge from the Royal Ulster Yacht Club. It was first mooted to be connected with the club's Commodore, the Marquis of Dufferin, a distinguished diplomat, but on August 2, 1898, it was announced that the boat would be sponsored by Sir Thomas Lipton, the showman-grocer.

His yacht *Shamrock* was designed by William Fife and was 128 feet long on a waterline of 90 feet; she met *Columbia,* 131 feet of Herreshoff design, which was owned by a syndicate that included Iselin and J. Pierpont Morgan, the Commodore of the NYYC and possibly the most powerful man in the world.

Columbia won the first race by 10 minutes and then took the second race when *Shamrock* pulled out after her topmast had snapped. In the third race, *Shamrock* led at the running start by 1 minute, but the defender sailed through her lee to lead by 17 seconds as they headed home on the wind. The final margin of *Columbia's* win was 6½ minutes. Lipton returned home in partial triumph. While he had not won the America's Cup, he had won the hearts of the people and restored the friendship of the NYYC.

He returned with *Shamrock II* just two years later. The 137-footer was designed by G. L. Watson and skippered by Edward Sycamore. *Columbia,* with Charlie Barr at the wheel, was chosen to defend again, having beaten *Constitution* and *Independence* in trials. Barr's

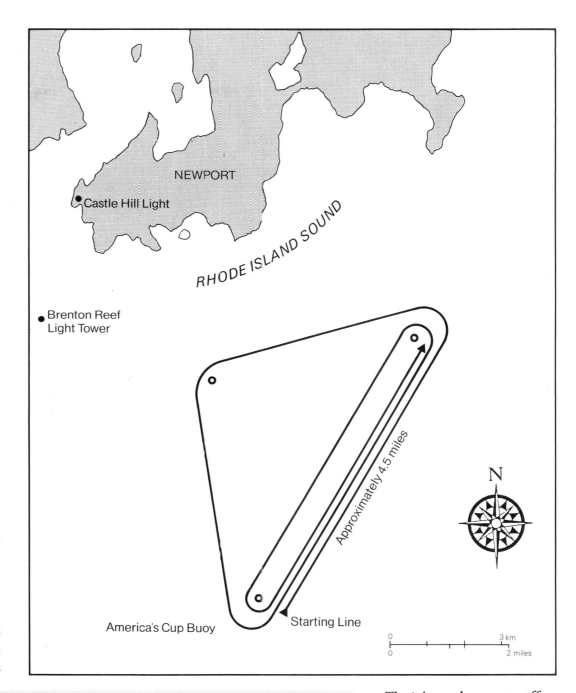

The triangular course off Newport, Rhode Island, for the 1983 America's Cup.

Weatherly, *rejected in 1958, defended the Cup in 1962. It was only the skill of skipper Bus Mosbacher which took the slower boat to a four-to-one win over* Gretel.

crew was well trained, and this was the forte of the American boat. *Columbia* won the first two races, the first by 1 minute, 20 seconds, the second by 3 minutes, 35 seconds, helped by a time allowance of 43 seconds. *Shamrock II* beat her home by 2 seconds in the final race but lost it on handicap. She had led by 1 minute on the run out, but Barr had pulled *Columbia* back to her on the beat with eighteen tacks to luff across the line with only feet of *Shamrock's* bow in front.

Lipton wanted to challenge again the following year with *Shamrock II* but the deed of gift prevented him. He was back the following year with a new boat, designed by Fife with help from Watson. Like *Shamrock II,* the new boat was tank-tested before the design was finalized. *Shamrock III* and the original *Shamrock* were towed to the United States for tuning up before the match with *Reliance* began. To defend, a syndicate of millionaires including a Rockefeller and a Vanderbilt commissioned a new boat from Herreshoff. *Reliance* was the biggest single-masted yacht ever built, 144 feet long on a waterline of 90 feet, with 16,159 square feet of sail. She was, however, a floating battery, electrolysis wreaking havoc in her steel-framed, bronze-plated hull with aluminum decks! She won all three races: the first by 7 minutes; the second by just over 1 minute; and the last when *Shamrock III* got lost in fog and retired.

Reliance was not a pretty boat, but she was effective. Lipton realized how effective and yearned for a boat like her. He got one from Charles E. Nicholson in 1914, a snub-ended 110-footer with a 75-foot waterline. She was on her way to the United States as war was declared with Germany. It postponed Lipton's fourth challenge until 1920.

This challenge was the first time in the history of the Cup that the boats were steered by amateurs. On *Shamrock IV,* there was Sir William Burton, while on the Herreshoff-designed *Resolute,* there was Charles Francis Adams, a descendant of two presidents and generally reckoned to be the best sailor in the United States. He took *Resolute* into a 5-minute lead at the halfway stage of the first race, only to lose it when the throat halyard of the gaff parted and the gaff jumped off the mast. *Resolute* retired.

In the second race, *Shamrock IV* sailed away from her opponent and despite a 7-minute handicap penalty, won by a clear 2½ minutes. Lipton had to win only one more race to achieve his ambition. *Resolute* was 2 minutes up at the turn of the third race, but *Shamrock IV* came right back to her, only losing by her handicap difference; the race was tied otherwise.

The next race was *Resolute's* by a big margin of 10 minutes, although 7 of these were from her handicap. It was hoped that the final race would be a good one. Light airs, however, saw to it that the race was anti-climactic, *Resolute* going into a definite lead half way up the first leg and extending it to 13 minutes at the finish. But Lipton's boat had won races, and although he was seventy years old he was keen to try again.

It was to be ten years before he did. Gone were the days of handicaps, of gaff rigs, and of the course off New York. The eighty-year-old Sir Thomas was treated to level racing in the J-Class boats of the Universal Rule, and Newport, Rhode Island, was where the race was held.

For his challenger, Lipton turned again to Nicholson, and the first British boat built to the J-Class rule was 119 feet long on a waterline of 81 feet. *Shamrock V* was built over a steel frame.

The Americans built four boats which raced together in a selection series to defend the Cup. Harold "Mike" Vanderbilt's *Enterprise,* a yacht appropriately named for the economic downturn that was then current, was at the time a masterpiece of technology, particularly her rig. She had a duralumin mast that was riveted together and weighed only two-thirds that of the steel one of *Shamrock V.* In addition, she had a "Park Avenue" boom with athwartships tracks that allowed perfect control of the shape of the foot of the mainsail. Her winches were mainly below the decks, and her crew wore numbered jerseys like a football team. All the commands for sail trim were done by calling the crew's numbers; Vanderbilt was better organized than any of his defense rivals and, when it came to it, than the skipper and crew of *Shamrock V.*

Lipton had the 23-Metre *Shamrock* in Newport as a trial horse for his challenger, and according to Tom Diaper, who was mate aboard her, she had the better crew. After the Cup races, Lipton went on to his own sparring partner and admitted to the crew that they should have been

opposite page:
Constellation, *the defender in 1964 when she thrashed* Sovereign, *subsequently became British registered, and is here steered by Guy Gurney as a trial horse to* Lionheart.

The 1964 British trials. Kurrewa *(K3)* leads Sovereign *(K12)*.

The 1964 British trials. Kurrewa (K3) leads Sovereign (K12).

the men who had crewed the Cup challenger. They might have made up some of the difference. *Shamrock V* lost the first race by 2 minutes, 52 seconds and the second by 9 minutes, 34 seconds, and retired from the third with a broken main halyard. *Enterprise* won the final race of the best-of-seven series by 5 minutes, 44 seconds.

Public donations paid for a huge loving cup which was presented to Lipton for his sportsmanship throughout his five challenges. He took it home but was dead within a year.

The technological advance of *Enterprise* did not go unnoticed by the airplane tycoon Sir Thomas Sopwith. When he entered the scene, his J-Class racer *Endeavour* was a 131-foot overall, 83-foot waterline, steel-hulled boat with an aluminum alloy mast.

Vanderbilt built new (*Enterprise* was scrapped shortly after her 1930 win) and went again to Starling Burgess to design him a boat; it was 127 feet long, with a waterline of 82 feet, and called *Rainbow.* She lost many races to the Frank Paine-designed *Yankee* and was within an ace of being rejected by the NYYC's selectors when *Yankee* dropped out of a race after some rigging parted. Tons of ballast had been added to *Rainbow,* and with several rig alterations, including a controllable bendy boom, she began to improve. In the final trial, she beat *Yankee* by 1 second and got the selectors' nod.

Endeavour was a vast improvement on *Shamrock V,* whereas *Rainbow* might well have been slower than *Enterprise.* It seemed that way when they met in the first race, and *Endeavour* rounded the windward mark 18 seconds behind and then sailed past *Rainbow* to win by just over

2 minutes on the run home. *Endeavour* won the next one, by 51 seconds, and the Cup had never teetered like this. At the turning mark of the third race, with only a starboard tack close reach to the finish, *Endeavour* was more than 6 minutes ahead. Vanderbilt went down below, and then began a series of events that were to change the face of the series.

Sherman Hoyt was left at the wheel, presumably to sail *Rainbow* home to another defeat. Instead, he sailed her a little high of the course in search of wind. Sopwith saw this and tacked to cover him. By the time he had tacked back and had *Endeavour* up to speed again in the light wind, Hoyt had taken *Rainbow* through to leeward and into a 3-minute lead.

The next race was decided by protest. *Endeavour* led at the weather mark, and when *Rainbow* sailed to windward of her on the reach home, Sopwith luffed but *Rainbow* did not respond. Following British racing practice, Sopwith bore off to avoid a collision and hoisted a protest flag as he crossed the finish line. The race committee (of the NYYC) disallowed the protest because the flag had not been flown immediately, as the club's rules required. The decision did not go down well with those who felt that it was unnecessary, unfair, and an unjust means of keeping the Cup. It was then that a commentator of the day wrote: "Britannia rules the waves and America waives the rules."

The fifth race went to *Rainbow* by 4 minutes; in the sixth race *Rainbow* was behind after a 10-mile reach but led after a beat of the same distance. On the final run, Hoyt took over the wheel and lured Sopwith off to leeward of the

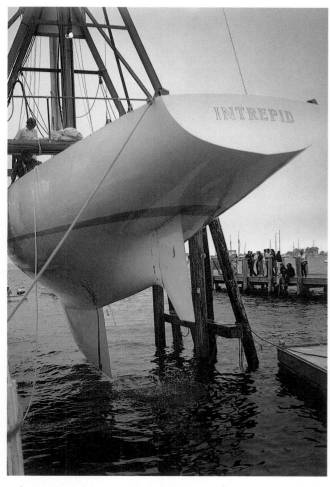

far left: Intrepid, *the defender in 1967 and 1970, came close to making it three in a row in 1974 until she lost the defense trials in the final race after a running backstay parted.*

left: *The defender in 1974,* Courageous, *just beat* Intrepid *in the final trials and went on to beat the challenger,* Southern Cross, *by four races to nil.*

below: Southern Cross, *the world's first aluminum 12-Metre, designed by Bob Miller (later Ben Lexcen) and skippered by Jim (later Sir James) Hardy.*

course. His tactic paid off, and the defender crossed the line 55 seconds ahead to keep the Cup safe from the fifteenth challenger, the one that had come closest to winning it. Had Sopwith taken his entire professional crew with him, things might have been different. Many of them refused to go because it meant that they would lose their winter jobs – fishing – and they went on strike when Sopwith refused to guarantee them their wages if they sailed on *Endeavour*.

He was to challenge again three years later with another Nicholson-designed J-Class boat, *Endeavour II*. She was the biggest of the Js, 136 feet overall on a waterline of 87 feet. Vanderbilt also commissioned a new boat – he had been scared by the previous British boat.

His *Ranger* was the result of the combined skills of Burgess and the young Olin Stephens. They tested models at the towing tank of the Stevens Institute in Hoboken, New Jersey, and came up with a radical design that was startlingly fast, yet both admitted that they would have rejected the design but for the results of the tank. In her only summer afloat, *Ranger* sailed thirty-four races and won thirty-two of them by an average of more than 1 mile. Against her, *Endeavour* hadn't a chance.

The first race was *Ranger's* by 17 minutes and the next by 18½ minutes. One cannot help

but wonder whether Vanderbilt kept himself in check in the next two races, for his winning margins were only 4 minutes, 27 seconds and 3 minutes, 37 seconds. The Cup remained in the New York Yacht Club.

The clouds of war were already gathering, and an era was over. The redistribution of wealth and inflation were to ensure that there would never again be racing in yachts of the J Class.

It took years of negotiations between the Royal Yacht Squadron and the New York Yacht Club before there was a move to change the deed of gift of the Cup in order that it could be raced for by boats of waterlines less than 65 feet. By 1956, the NYYC Commodore Henry Sears produced a fourth deed of gift, which was approved by the Supreme Court of the state of New York. In essence, it allowed boats to race if they had waterlines no smaller than 44 feet and could be shipped, rather than sail on their own bottoms, to Newport for the racing. It was aimed at holding Cup races in boats of the 12-Metre class of the International Rule. Within three months, a challenge had been received from the RYS and the date set for racing in 1958.

There were four American Twelves to compete for the right to defend: the pre-war *Vim*, owned by Vanderbilt, now seventy-four years old and sailed by Bus Mosbacher; Chandler

The Ian Howlett-designed Lionheart *was a "heavy" 12-Metre. Her challenge was finally strangled by bad management.*

opposite page: Lionheart *(K18) and* Sverige *(S3), two of the 1980 contenders for the Cup, racing in Sweden.*

29

right: Freedom *and* Australia *had a tough battle in 1980. Australia's speed was enhanced when designer Ben Lexcen adapted* Lionheart's *whippy topmast design for his boat to give* Australia *more area in her mainsail.*

below: Defender, *the David Pedrick-designed defense candidate, never did reach the required pace, despite several major hull alterations.*

Hovey's *Easterner; Weatherly,* skippered by Arthur Knapp; and the new S&S-designed *Columbia.* It turned out to be a *Columbia* versus *Vim* series, and only the fast improvement of *Columbia* got her the selection.

Columbia was sailed by Briggs Cunningham, and even he must have been disappointed by the poor showing of *Sceptre,* the British David Boyd-designed 12-Metre. The American boat won the seventeenth defense by four races to nil, with never less than 7 minutes as her winning margin. It was a whitewash.

While the Royal Thames Yacht Club planned to do better in 1962, a group in the Royal Sydney Yacht Squadron had the same idea, and it was this challenge that the NYYC accepted. It was led by Sir Frank Packer. He bought *Vim* for his syndicate as a trial horse and put Alan Payne to work to design *Gretel.* Payne tactfully gained the use of the Stevens Institute's tank and permission to use American sailcloth. He designed not only the boat, but also the first cross-linked coffee-grinder winch system, which allowed four men's power to haul in the genoa sheets at once. That alone was a breakthrough which stood the challenger in good stead. The NYYC did not take this challenge seriously.

Only one new boat was built, *Nefertiti,* to designs of Ted Hood, while *Weatherly* was redesigned by Luders, with Mosbacher as skipper. He got the selection to defend. When it came to the Cup races, it was readily apparent that Mosbacher had the slower boat.

With the wrong mainsail set, a broken backstay, and being over the line early at the start, *Gretel* was less than 4 minutes down at the finish of the first race. Three days later, in a goodly breeze, *Weatherly* led by 12 seconds at the end of the 8-mile windward leg and held it on the first reach. Then after a bad spinnaker set on

The close fight between Liberty *and* Courageous *in 1983 most certainly prepared the US defender for what was in store.*

Weatherly, Gretel went through to windward with a war cry to a win of 47 seconds. Newport went mad, and the song was "Waltzing Matilda"!

The rest of the races were in light winds, and Mosbacher used all his guile to win them. Had the Australians been aware of their potential and had Sir Frank Packer not interfered with the crew organization, *Gretel* would have won the Cup.

It must have been embarrassing for the New York Yacht Club to deal with the 1964 challenge from the Royal Thames Yacht Club. Its David Boyd-designed *Sovereign* for Tony Boyden was little better than *Sceptre,* whereas the new S&S-designed *Constellation* was the result of the nasty shock the Americans had had with *Gretel.*

Constellation had been fired to improvement at sea by close racing with the Luders-designed *American Eagle,* which won most of the early races, and she came to the Cup with speed to spare. Her helmsman, Bob Bavier, took over the job in mid-season and added the extra fire that was needed. His job in the Cup races was simple. *Constellation* beat *Sovereign* by huge margins, once by over 20 minutes, to win by four races to nil.

In 1967, it was the turn of the Australians again. They went to Newport with a boat designed by Warrick Hood which was not as good as *Gretel.* The Americans, however, had progressed. In *Intrepid,* they had a "wonder-boat." Olin Stephens had detached the rudder from the back of the keel and hung it on its own separate skeg. Then he put a trim tab on the back of the keel to increase its efficiency. With Mosbacher steering, the new boat had no problem in dealing with the challenger and was four to nil up in the series, with margins of between 3½ and 6 minutes.

There were four challenges for 1970, but those from Britain and Greece petered out, leaving those from France and Australia. The French boat was Baron Bich's, and it lost the elimination series by four races to nil. The Australians were better prepared.

Their new Alan Payne design for Sir Frank Packer carried great hope. She was fast, and her crew was well marshaled. Sir Frank was less interfering. She had all the potential to win and displayed it in her summary dismissal of France.

The new S&S 12-Metre had flopped. *Valiant* was a big, heavy boat which had shown well in the tank but not on the course. *Heritage* was designed, built, had its sails made, and owned and skippered by Charley Morgan. Somewhere – maybe everywhere – along the line, he got things slightly wrong. It left only a rebuilt *Intrepid,* with alterations by Britton Chance, Jr., as a defender. For the second time, the Americans had the slower 12-Metre, but the talent of skipper Bill Ficker was the telling factor.

He won the first race, when a crewman from *Gretel II* fell overboard, by 6 minutes. At the start of the second race, Ficker began by squeezing between *Gretel II* and the committee boat, and Martin Visser, *Gretel II's* starting helmsman, luffed up and hit *Intrepid* just after the starting gun. *Gretel* passed her on the run and finished first, only to lose the race on protest. The cries of anguish could be heard all the way back to Sydney. "Protesting to the New York Yacht Club's race committee," suggested Sir Frank Packer, "is like complaining to your mother-in-law about your wife."

Gretel did win one race, but the series went to *Intrepid* by four to one. Jim Hardy, *Gretel II's* skipper, said later that he had not realized how much faster she was than the rebuilt *Intrepid;* he would have tackled the races differently.

Hardy was back in 1974, displacing Olympic-gold-medalist John Cuneo from the skipper's berth aboard Alan Bond's *Southern Cross.* The west coast of Australia made its first challenge from the Royal Perth Yacht Club with the Ben Lexcen (then Bob Miller) design.

The realization that a new fast 12-Metre was needed to defend was an ever-present thought in the minds of the members of the New York Yacht Club, and this time there were four trialists. There was a new boat of radical design by Britt Chance in *Mariner,* with a revamped *Valiant* as a running mate. *Intrepid* was back, much remodified by Stephens, and there was the new S&S creation, *Courageous. Mariner* was Ted Turner's; even after a back-end rebuild, she was never fast, and Turner was even displaced as skipper by Dennis Conner.

Intrepid did go fast again with Gerry Driscoll as skipper, and it was she that gave *Courageous* a run for her money, only losing the selection in the last race when a running backstay gave way and the mast-ram hydraulic packed up in a good breeze when she was leading. The *Courageous* syndicate had problems of personnel which were only resolved at the eleventh hour when Ted Hood became skipper and Dennis Conner became tactician.

There was never any doubt in the Cup races. It was always *Courageous* in the lead; four to nil was a clear victory for Hood and Conner.

Bond was not dismayed and planned his next effort with care. So, too, did the Americans. Ted Hood designed his own new boat, *Independence,* while his rival sailmaker Lowell North had charge of the S&S new boat, *Enterprise.* Turner, at a late stage, got hold of *Courageous* for the trials. In the battle of the sailmakers, Turner got the selection.

Bond had Lexcen combine his talents with Johan Valentijn, a Dutch-born alumnus of the S&S office, and between them they designed *Australia.* She was aimed to be fast in light winds and steered by Noel Robins. He first had to win the eliminations trials, but that was not difficult. The Pelle Petterson-designed and -skippered *Sverige,* the first Swedish challenger, beat *Gretel II,* back in Gordon Ingate's hands, by four races to three, while *Australia* smashed *France.* In the final *Australia* had little difficulty in beating *Sverige* by four to nil.

It was the same scoreline in the Cup races, but this time it was Turner in control, while Robins appeared to have no answers. The

previous page: Victory '83 *and* Australia II *tuning up in 1983 prior to the challenger selection trials.*

opposite page: Victory '83 *in early trials.*

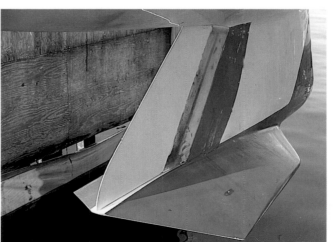

far left: Azzurra, *the first Italian challenger, designed by Andrea Vallicelli, was one of the best prepared of the 1983 candidates and promised future serious challenges from Italy.*

left, above: *Removing the "winglets" from the keel of Victory '83.*

left, below: *Finally unveiled, the keel of Australia II revealed two huge wings which gave her a more efficient keel of greater stability. The keel was the talking point of Newport throughout the summer of 1983, when no one outside the Australian camp knew exactly what the keel looked like and speculation was rife.*

Dennis Conner at the wheel of Liberty *with navigator Halsey Herreshoff (grandson of the Wizard of Bristol) at his shoulder and tactician Tom Whidden (in white cap), just prior to the fourth race in 1983.*

opposite page: Liberty *on her way to winning the fourth race.*

S&S-designed *Freedom* won most of her races.

The challenge from abroad brought Britain back in with the Ian Howlett-designed *Lionheart* skippered by John Oakeley. A syndicate decision put Lawrie Smith in Oakeley's place at the start of the final trails. One of *Lionheart's* innovations was a very bendy topmast which enabled her to set a mainsail with some 200 square feet more sail in it. It was snapped up by Lexcen, who made a similar mast for *Australia.*

She had been altered by him in the intervening time and had James Hardy back as skipper. In the trials, she easily beat *Sverige, France 3,* and *Lionheart* to take on Conner.

Australia lost the first race to *Freedom* by nearly 2 minutes, and Conner never looked in trouble. In the next, when it was light, *Australia* had gone into a mile lead when the time limit ran out. Then *Australia* leveled the scores with a race that went on past dusk and was finished only 7 minutes inside the time limit. Conner then took control of the situation and won the next three races comfortably. The Cup was safe.

Such security, however, cannot cope with all the onslaughts. The measure of that security had been in the ability of the NYYC to encourage several syndicates to defend the Cup. The world economic depression and the quantum jump that Conner had made in his preparations together reduced the number of possible syndicates and the number of available personnel. Where could syndicates capable of raising upward of $5 million be found, and where could a squad of twenty-five reasonably experienced big-boat sailors be obtained who were prepared to devote the best part of three years to a Cup campaign? These were the unobtainables which saw the 1983 defense reduced to two syndicates with a total of three 12-Metres in line for candidacy. Piled against the Americans were seven syndicates resolved to wrest the Cup from its long-time place of residence. All were full of enthusiasm; most were prepared to match Conner for time; some prepared to put in more; at least three had the relatively limitless funding that is so important; and there was a wealth of experience which was regularly increased from all possible sources.

Every previous British 12-Metre challenge had proved disappointing, but with the promise of $8 million from Peter de Savary, his *Victory* syndicate had one of the shortcomings eliminated. In the end, it came close to selection, fighting out the final trials with *Australia II* before succumbing to a four-to-one scoreline.

The Italians were challenging for the first time, but the *Azzurra* syndicate, headed by the Aga Khan, went about things in the right way. They had money; they bought *Enterprise* from Dennis Conner's squad; and they had, in Andrea Vallicelli, a fine designer who understood the way 12-Metre progress had gone.

margins increased from just over 1 minute to 2½ minutes and the Cup remained secure. Turner staggered into the final press conference still celebrating with a bottle of rum and fell backward from his chair. He was having fun, something that had long gone from the Cup.

There was not too much of it in the summer of 1980 when Dennis Conner altered the game plan in the Cup. He had spent three years sailing nearly 300 days a year preparing himself, his boats, and the sails he needed to win. It was a program that few could, or would even try to, match. Turner did not – he had done it before, and it seemed as if that once was enough; he was there to give the 12s some racing practice and have some fun. Then there was Russell Long, who had *Independence* carved up and rebuilt as *Clipper* to Dave Pedrick's designs. Turner was the first to go, and it was not long before Long went too. Conner was just too good, and his new

The French effort was to stay in Cup racing with minor alterations made to *France 3* by the new syndicate headed by Yves Rousset Rouard. *France 3* was quickly eliminated, but the effort kept the French abreast of developments.

Advance went quickly from the scene too. The Royal Sydney Yacht Squadron's syndicate commissioned a radical design from Alan Payne, but his years away from the scene showed. *Advance* crew members stayed on to help with the Australian campaign.

The same was true of many of those from *Challenge 12,* the other new Ben Lexcen design. She was possibly the second-fastest 12-Metre in Newport that summer, but she failed through lack of sufficient finance at the right time. So did the Bruce Kirby-designed *Canada 1.*

The real breakthrough came from Alan Bond's syndicate, with the Lexcen-designed *Australia II.* Secrecy surrounded the boat like the screen that hid her keel all summer, and the speculation about her performance got to even the America's Cup Committee of the New York Yacht Club. There was no denying that *Australia II* was fast. She was beaten on only five occasions all summer until the Cup, and the only worry of her syndicate seemed to be that her crew were getting insufficient competition.

For the defense, Conner had initiated a huge program starting with two new boats, the S&S-designed *Spirit of America* and the Valentijn-designed *Magic.* "Spirit" was a relatively heavy displacement boat, while *Magic* was the smallest 12-Metre ever built. Neither worked successfully. *Magic* was the first to be altered, and then a complete new keel and underbody was fitted to *"Spirit."* Both were pensioned off in favor of a new boat, *Liberty,* to Valentijn designs.

Tom Blackaller raised a syndicate with a new boat, *Defender,* designed by David Pedrick. It ran into problems with certification, underwent surgery around the rudder stock area to reduce the waterline length, and then had a wedge-shaped slice taken from the mid-section forward of the keel. She never did have the edge of her rivals, not even her running mate, *Courageous,* which in the hands of John Kolius looked a possible defender. Some minor alterations had been made to her, and these gave her a new lease on life — not enough, as it happened, to beat a well-cranked-up *Liberty.*

From the very first race, it appeared that an upset was on the cards. *Australia II* led at the first mark by eight seconds and increased that by 2 seconds on the first reach. On the second reach, Conner attacked, and *Liberty* went past to windward into a 16-second lead which she increased to 29 seconds on the second beat. On the run, *Australia II* came back and was attacking near the leeward mark when part of her steering failed. *Liberty* won by 70 seconds.

opposite page: Australia II *on the final beat of the sixth race. The blue-painted disguise of her keel does not totally hide its shape.*

John Bertrand, skipper of the victorious Australia II, *the man who took the America's Cup from the New York Yacht Club after 132 years.*

She won the next, too, but not until she had passed *Australia II* on the second beat. *Australia II* suffered from the start, with her mainsail pulled 18 inches down the mast in its headboard traveler, a fault which could not be corrected.

Then came a race in a dying northeaster in which *Australia II* showed her true potential. *Liberty* closed 24 seconds on the two reaches, but the Aussies were a long way ahead, finishing a record 3 minutes, 17 seconds in front. Conner pulled a masterly port tack start in the fourth race, just clearing *Australia II's* bow as John Bertrand brought her up to course as the gun fired. It was the confidence boost that Conner and his crew needed to give the Australians a sailing lesson. *Liberty* won by 43 seconds.

Just over an hour before the start of the fifth race, a hydraulic ram at the end of the port jumper strut on *Liberty* fractured. High-speed launches brought a spare from the shore, and two men were up the mast for the best part of an hour clearing the old one away and fitting the new one when it arrived. As the 10-minute gun went off the repair was completed, and then a genoa was ripped as it was hoisted and a replacement set. Despite all these problems, Conner got the better of Bertrand in the pre-start maneuvers, forcing him over the line early, and led away by 37 seconds. *Australia II,* however, led at the weather mark by 23 seconds and went on to win the race by 1 minute, 47 seconds. Bertrand, like Sopwith, had won two races.

Conner won the sixth start, but by the weather mark with the benefit of a huge wind shift, Bertrand took *Australia II* round 2

minutes, 29 seconds ahead. In a 15- to 18-knot breeze, it was an unbelievable margin, and the white-hulled boat went on to win by 3 minutes, 25 seconds to level the series. All hell broke loose on the dockside when *Australia II* returned to Newport; spectators, media commentators, and sailors crammed around to see the boat that had gone farther than any other in a quest to win the America's Cup. Somewhat strangely, with their tails up, Bond opted for a lay day for *Australia II*.

It was then that Conner made the decision to lighten *Liberty*. He had the benefit of three ballastings recorded on three certificates, and he had only to be checked for remeasurement by 20:00 hours on the day before the race; a lay day gave him the time to complete the alterations and remeasurements. Bond did not approve and said so: "We're here to race one boat, not two!" His pleas were in vain. But then there was another delay when the wind on the Saturday scheduled for the race was not steady enough to get them away cleanly. It was Conner's turn to call for a lay day, and he threatened to change

ballast again. Bond was cross, very cross. Conner kept him on a string, took his boat to the yard at Cove Haven where such alterations take place, removed the mast and checked it through, but left the ballast. Pure gamesmanship.

The race, when it came, was dubbed "The Race of the Century." And it was.

The start of the race was delayed for 55 minutes. Conner wanted the right-hand side of the course, and got it. The early tacks as the yachts came together saw *Australia II* making gains of 5 feet each time until Bertrand was able to slap a tack right on *Liberty's* bow. When they converged the next time, Conner dipped the stern of *Australia II* and went to the left-hand side of the course. Bertrand went with him, but this day Conner was sailing brilliantly. He was making each move pay, and he said afterward that it was because Bertrand had not had the hard-match racing experiences during the summer that he was able to outsail him. And he did. *Liberty* was much of a match for speed with *Australia II;* then the luck, for once, ran Conner's way, and the header came as he was thinking

about tacking. It enabled him to tack, on port, across *Austrialia II's* bow and lead by 29 seconds at the weather mark.

The first reach was quite shy because of the wind shift. *Liberty* stretched her lead to 45 seconds, but on the broader reach, *Australia II* narrowed the gap to 23 seconds. On the second beat, Conner was nothing short of brilliant and rounded the weather mark 57 seconds in the lead. Very soon, *Liberty* gybed on to the best slant of the wind to take her closest to the rhumb line. *Australia II* held off gybing, heading for a darker patch of water out to the right. When she got there, the 6 knots of breeze were increased to 8 and *Australia II* gybed and sailed faster than *Liberty*. When the red-hulled boat gybed back to defend her lead, it had gone; as the two boats paralleled, it was obvious to those on board *Liberty* that *Australia II* was able to sail closer to the rhumb line and faster. It brought the query from Conner to his crew: "Does anyone here have any ideas?" When he said that, his crew knew there was trouble.

Australia II rounded the bottom mark with a 21-second lead. Conner tried all he knew to get past, but Bertrand was master of the situation and covered him like a blanket. At the finish, there were just 41 seconds between them. *Australia II* had won the America's Cup. History had been made that day. The Cup that had been thought to be the property of the New York Yacht Club forever had fallen to the challenger from Perth, Western Australia. The streets of Newport saw more than one inebriated Aussie supporter that night, and there were more than a few tears on the cheeks of Americans. It was the end of an era.

John Bertrand, Alan Bond, Warren Jones, and Ben Lexcen head the Australia II *team to receive the America's Cup at Marble House, Newport (where Mike Vanderbilt lived throughout his three successful defense campaigns) — the moment of triumph that ended the 132-year run of the New York Yacht Club.*

Fastnet Race and the Admiral's Cup

Ocean racing started in Britain because of the efforts of a handful of men who prompted the Fastnet Race. Public opinion was against it; questions were asked in the Press about its advisability. Even some of the most hardened and experienced yachtsmen opposed it, and said so. Claude Worth, a founding member of the Royal Cruising Club, wrote in *The Field:* "At the risk of making an unpopular suggestion, I venture to express a doubt which arises in my mind — are our latitudes suitable for a public ocean race? If two owners, experienced in ocean cruising, arrange a match involving several hundred miles of deep water, they know exactly what they are doing. But a public race might very well include some owners whose keenness is greater than their experience." Worth's comments rang true in 1979 when Force 11 winds ripped the Fastnet fleet apart. In that year, when 303 boats started from Cowes, several skippers and crews were not sufficiently experienced to deal properly with the conditions. Fifteen people were to lose their lives in that race.

The idea for the race came from Weston Martyr, a British yachtsman who lived for some years in the United States, where he had been introduced to the Bermuda Race. He wrote to a British yachting magazine in a fulsome manner, suggesting that unless British yachtsmen started taking an interest in ocean racing immediately, they would never catch up with developments in America.

He also suggested the course the race should take: "... from the Solent, down the English Channel, across the Irish Sea to the Fastnet Rock, and back to Plymouth." When, with George Martin and Malden Heckstall-Smith,

the editor of *Yachting Monthly,* he formed the committee of three to organize an ocean race, Martyr had to fight for his course. Other alternatives were offered, but he insisted that an ocean race had to have open ocean in it. Support was not universal. The Royal Yacht Squadron was not enthusiastic, so the race was started from Ryde rather than Cowes. The Royal Victoria Yacht Club at Ryde fired the gun on August 15, 1925, and the Royal Western Yacht Club organized the finish at Plymouth. The early rules were few. The race was open to any yachts of 30- to 50-feet waterline. One restriction was that "no more paid hands will be permitted than can normally be accommodated in the fo'c'sle."

Seven boats answered the starter's gun from an entry list of sixteen. All were deep-drafted cruising boats, and all but one, *Jessie L,* were gaff-rigged. The race was won by Martin's 56-foot converted Le Havre pilot cutter *Jolie Brise,* which took just over 6 days to complete the course. Five yachts finished. At the party after the race the Ocean Racing Club was formed, and it was agreed to race again in 1926. The conditions had been favorable, with enough fresh breeze to give everyone who took part a taste of what they had been told to expect.

There were nine entrants for that second race, four of which had been in the first. The first foreign entry to the Fastnet was attracted – the American schooner *Primrose IV.* The race had become international. A new Fife-designed Bermudan cutter, *Hallowe'en,* was the first to finish in 3 days, 19 hours, 5 minutes – a time which stood until 1939 as the course record. The race was won by the Royal Engineers Yacht Club's new boat, *Ilex,* which had a nasty moment or two on the way back from the Fastnet Rock in near gale force conditions. It was decided that *Ilex* would go faster with two reefs in the main and the yacht was hove to for this to be done. During the shortening of sail, three men went overboard. All got back on board and the matter was treated quite lightly. *Ilex's* winning margin was a mere 13 minutes, 8 seconds. Had not *Primrose IV* blown out her balloon jib shortly after rounding the Fastnet Rock, the Americans might easily have won.

The race drew fourteen starters the following year, including two American schooners. It was to be a severe test of men and boats. It started in a near gale and the conditions worsened, forcing twelve boats to retire. *La Goleta,* one of the American schooners, which had been built to Alden designs in Britain, leaked badly throughout the race, but battled it out with Lord Stalbridge's *Tally Ho,* a cutter built on the lines of a Falmouth Quay punt. They finished forty-two minutes apart after five and a half days of racing, with *La Goleta* ahead, but not by enough to stop *Tally Ho* taking the Fastnet Cup on handicap. On board the schooner there had

top: *Edward Heath at the wheel of his third* Morning Cloud.

above: *Arthur Slater's* Prospect of Whitby *leads Dave Johnson's* Superstar of Hamble *in the 1973 British trials.*

been plenty of excitement as the crew crammed on the canvas for the run home. Fourteen miles were logged in eighty minutes on one occasion. One man was washed overboard, but clung on so that other crew members were able to get him back on board.

The heavy weather of that race did not deter twelve skippers and crews from entering a year later, when again there were two American schooners and the first entry from France. One of the British boats, *Noreen,* was a converted 12-Metre; she was one of the four which retired. This year, 1928, the entry had been restricted to yachts of over 35 feet waterline. One of the American yachts caused considerable comment because she had been designed by Starling Burgess specifically to the ocean racing rules in order to win races. It was an attitude considered a touch unsporting by some who viewed the sport as merely an adjunct to cruising, and who

raced whatever boat they happened to have at the time.

Nina was definitely different. Her owner, Paul Hammond, had lavished a great deal of time and effort on his boat and she came to Britain after the Transatlantic Race to Santander, which she had won. A 50-foot waterline yacht, her rig was somewhat controversial, as it was not quite within the parameters of the Universal Rule as a schooner; her mainmast was a few inches too far forward. She was described by Alf Loomis, who had navigated *La Goleta* the previous year, as a two-masted cutter. She had a crew of eleven, far more than would have been found on an equivalent-sized British boat, with a wide variety of staysails to hoist and trim with the eleven two-speed sheet winches and four halyard reel winches. Her skipper, Sherman Hoyt, argued constantly with the navigator, Warwick Tompkins, and took over the navigation after the

taffrail log had been washed away on the way to the Rock. Despite this, *Nina* was first to round the Fastnet, was first home, and was first on corrected time, beating the first-ever winner of the race, *Jolie Brise,* by more than 5 hours.

Jolie Brise won the next two races, with the race in 1930 as windy as the 1927 race. Both wins were from small fleets of ten and nine respectively, but she remains the only triple winner of the Fastnet Cup.

The race took a step forward in 1931, when the Ocean Racing Club was granted the Royal Warrant and became the Royal Ocean Racing Club. That year Olin and Rod Stephens first brought their 52-foot yawl *Dorade* to Britain. She was one of six American yachts among the seventeen starters, and she had previously won the Transatlantic Race.

It was a race of heavy winds, which brought the first fatality. Colonel Hudson, the joint owner

of *Maitenes II,* was clearing an oil bag from the starboard after stanchion (no pushpits were fitted in those days) when the yacht lurched and he was thrown into the sea. *Maitenes II* was running with bare poles and a sea anchor trailed. Colonel Hudson, who was wearing heavy oilskins and boots, managed to grab the warp of the sea anchor but was unable to maintain this grasp. He disappeared beneath a wave and was not seen again. At the time the skipper, Bill Luard, recorded that the wind was Force 10.

At the front of the fleet the race was extremely close. The scratch boat was a Nicholson cutter, *Patience,* which crossed the line just 78 seconds ahead of *Highland Light,* one of the American yachts. *Dorade* was fourth home, just over 1 hour behind the leaders, but on handicap she was the winner by 8 hours!

It was decided that after this race the Fastnet would be a biennial event, alternating with the

Yeoman XX – *"Kiss Kiss"* – *Robin Arsher's Doug Peterson-designed Two-Tonner, which made the British team on two occasions, 1975 and 1977.*

Bermuda Race, and it was expected that by 1933 there would be a big fleet. But it was the smallest ever, of six, three of which were American, including *Dorade.* The race was extended by returning to Cowes, increasing the distance from 605 to 720 miles. Charles E. Nicholson skippered his own design, *Flame,* to be first home, but the race was once again *Dorade's.* She won by a large margin.

Rod Stephens was back in 1935, as skipper of *Stormy Weather.* Again he won, and easily. There was another foreign win two years later, when the fleet had grown to twenty-nine. Kees Bruynzeel's *Zeearend* was a Stephens-designed yawl, which the Dutchman sailed extremely well to win by 2¼ hours. The considerable opposition included many new boats, such as Ikey Bell's *Bloodhound,* a sister hull to his *Foxhound,* from Nicholson, but benefiting from the rating allowance given to the yawl over the cutter.

John Illingworth, who had skippered the yawl *Thalassa* in the previous race, had gone to Laurent Giles full of ideas which he wanted incorporated in a new yacht. Giles honored Illingworth's requirements and *Maid of Malham* was the result. Other new boats included the Robert Clark-designed *Ortac,* and *Stiarna,* another *Foxhound* hull with a cutter rig. They were boats that were to be seen around the ocean races for many years to come.

Despite the gathering clouds of war, there were three German boats in the 1939 race, including *Nordwind* from the Kriegsmarine, which broke the thirteen-year-old course record, and *Walkure* from the Luftwaffe. *Zeearend* was there to defend the Fastnet Cup.

Nordwind's time was 3 days, 20 hours, 58

above: Acadia, *in the Argentinian team, rounding the Nab Tower in the 1979 Channel Race.*

left: *The course for the Fastnet Cup Race, from Cowes on the Isle of Wight, around the Fastnet Rock, and back to Plymouth.*

opposite page: Mandrake *(Giorgio Carviero) chases her Italian teammate* Guia *(Giorgio Falck), both in pursuit of* Noryema X *(Ron Amey) in an inshore race in 1975.*

above: *The fifth* Morning Cloud, *with a 2.2-ounce spinnaker set, follows* Golden Apple of the Sun *eastward to Hill Head.*

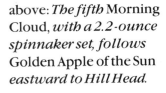

previous page: *The 1979 series was one of wind and there was plenty of opportunity for boats to get into trouble in the Solent before the gale-struck Fastnet Race.*

minutes, which was to remain unbeaten for twenty-six years.

That 1939 race was, however, a home win, albeit for an expatriate American living in Britain. *Bloodhound* beat *Zeearend* by just over 1 hour on corrected time. *Nordwind* sailed home only three weeks before the declaration of the war with the Erivale and Inter-Regimental Cups aboard. These two Fastnet trophies were lost during the conflict, but have been subsequently replaced.

There was one common factor in the first two postwar Fastnets: the winner. John Illingworth had gone farther with his design deliberations with Laurent Giles to produce *Myth of Malham,* a boat with her ends cut off in a most extreme manner. The bow was nothing more than a rounded-off transom, with a flatter one at the stern, just aft of the waterline. "Ugly boat" and "dreadful-looking monstrosity" were only two of the insults leveled at *"Myth"* when she first appeared, but her effectiveness was obvious. She won her first Fastnet by nearly 6

hours from twenty-five starters in a race that was held mostly in light winds. Two years later, when it blew hard, *Myth of Malham* won by 8 hours. Both times she was followed on corrected time by Michael Mason's *Latifa* and Myles Wyatt's *Bloodhound,* although *Latifa* was second on one occasion and *Bloodhound* was second on the other.

"Myth" won in 1949 despite the fact that the RORC had revised the rating rule in an effort to plug the sort of loophole which Illingworth had exploited. The new rule required all yachts built after January 1, 1940, to be re-rated, but that did not stop other boats like *Myth of Malham* being built. *Gulvain,* an aluminum 43-foot waterline cutter, and *Fandango,* a 33-foot waterline yacht, both came from the board of Laurent Giles and were among the twenty retirements in the twenty-nine-boat fleet.

There was the same number of starters for the next race. The Americans were back again with Rod Stephens skippering the Swedish yawl *Circe,* and Kennon Jewett aboard the Havana-

52

Santander winner *Malabar XIII*. One of the foreign yachts had gone further along the *"Myth"* line – the van de Stadt-designed *Zeevalk* of Kees Bruynzeel. She was a plywood hard-chine light-displacement sloop, that was one third of the displacement of a conventional boat of her size! She was not to race against *"Myth"* as Illingworth was abroad. Neither was she to win; she was, however, second to Owen Aisher's *Yeoman,* a new Nicholson design. The race started in a gale and there were many early retirements. *Yeoman* and *Zeevalk* were always up with the bigger boats, the former finishing fourth only 3 hours behind *Circe,* to take the overall win from *Zeevalk.*

In 1953 it was decided to allow yachts of 24-feet waterline to take part in the Fastnet, rather than hold the Wolf Rock Race for boats of 24- to 30-feet waterline. But there was not a mad rush of entries; nine started in the small class out of a total of thirty-eight. Six foreign countries were represented, the United States having a Bermuda Race winner in every class. Indeed, it

was the presence of Gifford Pinchot's 38-foot yawl *Loki* in Europe which had prompted an American plea for a reduction in the size of boat allowed to race. The other two Bermuda Race winners were the 57-foot *Gesture* and the 46-foot *Carina.* It was, essentially, a light-weather race, in which the small boats were to do well. *Loki* had been up with the front-runners for much of the time but became becalmed at the Wolf Rock on the way home, and her even smaller rivals caught up with a northwesterly. Sir Michael Newton's *Favona,* one of the tiniest boats in the race, emerged as overall winner from Franklin Woodrooffe's *Lothian.*

The weather pattern was repeated two years later when the fleet had grown to forty-six. The wind never exceeded Force 4, yet for the leaders it was a fast race. Dicky Nye, whose *Carina* came second in Class II in 1953, had a longer and beamier Rhodes-designed yawl, *Carina II.* He won comfortably, 48 minutes clear of Huey Long's *Ondine* on corrected time. One of the more remarkable boats in the fleet was the

above left: *Admiral's Cup racing is always close, but never more so than when there is a steady breeze.*

above: Apollo IV, *racing for Singapore, had more than enough wind and broached violently as she gybed.*

53

latest of John Illingworth's. He and Peter Green
had an ultra-light displacement yawl capable of
setting a mizzen staysail a third as big again as the
mainsail. Had there been any reaching in this
race, their tiny *Mouse of Malham* would
undoubtedly have done better in fleet, but she
did win Class III from twenty-one others.
Illingworth had reasoned when planning her that
most ocean races contained a large proportion of
reaching and the performance of *"Mouse"* in
other races that season more than bore that out,
as she was very successful.

The year 1957 was the first of the Admiral's
Cup. This was donated by five senior members of
the RORC – the Admiral, Sir Myles Wyatt; Peter
Green; John Illingworth; Selwyn Slater; and
Geoffrey Pattinson – to promote foreign
competition in the Fastnet and Cowes Week. It
was for national teams of three boats per team.
Points were awarded for placings in the Channel
Race; two races in Cowes Week (the Britannia
Cup and the New York Yacht Club Cup), and the
Fastnet; double points for the Channel Race and
triple for the Fastnet. The British team led by 8
points before the Fastnet, with a team composed
of Slater's *Uomie,* Pattinson's *Jocasta,* and
Illingworth's and Green's *Myth of Malham.* A
radical modification to the RORC's rating rule
had further hit the remarkable boat which had
won the Fastnet ten years earlier, yet still she was
competitive. The British team faced stiff
opposition from the United States: *Carina II*
together with Bill Snaith's *Figaro* and Blunt
White's *White Mist.* It was a Fastnet that no one
who took part will forget. It started and ended in
a gale as two depressions struck the area within a
few days of each other. It had been suggested
that the race started eastward to avoid the rough
and tumble of the Needles Channel. That
instruction was written into the sailing
instructions two years later.

Illingworth records the wind as Force 9 at

the start, and it came from the southwest,
blowing straight into the Needles Channel. It was
more than a shakedown, and the retirements
among the forty-one starters were heavy. Only
twelve eventually finished the race, among them
five of the six Admiral's Cuppers; *Uomie* was the
odd one out. *Carina II* scored her second win,
but *Myth of Malham* remarkably won Class II,
and with *Jocasta's* time bettering the other two
Americans the Cup was won by Britain by the
narrow margin of 2 points. The two survivors in
Class III were in sight of each other for most of
the race. Adlard Coles's *Cohoe III* finished half an
hour ahead of Gustaf Plym's *Elseli IV;* the latter
much damaged and minus a spinnaker boom
which she lost overboard in the Portland Race, a
loss which probably cost her the race.

Carina II went for three in a row in 1959,
but there was no American team in the Admiral's
Cup; only French and Dutch teams took up the
challenge. Dick Nye came close to winning, but
two Class II boats were able to beat him in a race
that was notable only for the long period of calm
early on. Sven Hansen's yawl *Anitra* was the
winner from the RORC's *Griffin II,* with *Carina
II* third, 2½ hours astern. Britain easily retained
the Admiral's Cup.

By 1961 some new boats were built with
the Admiral's Cup specifically in mind. One of
them, Ren Clarke's *Quiver III,* made the British
team, joining *Griffin II* and *Myth of Malham.*
The United States was back for the Admiral's Cup
and the team piled up some points in the
Channel Race; Jakob Isbrantsen's *Windrose* won
it, while *Figaro* and Henry du Pont's *Cyane* were
fourth and fifth. Swedish, French, and Dutch
boats helped to keep the British trio back at
sixth, ninth, and tenth. *Quiver III* performed a
magnificent double win in the Britannia Cup and
the New York Yacht Club Cup, and by the Fastnet
Britain was only 13 points behind the United
States.

Quiver's luck ran out in the Fastnet; she looked set to win until the wind died for her between the Bishop and the Lizard, and first place went to the Dutch *Zwerver*. And while the British team had the best points, they were not enough to overtake the United States, and the Cup left home shores for the first time.

With Germany joining in, the 1963 Admiral's Cup field had grown to six nations. Britain started badly when Ron Amey's *Noryema III* was penalized 5 percent of her elapsed time for a start line incident in the Channel Race, but after the two inshore races there was very little between the three leading teams, with Sweden on 134, Britain on 130, and the United States a point behind. The Fastnet start saw Britain's *Clarion of Wight* involved in a collision and *Figaro* rip her mainsail right across. Bill Snaith's crew repaired it as they headed out of the Solent

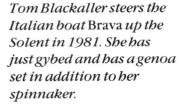

Tom Blackaller steers the Italian boat Brava *up the Solent in 1981. She has just gybed and has a genoa set in addition to her spinnaker.*

under genoa and mizzen. The *"Clarion"* crew had to await the outcome of a protest.

It was a bad start for some in a Force 6 westerly as the 125 boats beat down Channel, but this was the sort of weather that the Illingworth- and Primrose-designed 48-footer *Outlaw* wanted, and she romped into the lead, but by the Rock *"Clarion"* was ahead on corrected time. The wind then went fickle but a depression brought more again as the fleet neared Plymouth. *Figaro* took Class I from *Carina,* but it was Class II and III boats that were to take the major honors. *Clarion of Wight* won her protest and was the overall winner of the race, and with *Outlaw* and *Noryema* finishing seventh and ninth, the Cup returned to Britain when *Windrose* could finish only thirteenth for the United States.

The Australians arrived for the first time in

1965. With them on their debut in the Cup was Ireland, but one of their boats was no stranger to the competition: *Myth of Malham,* now 18 years old, was back, with her new owners Brigit and David Livingstone. But it was another relatively elderly yacht that was to make the headlines in this series, although not in the Fastnet itself; Gordon Ingate's thirteen-year-old *Caprice of Huon,* a Robert Clark design, won the Channel Race and both the Britannia Cup and the New York Yacht Club Cup. The Australians appeared unstoppable; they had displayed a new attitude toward the sport – they practiced! They did not, however, understand the complexity of the Cowes Week sailing instructions, and lost a lot of valuable points by going the wrong side of a limit mark in the first of the inshore races. Ron Swanson and his crew on *Camille,* on discovering this after the race, went out again

and sailed the course to retrieve what points they could. As five boats were disqualified and there was one non-starter, they gained six valuable points for their trouble. The Aussies did not like the Fastnet weather that year. There was a light downwind leg to the Rock and a beat home to Plymouth. The British team did more than enough to retain the Cup when *Quiver IV* scored top points and *Noryema IV* and *Firebrand* were third and ninth. The Fastnet was won by Dick Carter's own design, *Rabbit,* three quarters of an hour ahead of *Quiver IV. Gitana IV* was first to finish in a new record time of 3 days, 9 hours, 40 minutes.

The hope of success was enough to have the Australians back two years later. *Caprice* returned, and with her were two new boats, the 46-foot *Balandra* and the 40-foot *Mercedes III.* This time, however, they did not get things all

Outsider, *one of the winning German team in 1983, appropriately astride* Shenandoah *of the United States team.*

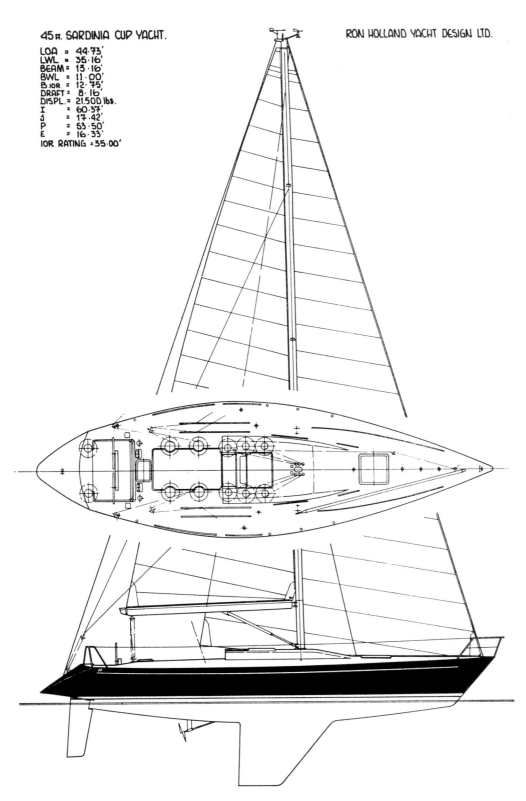

45 ft SARDINIA CUP YACHT.
LOA = 44·73'
LWL = 35·16'
BEAM = 13·16'
BWL = 11·00'
B IOR = 12·75'
DRAFT = 8·16'
DISPL. = 21,500 lbs.
I = 60·37'
J = 17·42'
P = 53·50'
E = 16·33'
IOR RATING = 35·00'

RON HOLLAND YACHT DESIGN LTD.

Sail plan and general deck arrangement drawing of a Ron Holland-designed 45-footer.

their own way from the outset. Eric Tabarly, with *Pen Duick III,* was in the French team, and he won the Channel Race with his wishbone schooner, but the Aussies were the top team with third, fourth, and seventh places. After the inshore races they led by 41 points from Britain, and the outcome depended on the Fastnet.

It was not a spectacular Fastnet and the Australians were not unhappy that Tabarly won the race. They finished in third, fourth, and seventh places and the celebrations in Plymouth had a justifiably Antipodean flavor. To rub it in even more, the three Australian boats were the three top scorers individually!

The Australian plans to defend the Cup were meticulous. This was in sharp contrast to the United States challenge; their team was picked on a "who's going" basis with Dick Carter's *Red Rooster* being built in Holland and being finished only just in time. There was still space for the

genuine Corinthian in a year when eleven teams raced for the Cup.

The Australians opened in style with Syd Fischer's 48-foot S&S *Ragamuffin* winning the Channel Race from *Red Rooster* and the team taking top points. They stretched it in the Britannia Cup, although Arthur Slater's *Prospect of Whitby* won for Britain, and again in the New York Yacht Club Cup, even though Dick Carter won the race with *Red Rooster.* It was a gloomy Fastnet with the wind tailing off after the start to make it a slow race. *Red Rooster* won the Fastnet by 68 seconds from Sir Max Aitken's *Crusade,* and there is still argument about a timing discrepancy which may have robbed *Crusade. Red Rooster's* win, *Carina's* third, and *Palawan's* eighth gave the Cup to the United States as the Australians were thwarted by the calms.

The conflict of running both the country and its Cup team was something of a problem for

Prime Minister Edward Heath in 1971. His *Morning Cloud* was an automatic choice for the team, from twenty-seven trialists; a team that would face the additional pressure of the media because of Heath's position. The number of countries taking part increased to seventeen and the inshore races were separated from the other Cowes Week races for the first time. The IOR rule was adopted and the range was wide — boats of between 29- and 60-foot rating were eligible for the Cup.

First, third, and fifth by *Prospect of Whitby, Morning Cloud,* and Bob Watson's *Cervantes IV* gave Britain the lead after the Channel Race. Fortunes were mixed in the inshore races, but going into the Fastnet the top scorers were Britain 480, Australia 458, and the United States 419. It was a truly testing Fastnet with conditions varying from calm to gale. The run, in gale conditions, from the Rock to the Bishop was the

telling part of the race. Syd Fischer's *Ragamuffin* was driven like a surfboat, flying home under spinnaker when more prudent skippers opted for boomed-out headsails. It was a relentless headlong charge, and though they had one bad broach the Australians sensed that this was their big chance. *"Rags"* averaged more than 9 knots for the 106 miles to the Bishop, and continued up Channel in the same vein. She won the race by 2 hours, 23 minutes, and created her own legend. Had *Koomooloo* not lost her rudder, the Australians would have taken the Cup with *Salacia II,* the S&S "improvement" of *Ragamuffin,* eighth. *Cervantes IV* was second and with *Prospect of Whitby* and *Morning Cloud* twelfth and fourteenth the Cup was back in Britain.

There was a German invasion of Britain, at least in offshore racing terms, in 1973. Their team of *Saudade, Rubin,* and *Carina* (two from

Container, *Udo Schutz's Judel and Vrolijk design which failed to make the German team and sailed for Austria.*

59

Steve Benjamin puts the tiller to leeward to start Shenandoah *around the bottom mark in the third inshore race of 1983, held in Christchurch Bay. At his shoulder Dave Ullman calls the shots on this United States team boat.*

S&S and one from Carter) looked perfectly ordinary until they showed their hand in Britain; then it was almost too late. The focus, until then, had been on the two Bob Miller-designed sister ships in the Australian team, *Ginkgo* and *Apollo II.* They had cleaned up everything in sight at home and began to do the same in Britain before the Cup races. Even so, Edward Heath, asked his opinion of the German prospects, replied: "None at all." Sixteen nations took part that year, represented by forty-eight boats.

A goodly breeze for the Channel Race gave all the crews a tough opener, although the course was not demanding. A run to the *Royal*

Sovereign, a reach across to Le Havre, and a fetch back to the Nab was not onerous. The top honors went to Jean-Louis Fabry's Finot-designed *Revolution,* which hoisted a spinnaker for the leg home when the wind freed and surfed across the Channel. Robin Aisher's Carter-designed *Frigate* was second with Ted Turner and the uprated One-Tonner *Lightnin'* third. Germany, however, took the team lead, 8 points ahead of Holland.

The first inshore was a classic. All other Cowes Week racing was canceled because of the forecast gale, but the Royal Yacht Squadron decided to send the Admiral's Cuppers off into

the 35-knot westerly. *Saudade* won, staying with higher-rated boats all the way around, while the first-to-finish *Saga* from Brazil was second and Britain's *Quailo II* of Donald Parr third. It was, however, Australia's day with *Apollo II, Ragamuffin,* and *Ginkgo,* fourth, fifth, and seventh. *Saudade* won again two days later, but the British team were best, and so going into the Fastnet the German lead was 6 points over Australia and 30 over Britain, not a large deficit for either country to overcome, and the hopes of both were high. The Fastnet had the largest number of entries till that time, 258 boats starting.

The Fastnet was an anticlimax. Light airs and fog . . . more light airs . . . more fog. Germany's consistency brought its reward and a new name had to be engraved on the trophy.

Fifty years of Fastnet racing was marked by another light airs race in 1975. The Admiral's Cup, too, suffered from the high-pressure-inspired weather; one inshore race finishing in Cowes as darkness fell. It really was not what the New Zealanders, taking part for the first time, were expecting. The Fastnet took the leaders even longer than the previous one. It was won by Richard and Harvey Bagnall in the Holland-designed Three-Quarter-Tonner *Golden Delici-*

There is no room for mistakes in the close-quarter combat of Admiral's Cup inshore racing.

Benjamin steers as
Ullman eases the running
backstay to flatten the
mainsail of Shenandoah.

ous. Britain's trio of *Noryema X, Yeoman XX* and *Battlecry* took the Cup, for which nineteen nations had entered, with the previous winners, Germany, finishing second.

However bad the racing might have been, there were still nineteen teams for the Cup two years later, including a team from Japan. There were then five races; an additional inshore race was held in the Solent prior to Cowes Week. Again the winds were light for the series, and one race was abandoned to be sailed again. Even the Fastnet was a bore. It was the slowest on record since the 1930s and the first of the Cup yachts, the British *Moonshine,* rounded the Rock some 12 hours after she might reasonably have been expected to finish at Plymouth!

It was the year of *Imp,* Dave Allen's 40-foot

Holland design, that had had the best points score at the SORC and now added the Fastnet win and the top Admiral's Cup points score to her record. She beat *Moonshine* by only 5½ minutes, but with *Yeoman XX* third and *Marionette* ninth, the Cup remained at home, the seventh win for Britain in the eleven races for the Cup so far.

The Admiral's Cup series of races from 1977 consists of a Channel Race of 220 miles, three inshore races of 35 miles each, and the Fastnet Race of 605 miles. The points scored in the Channel Race are doubled and those in the Fastnet tripled. The Channel Race begins at Plymouth, follows the English coast past the Owers lighthouse, and crosses the Channel at the lightship *Royal Sovereign.* From Le Havre the

course returns across the Channel to the finish at the mouth of the Solent, thus forming an equilateral triangle. The direction can be reversed if the winds are not favorable.

The five races are thus suited for different types of yacht. The inshore races over the difficult waters of the Solent and in Christchurch Bay are ideal for the small boats, the Channel Race is best for medium-sized yachts that can adapt to the changing wind conditions inshore, while the Fastnet Race can be one of the toughest of ocean races, where the big boats have an advantage while the small boats face the buffetings of the storms.

The contrast in conditions between 1977 and 1979 was as undeniable as it was unbelievable. Ted Turner described the Fastnet

that year as "the roughest race in the history of ocean racing." It was a race that was to claim the lives of fifteen competitors in a storm of the fiercest proportions; a race which Turner won and in which Bob Bell's 79-foot *Condor of Bermuda* broke the record for the course; a race in which a record number of 303 boats started and five of the twenty-four abandoned sank.

The inshore races that year gave an indication of the frailty of the craft as masts went and rudders shattered, and that within the confines of the Solent. After four races, Ireland led, 9 points ahead of the United States, with Australia another 9 points astern. When the gale-strewn Fastnet was over the Cup was Australia's; *Impetuous* and *Police Car* were third and fourth, while *Ragamuffin* was eighth. Jeremy Rogers'

top: *The crew of* Hitchhiker *fold a genoa after a sail change in Christchurch Bay.*

above: Formidable, *Peter Vroon's Dutch team reject, racing for Japan.*

Eclipse was best of the Admiral's Cuppers, and became top individual scorer, while Turner's 61-foot *Tenacious* gained the Fastnet Cup.

It was back to light winds for the 1981 series and the Fastnet Race, yet somehow Jim Kilroy's *Kialoa,* the 80-foot Holland design, found enough wind to be on schedule for the course record at the Rock; but not by the time she got home! She finished only just ahead of the Admiral's Cupper *Victory of Burnham,* Peter de Savary's first yachting venture. The British team won the Cup, and the Kiwi boat *Swuzzlebubble* just edged out *"Victory"* to be top individual boat.

There were again differences in the structure in 1983. Now all the inshore racing was divorced from Cowes Week. The first two races were held in the Solent prior to Cowes Week and the Channel Race, the third was held around an Olympic course in Christchurch Bay during the Week. And that was a definite success for the Champagne Mumm-sponsored event; their Cup, and the skipper's weight in champagne, went to Victor Forss with the Swedish Frers 51-footer *Carat.* By the end of that race, however, the German team had a 57-point advantage–19 Fastnet places ahead of the United States, whose *Scarlett O'Hara* had won the trophy for the best points in the inshore races. The Germans held together for the Fastnet, *Sabina, Pinta,* and *Outsider* finishing fourth, sixth, and eleventh to take the Cup for the second time.

The wind was not strong at any time, but it came from just the right direction for Bob Bell's 80-foot Holland-designed *Condor* to reach out and back to the Rock, apparently generating her own wind, sufficiently fast to break the course record. Not only that, she was able to save her time on handicap and Bell thus achieved a rare double win.

After the America's Cup, which has been held spasmodically as challengers appear, the

Indulgence *(Graham Walker) clears ahead of "Shorty" Trimmingham's* Flirt of Paget *and begins her tack in to starboard.*

Admiral's Cup, held every two years, is the race which attracts the most attention from yachtsmen. It was the first series in the world to incorporate inshore and offshore racing, and since its inception other competitions have followed its example, including the Onion Patch Trophy and Southern Cross Cup. Additional competitions to adopt the inshore and offshore scheme are the Rio Circuit in Brazil and the Ton Cups.

Like the America's Cup, it has sometimes attracted criticism of its organizers. Although Britain has not held the Admiral's Cup continuously for a long period of time, as the United States held the America's Cup until 1983, there have been charges of unfair competition and bias among the judges. However, the number of entrants has continued to grow, and disappointed and supposedly indignant challengers return for further attempts. With a maximum of three boats in each national team, more nations and yachts compete than in any other race.

Part of the attraction lies in the delights of Cowes Week, although the small harbor on the Isle of Wight has increasingly found the influx of visitors difficult to accommodate. This annual regatta, which dates back to a race in 1826, is generally considered the most important in the calendar. It is now a part of the English social season, and the festival atmosphere is a draw to sailors from all parts of the world, including those who take part in the ocean racing for the Admiral's Cup.

The amazing technological progress seen in sailing over the past quarter of a century or so since the first Admiral's Cup has been helped by those sailors who are constantly seeking to sail their boats with more speed and safety. For many of them the Admiral's Cup is the world championship in ocean racing.

Storm clouds darken the skies in Christchurch Bay as Brian and Pam Saffery Cooper's Dubois-designed 40-foot Dragon *rounds the leeward mark in the third inshore race of the 1983 Admiral's Cup.*

Bermuda Race
and the
Onion Patch Trophy

previous page: *A blustery spinnaker start to the 1982 Bermuda Race.*

A more leisurely start in 1970, the year Dick Nye scored his second success.

"Bermuda is Paradise," said Mark Twain, "but one has to go through Hell to get there." That same thought must have been echoed often by yachtsmen competing in the biennial race from Newport, Rhode Island, one of the oldest races in the international calendar and one which has considerable influence on handicapping systems.

A race to Bermuda was natural enough for American yachtsmen. The island formed by thousands of years of coral activity on an extinct undersea volcano is a natural point at which to aim yachts from the eastern seaboard of the United States. It has often been a staging post for transatlantic yachts and for many who head for the Caribbean islands from the New England and Middle Atlantic states. Bermuda has long stood as a challenge to the cruising yachtsman and, since 1906, as one to the offshore racer.

Thomas Fleming Day, the editor and founder of the magazine *Rudder*, was a forthright man, one who was prepared to back ideas, of which he was never short, with practical and enthusiastic development. Virtually single-handed, Day championed the cause of offshore sailing and, more specifically, racing in "relatively small yachts," soon after the turn of the century. When he began to use *Rudder* as a mouthpiece for his cause, in 1904, there had been three real ocean races – all of them transatlantic and all of them involving yachts of more than 100 feet long. The first, in 1866, saw the winner home in 13 days, 21 hours, 45 minutes, a time which even now would not go unappreciated.

Day, however, wanted racing for boats of less than 40 feet overall. His opinion was that offshore racing in these boats, without the aid of

professional crews, would make yachting "what it should be, a sport for men – real men." Therefore, he promoted a race from Brooklyn, New York, to Marblehead, Massachusetts, a distance of 330 miles, which drew an entry, in 1904, of nine starters, of which six finished. Even though he was the last of the six finishers himself, Day persisted with a similar race the following year, one of 250 miles from Brooklyn to Hampton Roads, Virginia. He had achieved a beginning for his sport.

For that race, three of the twelve boats that came to the line were specially built. Day toyed with the idea of a transatlantic race for his size of boats but mercifully was dissuaded. He did not let his ideas rest, however, and in the issue of February 1906 announced in *Rudder* a new race – one to Bermuda.

Sir Thomas Lipton had given Day a trophy for a long-distance ocean race (there are perhaps more Lipton Trophies in yachting than any other named Cup). Day got together with the Brooklyn Yacht Club again to organize this race, and at three o'clock on May 26, the three boats specifically built for the Hampton Roads race started for Bermuda. Day was skipper of the eventual winner, *Tamerlane*, a 38-foot yawl.

The early Bermuda Races lasted for just five years. There have been many theories as to why they died. Day had certainly proved that it was possible to race small boats offshore and particularly that they could be raced to Bermuda. In the last of these races, Harold S. Vanderbilt's 76-foot Herreshoff-designed schooner, *Vagrant*, was the winner – Day had long since lost his objectivity in size and had opened the 1907 event to vessels under 90 feet and had also removed the amateur qualification.

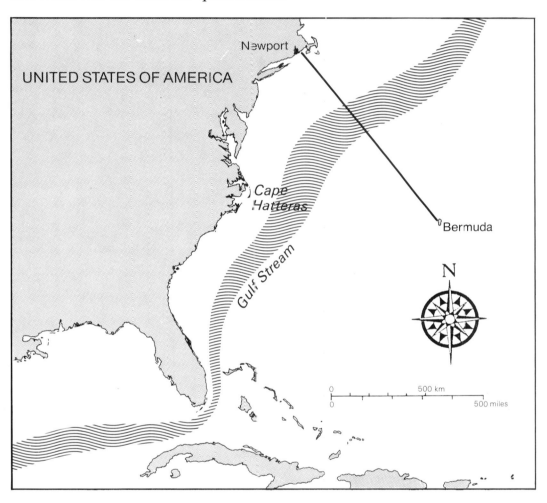

It was not until 1923 that Day's ideas were again revived, this time in *Yachting* magazine. The January editorial, written by Herbert L. Stone, proposed "a race for small craft from New York to Bermuda," suggesting that many of the new type of small cruisers that had been recently developed would be ideal for the purpose and that while "many of the fleet were designed to go offshore – yet but few of their owners have ever taken them off soundings."

Stone, unlike Day before him, had the support of others. He had already formed a committee of five Americans with a Bermuda representative to organize the race. All five of the Americans were members of the Cruising Club of America (CCA), formed the previous year by

The straight rhumb line course from Newport to Bermuda is drastically affected by the Gulf Stream's meanders. The Gulf Stream flows, like a river in the sea, at 2 to 4 knots.

right: *Burt Keenan's Frers-designed* Acadia *in 1978.*

far right: *The Ron Holland-designed* Marionette, *member of the British team in 1978, owned and skippered by Chris Dunning.*

William Washburn Nutting, and that club's association with the Bermuda Race has persisted to this day, although not all the members at that time were sure that racing was any part of the Club's countenance. One of the charter members, Frank B. Draper, went as far as presenting a report which stated: "I am of the opinion that the whole spirit of racing is radically opposed to the spirit of cruising. They are as oil and water."

Strangely, that same Frank B. Draper was to be found sailing on board the cutter *Flying Cloud* in the race, which started from New London, Connecticut – a compromise of the two centers of the embryonic CCA, New York and Boston. Twenty-two yachts in three classes came to the line. The race marked the first of the CCA's handicap systems.

The three classes were Class A for two-masted boats from 35 to 52 feet overall, excluding bowsprits and bumkins; Class B for two-masted boats of 53 to 70 feet overall; and Class C for sloops of under 60 feet. Each yacht carried a handicap of 1 hour per foot of overall length – a 70-footer would have had to have finished 35 hours ahead of a 35-footer to beat it.

It was a race of considerable importance for many reasons. The only Marconi-rigged boat in the race, Robert N. Bavier Snr's *Memory,* a New York 40 yawl, was nearly prevented from entering because many of the organizers believed the rig was unsafe and unseamanlike. Bavier proved them all wrong by being first to Bermuda. All the boats made it to the finish, and

the people of Bermuda were enormously enthusiastic toward the race (as indeed they still are today). It was sufficiently attractive as a race to persuade ten new owners to enter the race the following year. And from those who raced it in 1923, it was Bavier with a 59-foot Herreshoff-designed yawl who scooped the pool with line honors and a handicap win in 1924.

Bavier was back again in 1926, when the race was next held (a two-year break between races was decided in order to boost entries) with a radically designed 66-foot ketch. She was perhaps the first "rule cheater" in the offshore racing world. She had short overhangs compared with what was then fashionable and thus her waterline was proportionally greater than was that of any of the other boats; she was a bigger boat than the simple handicap system saw her to be. She had also been designed as a fast-reaching boat since the race generally had much of its wind from the southwest, across the path of the course. But in 1926 the winds were largely light and from ahead, and while Bavier's *Dragoon* was first to cross the line she failed to win on handicap (how often the radical boats, built with a specific race in mind, fail the first time out).

It was in that year that the first British entry was made into the race. George Martin's converted Le Havre pilot cutter, *Jolie Brise,* the winner of the first Fastnet Race a year earlier, sailed the Atlantic just for the race. In that race, too, several of the yachts carried radio receivers with which to check their chronometers – marine electronics were born at that time.

The limitations of the handicap system were readily appreciated by the CCA, which had officially fully adopted the race that year, and the Club made moves to rectify this before the next race. The Ocean Racing Club in Great Britain had already formulated a way of giving yachts a time allowance from a rating which took into consideration the major speed-producing factors of a yacht – length and sail area – and the speed-reducing factor – displacement – as well. This was further adjusted to compensate for the efficiency of the rigs of the boats – gaff schooners getting a further 10 percent allowance over Bermudan sloops and cutters. It was a rather arbitrary rule which set the CCA thinking of a more equable system of handicapping offshore racing yachts, and this search has, over the years, become a feature of the Bermuda Race.

By 1932, the start had moved to Montauk Point, New York, and the fleet was down from the forty-two boats of the previous race to twenty-seven. That year it was a tough race with a beat into three days of blustery winds in the Gulf Stream. It was won by John Alden's schooner *Malabar X,* but the victory was dimmed somewhat by the news of the loss of a life from the 78-foot *Adriana,* which had caught fire and sunk. Ten of her crew were rescued by *Jolie Brise,* this time in the hands of the Royal Ocean Racing Club's Commodore, Robert Somerset.

In 1934, the elapsed time record fell to *Vamarie,* which took 3 days, 3 hours, 37 minutes in the last race to start from Montauk Point.

Because of the predominantly light winds in Long Island Sound, the start of the 1936 race was moved to the Brenton Light Tower off Newport, Rhode Island, where the race has started ever since. The 1936 race attracted nine overseas entries among the forty-three starters. It was the roughest race since 1923.

The yachts sailed into a tropical storm as they entered the Gulf Stream. The winds gusted at more than 50 knots. There were eight retirements, for many and varied reasons, while another boat was disqualified for using her engine to maneuver when her topmast went over the side. Torn sails, broken headstay fittings, mast support fractures, and failing radio receivers were among the reasons why boats dropped out in the storm, but through it all came R. P. Baruch's *Kirawan,* a 53-foot cutter designed by Sparkman & Stephens, to win the race on corrected time.

Baruch took home with him the silver and gold model of St. David's Head Lighthouse, which is where the race finishes – the Bermuda Lighthouse Trophy. Unlike the winners of any other yacht race of note, the winner of this trophy receives a full-scale replica to keep – perhaps one reason why the race retains its popularity despite the politicking that goes on concerning which rating and which handicapping system should be used to determine the winner.

There was a severe contrast in weather two years later. Gone were the storm clouds and instead there were light winds and calms. The

Under the light of the Brenton Reef Tower, the S&S-designed fractionally rigged Siren Song *starts the 1976 race in a typical Newport fog.*

opposite page: *Seymour Sinetts'* Williwaw *leads her United States teammate* Scaramouche, *owned and skippered by Chuck Kirsch.*

S&S yawl, *Baruna,* a 72-footer, ghosted home to victory. And as if to prove that it was no fluke, her owner, Henry Taylor, won the Bermuda Race with her again in 1948 in a race when the competition and the winds were stiffer.

The race was not sailed in the war years, although some American yachtsmen were more fortunate than their counterparts in other areas of the world in that they still could get some passage racing, albeit in fresh water, on the Great Lakes. In the first race after the war the Madison Avenue design firm of S&S was again prominent. Their 57-foot sloop *Gesture* won in light airs.

In 1950 S&S were still ruling the roost.

William Moore's *Argyll,* a 57-foot yawl from Stephens, beat the famous *Bolero* by just over 1 hour on corrected time. For the larger *Bolero,* it once again proved how hard it is for a big boat to win under the CCA handicapping system. For John Nicholas Brown's boat to have beaten *Argyll* she would have had to average 8.5 knots.

The Gulf Stream has a huge effect on the Bermuda Race. It was not until 1950, however, that the Woods Hole Oceanographic Institute began to chart the progress of the Stream, and those who ventured forth into it had little or no idea of how to predict its effect. All they knew was that it existed as a body of water of different

temperature from the rest of the ocean and that it moved in a different direction.

The Gulf Stream has been described as a river flowing through the sea. It forms meanders in the same way that a river will form oxbow lakes in soft earth. Bearing that in mind, it is not surprising that sailors in the early Bermuda Races were in difficulties when they encountered it, frequently misreading its direction.

The Gulf Stream is a body of hot water from the Caribbean which flows north of Cuba and past the tip of Florida. It then hugs the coastline of the southern states to Cape Hatteras, North Carolina, where, many believe, the shape of that headland has the effect of causing the meanders which form on the stream's slowly expanding path as it heads northwestward into the Atlantic Ocean across the path of the course of the Bermuda Race. It is the meanders which have the greatest effect on the race. They are U-shaped, and their position varies. Like oxbow lakes, they can become detached to form dissociated circular whirlpool-like patches of current. In the meanders' more regular U-shaped form, the left-hand or western upright is the one that the Bermuda Race sailor looks for, since it has current going in the direction that he wants to go. The right-hand, or eastern, one he seeks to avoid. There are around 50 miles between them in an east-west direction, and there can be between 2 and 4 knots of current in the Stream. Getting it right and getting it wrong can mean the difference of a day in arrival time at St. David's Head. There is no difference in the water temperature of the two arms; that of the ocean is around 76°F, while in the Stream, it varies between 78° and 82°F.

It is relatively easy to see why the early Bermuda Race competitors were able to get the Stream wrong. They could tell by the temperature that they were in the Stream but had to wait a long time to tell in which direction it was going. In the prevailing southwesterlies, the seas in the westerly arm of the "U" would be rougher than those in the easterly arm, but that is a comparison that is not afforded to the competitors. They had to wait to see if their log readings were smaller than their celestial navigation plots to find their good luck; not for them the joys of today's Loran and Satnav, where the answer is delivered in minutes.

Today, the National Oceanic and Atmospheric Administration (NOAA) has continuous surveillance of the Gulf Stream, for, as much as anything, it affects the weather pattern of the eastern seaboard of the United States. Indeed yachtsmen have reason to be grateful to the NOAA, with its twenty-four-hour weather service on radio. Bermuda Race competitors have even more cause for gratitude. At pre-race briefings, the weather and Gulf Stream predictions are delivered by the NOAA

Gem (Bill Zeigler), Morning Star (John Ambrose), and Artemis (Arthur Emil) in the 1982 Bermuda Race soon after the start.

and include the position coordinates of the Stream gathered from the satellite observations, both visual and temperature delineated, of the administration. Anyone who now gets it wrong has only himself to blame.

There is no asking Dick Nye how he got it right in 1952 when he won the race with the 46-foot yawl Carina (all Nye's boats carried this name). He was able to get it right again eighteen years later. His first win was in dreadfully light winds, conditions which eliminated the bigger boats from the corrected time-prize lists.

By 1954, the fleet had grown to seventy-seven and was highly distinguished in terms of American yachting — all the big names were there, names evocative of the great days of American offshore racing: Bolero, Nina, Ticonderoga, Barlovento, Stormy Weather, Ondine, Gesture, and Caribbee among them. The weather was such as to turn the race into a pleasure cruise, with light airs for the first two days and nights, and just over 200 miles were logged before the breeze filled in. It meant that once again the smaller boats should win the race.

It needed, however, good reading of the Woods Hole Institute's Stream predictions to make the fastest passage to Bermuda. Dan Strohmeier found the southerly flow of the Gulf Stream correctly, farther to the west than many of the favorites, and took his 39-foot Malay, a Concordia yawl, to win on corrected time.

Light airs are not what most ocean racers want — there is still something of the shellback in their image and they feel thwarted unless the wind pipes up for at least part of a major race.

opposite page: Bill McAteer's Immigrant and Gerhard Moog's Dynamo of the Canadian team in the 1980 Onion Patch racing.

75

Nirvana, *the Dave Pedrick 81-footer which shattered the eight-year-old race record by over 5 hours.*

Sometimes they get more than they ask for, and there is some reluctance to go again the next time. The weather for the 1956 race was everything that the blue-water sailor could have asked for. The prevailing southwesterly blew strongly for the entire race, making the passage one of a close starboard tack reach. It meant a fast trip to Bermuda, and the 1932 record of *Highland Light* fell to the mighty yawl *Bolero*. Owned then by a Swede, Sven Salen, *Bolero* crossed the finishing line after only 2 days, 22 hours, 11 minutes, 37 seconds, for a course record that was to hold for eighteen years. *Bolero*, however, was not able to win the race or even its class. Remarkably Class A went to a schooner, *Nina*, built in 1928, which was owned by DeCoursey Fales, while the overall winner was Carleton Mitchell's 39-foot *Finisterre*, which sailed as close to the rhumb line as was possible.

It was a race that Harry Wise and his crew on *Edlu* will never forget. She hit the northeast breaker reef off Bermuda at 2:00 A.M. The coral tore along either side of the keel, and the boat filled quickly. The crew donned their lifejackets and clung to the rigging as the hull grounded. They were pounded by the waves breaking on the reef throughout the night but hung on, remembering the survival adage "stay with the boat." It saved their lives, since they were spotted by the coast guard in the morning, and life rafts were dropped to them from an aircraft. The experience has not stopped Wise tackling the Bermuda Race on subsequent occasions.

The 1958 race began in brisk north-westerlies, and the 111 starters appeared in disarray as they left the line at Brenton Tower.

Spinnakers were badly controlled as they rolled their way on the rhumb line course to Bermuda. It went on, with major improvement in the sail handling, for 450 miles until the northwesterlies died right away, with the smaller boats still charging along in the breeze until they reached the calms. The calm concentrated the field so that when the wind returned, the boats were all together. At St. David's Light, sixty-two boats crossed the line within 4 hours and 20 minutes. The smaller boats were to have a field day.

Once again it was Carleton Mitchell's *Finisterre*, driven as hard as her crew could go down the rhumb line, that took the major honors. She had finished only just over 3 hours behind the line-honors winner, *Good News. Finisterre*, another S&S winner of the Bermuda Race, was crewed by men handpicked by Mitchell to win the race – dinghy champions whom he knew would do their best to keep her going as fast as possible.

These were virtually the same men as he asked to do the next Bermuda Race with him. *Finisterre* had won twice in a row in conditions which had suited the smaller boats in the fleet. In 1960, she was to do it for a third time, but in this race conditions could hardly have been said to have been on her side. True, it had been light for the 135 starters for the first three and a half days, but then barometers began to fall like stones and the southeasterly wind blew with increasing intensity until it went up to 50 knots, ranging for much of the night between 45 and 60 with gusts exceeding 80 knots. It continued for more than 12 hours before the storm abated to 35-knot winds. Through all this, Mitchell and his crew

drove the little centerboarder with every ounce of skill and experience they had to win the race.

Retirements were aplenty. Headstays pulled out, rudders tore off, and masts fell down. At the height of the storm, Jack Westin went over the side of Charlie Ulmer's *Scylla* as he was changing over watches; he had unclipped his harness for that very purpose. Ulmer was ahead of his time in having a strobe light attached to the horseshoe lifebelt, and this was thrown overboard. Even so, very few of *Scylla's* crew thought that they would see Westin alive again. They dropped the sails and started the engine, but it was half an hour before they could get *Scylla* back to the strobe light – it was like looking for a needle in a haystack – but when they did they found that Westin had been able to swim to it, and they could recover him. Since that date strobe lights have been mandatory safety equipment for yachts in the Bermuda Race.

Six years after her Class A win, the thirty-four-year-old schooner *Nina* went one better. In 1962, the southwesterly held for the schooner to romp home to take the handicap prize for DeCoursey Fales. That year, the Royal Bermuda Yacht Club presented the Onion Patch trophy for biennial international competition in a series of races in Newport culminating with the Bermuda Race. It would be, like the Admiral's Cup, for teams of three boats, and was held for the first time in 1964.

Argentina joined Bermuda and the United States for the series, which was won by the American team. It was not an earth-shattering event, but by then the Bermuda Race fleet had grown to 143. That race was almost a classic for

weather. The moderate southwesterly winds gave out after 500 miles, and the fleet again piled up. From the pack, the lowest-rated yacht, Milton Ernstof's *Burgoo,* a 37-foot yawl, won top prize.

By 1966, the race fleet had reached 167, and there were teams from Germany and Great Britain to join the other three in the Onion Patch series. Britain, in the form of Ron Amey's *Noryema IV*, Dennis Miller's *Firebrand,* and Mike Vernon's *Assegai,* won the series. The Bermuda Race was won by Vince Learson in a stock Cal 40, *Thunderbird.*

The CCA had, that year, experimented with a performance factor in its handicap-correcting factor of elapsed time of each boat. It was complex enough to need an IBM computer (wasn't it convenient that Vince Learson was the president of IBM!), and when the corrected times were worked out under the conventional method using the North American Yacht Racing Union's tables, Learson's *Thunderbird* would have won by a bigger margin. The 1966 experiment was dropped.

The United States won the Onion Patch two years later when Canada joined in and Argentina dropped out. It was that year that Ted Hood won with his self-designed 51-foot steel yawl *Robin.* It was a down-the-rhumb-line race in moderate southwesterlies, which must have suited Hood's yawl to a tee. The American team won again in 1970, the year Dick Nye got his second Bermuda Race success, this time with a new McCurdy & Rhodes-designed sloop called *Carina.* That year there was more than a capful of wind, but nothing to compare with what the yachts had to face in 1972.

Off in the 635-mile dash across the Gulf Stream at the start of the 1982 classic.

Don Green's Evergreen *leads at the Weather Mark in one of the 1982 Onion Patch races off Newport, from* Infinity, Morning Star, *and* Artemis.

It was the roughest Bermuda Race on record. The record number of starters, 178, were lashed by a gale as they got halfway down the course. The smaller boats copped the worst of the gales, having to spend three days at sea in them, while the leaders were home after only 1 day of the blow. It was a crunching ride for the crews. Mountainous seas had built up and were taking a toll of men and boats; men because they were tired from not being able to sleep in the bucking yachts, boats because the pounding was searching out every little weakness. Spar damage and failure, gear breakage, and even a hull fracture were recorded, but through the storm, the Swan 48 *Noryema VIII,* skippered by Teddy Hicks, forged a clear path to Bermuda. Hicks had been Ron Amey's navigator for years, and in the owner's absence picked his course with even greater care than usual. He found the favorable meander of the Gulf Stream out to the east of the rhumb line and was on the right side of the shift when the gale struck. Even so, *Noryema* had to have two attempts to cross the finishing line because of bad visibility, yet she won, the first time a foreign boat had won the Bermuda Race in its long history.

Despite *Noryema VIII's* win, Britain could not stop the United States from winning the Onion Patch Trophy once again. Damage to the standing rigging of Sir Max Aitken's *Crusade*

forced her to heave to for eight hours, as she was unable to be sailed at all on port tack.

Had one been aboard David Powell's and Richard Martin's 48-foot S&S *Oyster* for the 1974 Bermuda Race, one might question why most of the fleet was reefed for much of the race in 20- to 30-knot southwesterlies. Like *Marionette* and *Noryema IX, Oyster* misread the Stream and headed down the rhumb line instead of going west and taking advantage of the Stream. The British team was, until then, dominating the points in the Onion Patch Trophy, although the 55-foot Frers-designed *Scaramouche* of Chuck Kirsch was top individual boat by the expedient of winning all three races. The Bermuda Race saw the British fall from grace in a big way — among the 167 starters, *Noryema IX* was 119, *Oyster* 137, and *Marionette* 143 — a salutary lesson to anyone who ignores the Gulf Stream. *Scaramouche* added to her earlier glories by winning the Bermuda Race, while Huey Long's new Britton Chance-designed 79-foot centerboard two-sticker smashed the race record with a time of 2 days, 19 hours, 52 minutes, 22 seconds.

Since then, the Onion Patch has lost much of its charm as a series; more international flavor is to be found at the SORC, and the choice of this latter event as one in the series for the Mumm World Cup has probably tolled the knell on the

Onion Patch, unless something is done to revive it. But to do so will need the old bone of contention to be sorted – that of which handicap system the CCA intends to use for the Bermuda Race. It has consistently flirted with alternative systems to the internationally favored International Offshore Rule (IOR), and this has doubtless reduced the foreign entry.

By 1974, the foment over the IOR had reached a peak, and with the backing of one of the "fathers" of the IOR, Olin Stephens, and the CCA, the Club's Commodore, Irving Pratt, set about raising funds to support a professor of naval architecture at Massachusetts Institute of Technology, who proposed a new handicapping system based more on speed prediction data. It took three years and $300,000 before the Measurement Handicap System (MHS) was complete – in time for the 1978 Bermuda Race.

Then there were only five machines capable of measuring yachts for MHS ratings–an electronic system which reproduced the hull shape on a computer printout and was able to give speed predictions on all points of sailing in all conditions. As a sop to the "cruising" element of the CCA, there were ancillary requirements which were intended to ensure that there were comforts suitable and proper for a cruising boat.

Since there were not enough machines available to measure the entire fleet in time, the competitors were offered the choice of racing under MHS or IOR–the top prize, however, going to the IOR winner. In any event, the race was won by a 40-foot yawl, twenty-three years old, and the promoters of the MHS were delighted. The yacht Babe was well sailed by her owner, Arnold Gay, who commented of his win: "We have set yacht design back thirty years"– not Gay perhaps, but the MHS. Second was a sister ship of Babe's, owned and skippered by the 1954 race winner, Dan Strohmeier. He offered the CCA Establishment comment: "With the MHS, I think we have recovered some of the spirit of the earlier Bermudas." He went on: "One could feel that the winner might be any yacht milling around the starting line." All of which is very well for a second-grade event, but not for a premier international race.

The CCA compounded its felony by announcing that the 1980 race would be held under the MHS only. What followed could be seen either to uphold the decision (if you are of the CCA ilk) or to display it as ridiculous (if you are an IOR supporter). The view of the IOR protagonists was put by two of the CCA's senior members, Pat Haggerty and Rod Stephens. They used the Club's newsletter to deplore the elimination of the IOR, Haggerty pointing out that there were more than 10,000 yachts with IOR certificates around the world. The outcry

opposite page: *Plenty of deck action at the start of the 1982 Bermuda Race.*

was sufficient for the Royal Bermuda Yacht Club, the co-sponsor of the race, to ask for an IOR division. The compromise reached was laughable. An IOR division was allowed with its own trophies as long as all the boats taking part in it were also measured for MHS!

What went hard against the IOR supporters was the disaster in the Fastnet Race of 1979 when five yachts sank, over forty were capsized, and fifteen lives were lost – all from IOR boats racing. It was a great lever for the CCA, anti-IOR lobby, which saw the IOR boats guilty of every sin of which they had believed them capable. The RORC's report of its inquiry did nothing to restrain their prejudices.

The winner of the 1980 race was the 40-foot ketch *Holger Danske,* the total antithesis of a modern ocean-racing yacht. She was sixteen years old and looked every bit a cruising boat. Her skipper, Richard Wilson, sailed her hard but would be among the first to admit his surprise at having won; a win that Donald Graul, writing in the magazine *Yachting,* said was helped by "a gift of perhaps 25 percent more time allowance than she would have had if the computations had been based on actual conditions encountered during the race." One of the much acclaimed virtues of the MHS, according to its protagonists, is its ability to include factors of wind speed and direction when calculating the predicted speed of a boat in a race. The predicted winds for the 1980 Bermuda Race, those used in the MHS calculations, were for head winds for much of the way. As it happened, it was a reach for most of the race, and the ketch configuration of *Holger Danske* was able to obtain extra benefit from the free-sail area of her mizzen sails.

By the time the race was held in 1982, in two divisions and after two delays because of a forecast storm, the matter was far from resolved, but an overall winner of the two divisions would be named. It would be the yacht which had the greatest margin of win, by time, in its division.

It was a fast race. The 81-foot *Nirvana* of Marvin Green, a design by Dave Pedrick, smashed the 1974 race record of *Ondine* by over 5 hours, yet she was only second in class and eighth in the IOR fleet. The winner in that division was the twelve-year-old *Carina* of Richard B. Nye, twice before winner of this race. It remained to be seen whether he could match Carleton Mitchell's record of three Bermuda Race wins, for Nye had to find out what the margins were in the MHS fleet. He had won his division by 16 minutes from Mike Swerdlow's *Aries.*

The MHS winner was Robert Morton's 57-foot *Brigadoon III,* a classic S&S design of 1968. Second was the Commodore of the New York Yacht Club, Robert Stone (to achieve great respect a year later for his handling of the handover of the America's Cup to the Royal Perth Yacht Club); his 61-foot *Arcadia* was 51 minutes behind *Brigadoon III.* That difference made Morton the overall winner of the Bermuda Race with *Brigadoon III.*

Until the next race, the controversy will continue. And it is unlikely to stop then. What the CCA has to decide is whether it wants the Bermuda Race to be a domestic affair or whether it wishes to see it take its rightful place again in the international racing calendar. Until the dual handicap status is resolved, the race is condemned to total domesticity.

John Ambrose's Frers-designed 46-foot Morning Star, *one of the 1982 United States Onion Patch team.*

Sydney-Hobart Race and the Southern Cross Cup

previous page: Hitchhiker *in the 1981 Southern Cross Cup – the Frers 41-footer went on to represent Australia in the Admiral's Cup and win the Two-Ton Cup in Sardinia.*

At the start in 1967, Rainbow II (C96), Chris Bouzaid's winner of the race.

It is easy to see why the Sydney–Hobart Race and its associated Southern Cross Cup series have achieved their enormous popularity; December in Sydney provides the key. The 630-mile "classic" is the only major ocean race which is held in the easterly trade wind belt and which finishes in the Roaring Forties. Now it has the addition of the maxi-raters' South Pacific Championship to complete a festival of ocean racing at Christmastime.

It all began with a chance remark from Captain John Illingworth, RN, stationed in Sydney in 1945. He was one of the first yachtsmen to speak to the membership of the recently formed Cruising Yacht Club of Australia, his reputation as an ocean racer having preceded him. At the end of his talk, he was chatting with one of the Club's founders, Peter Luke, and the conversation, according to the 1958 program of the fourteenth Sydney–Hobart Race, went as follows:

Luke: "Walker, Earl, and I are going to cruise down to Hobart. Why don't you come along?"
Illingworth: "Why don't we have a race?"
Luke: "OK, we'll make it a race."

There was very little time to organize the race, but in those heady, immediately postwar days, there was tremendous enthusiasm to overcome the problems. The Royal Yacht Club of Tasmania was recruited to help with the organization, a relationship which continues today; the RORC rating rule was adopted (as much as anything because there was no other readily available at the time, and perhaps because Illingworth had been heavily responsible for its formulation); and nine yachts entered for the race.

Those nine yachts were almost all heavy-displacement boats with bowsprits, quite unlike the racing boats of today. *Rani*, Illingworth's boat, was slightly different, and she was to be a constant reference point for Illingworth for the rest of his life. *Rani* was a short-overhang, double-ended, light-displacement 35-footer. She was designed by A. C. Barber in Sydney and built by the Steel Brothers of Lake Macquarie in New South Wales. Illingworth had an obsession about unnecessary weight in boats, and the stories of him insisting that his crews empty their pockets of small change before going on board for a race are now legend.

Boxing Day (December 26) seemed as good a time to start this race as any, and at eleven o'clock, the nine yachts set out for Hobart. Two

above left: *Arthur Slater's 45-foot* Prospect of Whitby *chases Syd Fischer's 48-foot* Ragamuffin *in the third race of the 1971 Southern Cross Cup.*

above: *Prime Minister Edward Heath's second* Morning Cloud *in the third race of the 1971 Southern Cross Cup.*

left: *Ted Turner's converted 12-Metre* American Eagle *leads Jim Kilroy's* Kialoa II *in the third Southern Cross Cup Race of 1971, when* American Eagle *led home by 18 seconds. In the Hobart race* Kialoa *was first home.*

far right: *Quailo III, one of the winning British team in the Southern Cross Cup of 1973, off Sydney Heads.*

right: *Johnson Wooderson at the wheel and John Hollamby in the cockpit of* Yeoman XXI, *being chased by* Ragamuffin *at the finish of the 1979 Hobart race.*

below: *Start of the 1979 Sydney–Hobart Race.*

days later, they had been scattered by a southwesterly gale, but still eight of them were to reach Hobart. The exception was the 52-foot ketch *Archina,* owned by Peter Goldstein, who might have preferred it had he been just cruising. He put the yacht into Jervis Bay after being hove to for 38 hours, and telephoned his family to tell them that the seas were the worst ever seen by most of the crew, that they were violently ill from the pounding of the seas, but that the yacht was undamaged and would sail to Sydney.

The "cavalry charge" to the mark off the South Head at the start of the 1981 Sydney–Hobart Race.

right: *The rhumb line course of the Sydney–Hobart Race – it often pays to be east of this line across the Bass Strait.*

Life was not all fun on board *Saltair,* owned by Richard Walker, which ran for shelter off Narooma, behind Montagu Island. Once there, the crew seemed determined to make up for their earlier privation and spent a day ashore, where they shot several rabbits, which were subsequently eaten. Out at sea, others were roughing it. Richard Bartlett's ketch *Horizon* was hove to for 24 hours with the hatches closed, Peter Luke's *Wayfarer* lost her mainsail and jib, while Illingworth soldiered on with *Rani's* mainsail torn and a jib blown out. Contrary to what everyone believed at the time, Illingworth never went far offshore, at the most 20 miles, all the way down the Australian coast, and he made his landfall on the northeast coast of Tasmania at Cape Forestier, right where he had planned to do so when he began.

There was some public concern for the yachts at sea, and a Royal Australian Air Force Liberator aircraft flew a sortie and spotted all but

two: *Rani* and *Horizon*. *Horizon* was not sighted until she was 50 miles off the Tasmanian coast, while *Rani* was not seen until the fifth day, when she was becalmed off Tasman Island, just 41 miles from the finish.

On December 30, a reporter flew in an amphibian Catalina and wrote of the fleet the next day in his newspaper: "The yachts were shipshape and appeared to have withstood the buffeting well. Their sails and paintwork glistened in the sun as they gracefully rode the moderating seas."

The wind did return for *Rani,* and she came across Storm Bay through the mist and heavy squalls to finish off Battery Point at 1:22 A.M. on January 2. Even at that time of the day, there were at least 300 people lining the Castray Esplanade to cheer *Rani* and her crew as the gun signaled her crossing the line. At 35 feet, *Rani* was the second smallest yacht in the fleet.

It had been expected that Percy Coverdale's *Winston Churchill* would be first into Hobart, and Illingworth wrote later of his surprise when coming up the Derwent: "A launch full of chaps came down the river to identify us and gave us a very hearty cheer. I hailed back and asked them how many boats were in ahead of us, which was greeted with more cheers and laughter. I could feel a sort of inaudible groan from the crew, as repeated inquiries only brought more laughter. We did not realise that they in the launch thought that they were having their legs quietly pulled, and it took us some moments to find out the truth – that we were the first home."

Peter Luke was last home with *Wayfarer;* she finished at 5:21 in the afternoon of January 6 (in modern times, most of the boats would have left to cruise home well before that, and only after some hefty celebrations in port). Luke told of "gales every second day" and of "when it

The ferro-cement 73-foot Helsal, *first to finish in the 1983 Hobart race, accompanied by spectator boats up the Derwent. She broke the race record, a remarkable performance by a yacht constructed in this material, the only yacht so built to perform well in racing.*

89

top: *On board* Condor of Bermuda *on the 1979 race to Hobart.*

above: *Lou Abrahams'* Challenge, *a 46-foot S&S design, was new for the Southern Cross Cup in 1979 – it took her until 1983 to win the Hobart race.*

opposite page: Police Car *leads* Southern Raider *in the 1981 Southern Cross Cup second inshore race.*

wasn't blowing a gale, it was almost flat calm."

That first race was an undoubted success, so much so that a year later there were twice as many starters, six of them from Tasmania. If the competitors in the first race had thought that they had been through a tough one, those that went the second time knew differently. This time, the storm hit when the yachts were in the Bass Strait. The sailing master on Frank and John Livingstone's *Kurrewa III*, Jim Rattenbury, a man who had spent his life at sea, said that it was the worst he had experienced in sixty years. Boats were driven up to 100 miles off course, and it is interesting to note that the last to finish of the eleven who did was Peter Luke with *Wayfarer.* There were, however, eight retirements. The 65-foot Fife-designed *Morna* was first to finish, as she was in the following two races. Owned by Sir Claud Plowman, *Morna* set a new record for the

course in 1948 of 4 days, 5 hours, 1 minute, 21 seconds, which stood for three years. The same boat, sold to the Livingstone brothers and renamed *Kurrewa IV,* was line-honors winner again in 1954, 1956, 1957, and 1960 – a record that will probably never be beaten.

The early races were undistinguished, except to those who took part, but they did mark the emergence of the Australians in the sport of ocean racing. Always inventive and willing to "give it a try," they quickly made inroads on the accepted norm and shortly were to enter the field of international racing. It was to be a long time before a foreign entry was again to win the Sydney-Hobart. One of those who took part in the first race, as a crewman on *Winston Churchill,* was Alan Payne, then a young naval architect, and it was one of his designs, an experimental light-displacement boat, *Nocturne,* that was to make an impressive showing in the 1952 race, although whether the impression was greatest on its crew or rivals has never been agreed.

Nocturne was designed for Sydney Harbor and occasional weekending up the coast, not for the rigors of a Hobart race. She was so light that she bounced from wave to wave and leaked a great deal. It was said that her owner, Bob Bull, spent time up in the bows trying to caulk the seams of the hull with the ball of wool that he had brought along for stopping the spinnaker. It was generally agreed on board that any way of stopping the water flow was worth a try. *Nocturne,* a 35-footer, beat many larger boats to Hobart and was placed third on corrected time, the old RORC rating formula heavily penalizing her light displacement. She did point a way, but Payne did not go down it again, reckoning that strength was much more important. To obtain strength, then, needed much heavier scantlings and therefore greater displacement.

The number of entrants remained around twenty for several years, and when it rose to twenty-eight starters in 1956, the year that Vic Meyer's 57-foot steel cutter *Solo* won on corrected time for the first time, the three gales of the race put some fear back into the event, so that the following year there were only twenty starters again. *Solo* won again in 1962, beating Huey Long's line-honors-winning *Ondine* by 39 minutes after the handicaps had been computed. But this race will always be remembered for the line-honors battle between *Ondine* and Peter Warner's 73-foot Fife-designed schooner *Astor.* They finished yards apart, with exactly 1 minute separating them. It was to be many years before there was another finish quite as exciting as that.

The next three years belong to the Halvorsen brothers, Trygve and Magnus. They had won the race before, in 1957 with *Anitra V,* when they arrived in Constitution Dock with the crew clean shaven and dressed in uniform

above: *Start of the 1981 Sydney–Hobart Race.*

right: Condor of Bermuda, *Bob Bell's 79-foot Sharp design, outside the Heads shortly after the start of the 1981 Hobart race.*

sweaters; it marked a new departure in elegance for the ocean-racing crews of Australia. That win, however, was only a prelude to the Halvorsens' domination of the Sydney–Hobart Race in the early 1960s. To win the race, with the same boat, three years in a row is inconceivable now, and it was only just possible then.

The Halvorsens' triple win was due to their total appreciation of ocean racing. They thoroughly prepared their boat for the Hobart race and sailed it as hard as they could. Joe Pearce, a sailmaker with the Hood loft in Sydney, did his first Hobart race on *Freya* in 1965 and after they had docked he said: "We made 48 sail changes during the race. It was a matter of getting the perfect combination. Although at times we had a headsail up for as long as four hours, the tension of the cloth in the sail could have been altered as often as every five minutes." It must be remembered that these were the days before headsail-luff grooves, when sails had to be hanked on and off a single stay with the consequent loss that meant. Then decisions had to be more certain than they are today as the effect of a mistake was felt longer. It was in the days, too, when few enough people understood what altering the cloth tension of a sail would do to its shape. Joe Pearce was not there just for the ride; the Halvorsens knew his value. Pearce, however, was to say of them: "I think their secret is that they can apply their experience in just the right places at just the right times."

That 1965 race marked the end of an era. The Halvorsen brothers stayed aboard *Freya* all day the next day, and when they emerged as 1966 began, they said that *Freya* would be put up for sale, as Trygve was heavily involved with the 12-Metre *Gretel* and the 1967 challenge for the America's Cup. That glorious era of the designer-builder-sailor brothers was over. Magnus was to win the Hobart race once more, aboard *Love & War* in 1974, and has gone on to compete in thirty of them.

It was in 1965 that Australia made its first challenge for the Admiral's Cup, and the effect was to be quite dramatic. No one gave the Australians a chance at Cowes, but they came so close to winning that their performance was something of an embarrassment in Britain. It also demonstrated the technical developments that were going on elsewhere in the world in a very practical manner, which Australian sailors were not slow to comprehend. Putting their own sailing expertise together with the new technology made them a very powerful force indeed.

The size of the fleet had begun to grow; there were more than fifty starters for the first time in 1965, and there was no doubt that the standard of competition was increasing at an even faster rate. By 1967, there was an added stimulus to international competition in the Sydney–Hobart. The Australian team had that year won the Admiral's Cup, and it was decided

Bernard Lewis' Vengeance *was first to finish in the 1981 race to Hobart but only thirty-third on corrected time.*

93

above: John Bertrand steering Alan Bond's Apollo V *– a member of the Australian team in 1981.*

opposite page: Jack Rooklyn's Lexcen-designed Apollo, *affectionately known by her crews as "The Green Gherkin."*

to run a similar event in Australian waters, the Southern Cross Cup. At first, the only overseas entries for the Cup were from New Zealand taking on the State teams. Just to rub salt into the wounds, it was Chris Bouzaid's One-Tonner *Rainbow II,* a Sparkman & Stephens design, which scooped the pool in the Hobart race, helping his side to a Southern Cross Cup win.

There was also European acknowledgment of the importance of the Southern Hemisphere "classic" with the appearance of Eric Tabarly's schooner *Pen Duick III,* which had won the Fastnet Race earlier in the year. The 57-foot schooner, with which Tabarly had exploited the RORC rule by gaining huge free-sail area with the wishbone foresail, was first to finish, but suffered from light airs in the later stages of the race, while the smaller boats had fresh north-westerlies down the Tasmanian coast and up the Derwent. *Rainbow II* finished nearly 16 hours behind *Pen Duick III,* but it was enough for the Kiwi One-Tonner to win by close to 1 hour on corrected time.

Sad to relate, a dock strike stopped the British team of three boats entering this first Southern Cross Cup. The same strike also stopped two of the triumphant Australian team from leaving Britain in time to take part in the Hobart race. And while they may have missed out because of a technicality, one other team made the Cup races by means of another

technicality, which has since been closed. The Australian Capital Territory, whose only sailing water is Lake Burley Griffin, a man-made area suitable for dinghies and small keelboats, entered a team. It did well enough to finish fourth of the six teams, beating Queensland and Victoria. Maybe it was the sailors from Brisbane and Melbourne who shut the gate on their fellows from the bush.

The following year, the Australians were keen to defend the Admiral's Cup, and the Hobart race was the final trial race for that team. The year brought a new force to Australian ocean racing, one which was to remain there for many years to come: Syd Fischer. He had two previous Hobart races under his belt with his boat *Malohi,* but it was with his commissioning the 48-foot Sparkman & Stephens-designed *Ragamuffin* from Cec Quilkey that Fischer was to make his mark.

Ragamuffin never did win a Sydney–Hobart Race, since Fischer never got the necessary breaks, but she did place consistently highly for the next six years and was a truly international force in the ocean-racing scene. In her first year, *Ragamuffin* came up against Dennis O'Neill's *Koomooloo,* a 41-footer designed by Ted Kaufman as a development of his own *Mercedes III,* and also built by Cec Quilkey, and it was to be *Koomooloo's* turn to win the Sydney–Hobart Race.

Helsal IV, Apollo, *and* Condor of Bermuda *lead the Hobart fleet out of Sydney Harbor on December 26, 1981.*

It was a year when it blew hard for much of the race. A fresh southwesterly on the second night increased to Force 9 as the fleet crossed the Bass Strait (it would appear to be a regular feature of the Hobart race to have a strong blow in the strait), but then there were calms around Tasman Island and in the Derwent (again regular Hobart race features). *Koomooloo* did everything right, winning by over 1 hour on corrected time. She joined *Ragamuffin* and *Mercedes III* in the Australian Admiral's Cup team; they were not to be successful, but their performance did ensure a full British team to the Southern Cross Cup the following December.

That team was led by Sir Max Aitken with the 62-foot Alan Gurney-designed *Crusade*. The 41-foot S&S *Prospect of Whitby* of Arthur Slater and the stock S&S 34 *Morning After,* owned by Rodney Hill, completed the British team. That is

except for the remarkable reserve. This was another stock S&S 34, the first of Ted Heath's *Morning Clouds,* which was a private entry for the Sydney–Hobart Race.

Ragamuffin totally dominated the first three Southern Cross Cup races, winning each of them on corrected time. She was a member of the New South Wales team. At the time, there was no Australian team as such, but the New South Wales team might just as well have been. Contemporary newspapers referred to it as Australia winning the Cup. The first race was abandoned following a protest from Rodney Hill that *Morning After* had been damaged by another boat and that it was no fault of *Morning After.* By the end of the first three races of the series, the New South Wales team had a handsome lead.

The year 1969, as almost everybody who

doing exactly what the only other Englishman to win this race, John Illingworth, had recommended: go well offshore and ignore the weather forecasts. Heath went well out to obtain the maximum benefit of the "Southerly Set," the ephemeral current which can help a boat to get to Hobart quickly. Heath had found that there were two ways of finding the current other than knowing it was beyond the 100-fathom line: the temperature of the sea would rise from 69°F. to 72°F., and there would be an increase in the incidence of the small blue jellyfish known as bluebottles. It is, however, of some doubt that going 60 miles offshore helped *Morning Cloud* in any way with a more favorable current than the rest; Heath said after the race that the temperature of the sea never rose much above 70°F., and that they did not see too many of the jellyfish. What going out there did was to give *Morning Cloud* longer in the favorable northerlies than most of the fleet and a good slant in to the Tasmanian coast when she made a landfall.

Morning Cloud had run with a spinnaker for 67 hours, sometimes planing over the long waves. On the morning of the fourth day, the wind fell away to nothing and then later filled in from the southeast, veering later to the south and blowing with full Antarctic-gale intensity. It was cold and wet, but *"Cloud"* made a landfall at the point of the Freycinet Peninsula and began a beat down the coast to Tasman Island, some 60 miles away.

At this time, three o'clock in the morning, the two leaders were sailing up the Derwent to cross the finishing line. Once in the dock, the party began, and not a little one at that, despite the hour of the morning.

The *Morning Cloud* crew was pleased with its landfall, but no one expected to hear just how well the boat was doing from a radio news broadcast the following day. As navigator Anthony Churchill was monitoring a local bulletin, he heard that if *Morning Cloud* could be in just before six o'clock that evening, she could be the overall race winner. At the time, the 34-footer was scooting across Storm Bay with a fair breeze. As they entered the Derwent, the breeze began to fail; and as they were in the last 2 miles, there was every threat that the wind would die away completely as they ghosted towards the finishing line under floater spinnaker.

When they were 150 yards from the line, skipper Heath had to call for a gybe to get inside the buoy at the outer end. Moments later, at three minutes to five, the gun fired to announce *Morning Cloud's* finish, and with it began a cacophony of car and boat horns and cheering. The twenty-fifth Hobart race had been won, like the first, by an Englishman, this time from a record seventy-nine-boat fleet.

has sailed has cause to remember, was the year in which Ted Heath won the twenty-fifth Sydney–Hobart Race. He won it in style and brought the city of Hobart into the international limelight for a couple of days.

As Heath and his crew loaded stores aboard *Morning Cloud* for the "classic," there was even greater activity aboard a boat moored at a nearby slip at the Cruising Yacht Club dock. Alan Bond's recently built 57-foot Bob Miller-designed (later to become Ben Lexcen-designed) *Apollo* was being completed by a small army of carpenters and joiners. They were finishing the furniture below, while on deck some of the crew were worried that they had not yet hoisted a spinnaker on the boat. Yet *Apollo's* line-honors battle with *Crusade* was one of this race's features. It went to *Crusade,* by 19 minutes.

Heath on *Morning Cloud* won the race by

It was a smaller fleet the following year, but there was a season-long needle match going on between *Ragamuffin* and her near sister ship, *Salacia II.* Arthur Byrne decided that he would take every advantage possible from the newly formulated International Offshore Rule and commissioned Sparkman & Stephens to design him a boat to the new rating parameters, based on *Ragamuffin*. One would not say that Syd Fischer was entirely delighted, but he accepted the challenge; the season leading up to the 1970 Hobart race was enlivened with the duels between *Ragamuffin* and *Salacia II,* duels that continued through the Admiral's Cup trials and on to the 630-mile slog to Hobart.

Neither of them was to win. That went to Bob Chrighton-Brown's big Camper & Nicholson ketch *Pacha,* in what was generally accepted as a big-boat race with moderate to fresh northeasterly winds for two days followed by a southwesterly gale. "*Rags*" and *Salacia II* fought out their own battle, and it was resolved in *Ragamuffin's* favor. She took second place, while *Salacia II* was third. Both made it into the Admiral's Cup team with *Koomooloo,* now owned by Norman Rydge.

Three months after that heavy-weather Hobart race, the New Zealanders held the One-Ton Cup, with a full-out defense planned on the trophy which Chris Bouzaid had won in Heligoland. The Kiwis were foiled though by a last-minute entry from Syd Fischer, who won with *Stormy Petrel*. The defeat acted as a goad in the side of the Kiwis, who put a huge effort into the Southern Cross Cup. They set the world talking after the controversy they began by setting light genoas flying free outside the spinnaker sheets – the first time the "big boy" had been seen.

The controversy began in the third race of the Southern Cross Cup series, for the Middle Harbor Yacht Club Cup. *Wai-Aniwa,* Ray Walker's One-Tonner with Chris Bouzaid as skipper, was running square to the finish inside Sydney Harbor when Bouzaid called for the drifter to be set to leeward of the spinnaker and its sheets. Members of the British team argued that they had been prevented from using a similar maneuver at home, but found that the only way to challenge the legality of this practice was to protest. With a certain reluctance, Sammy Sampson, the skipper of *Morning Cloud* in Heath's absence, lodged a protest alleging that *Wai-Aniwa's* action infringed IOR rule 860D, in that a headsail was set to fly kitelike over the spinnaker, that the headsail was set upside down, tacked on the centerline at the bow with the luff outside the spinnaker. It was also claimed that the halyard was slacked so that the head was 6 feet from the forestay and that it was sheeted to the end of the main boom.

It took a New South Wales Yachting Association protest committee two sessions, totaling nearly four hours, to dismiss the protest. It found that the sail was not upside down; the spinnaker was sheeted outside the forestay and inside the headsail, which was set as a spinnaker staysail. The tack of this headsail was in its

opposite page: Action for the crews as spinnakers are doused at the South Head turning mark.

below: The windward start of the 1981 Hobart race.

previous page: Pacific Sundance, *the Bruce Farr 40-foot design skippered jointly by Geoff Stagg and Peter Walker, which totally dominated the 1983 Southern Cross Cup racing and led the New Zealand team to victory.*

normal position, and it was sheeted legally to the end of the boom. It was hoisted to about 3 feet from the halyard sheave on the mast, and the sag was around 4 feet. The committee found that these facts did not make the headsail to be flown kitelike, and thus it did not contravene rule 860D. Chris Bouzaid's invention, the big boy, the blooper, call it what you will, was here to stay.

Until the Sydney–Hobart Race, the Southern Cross Cup had been a very close affair. The British team was that which had won the

Bradley's Head, and was disqualified. The scoreline after three races put Britain in the lead with 200, while New South Wales had 197 and the Kiwis, 196.

In the early stages of the Sydney–Hobart Race, with its record-equaling seventy-nine-boat fleet, the British team looked well set to win, but such are the vagaries of the wind along the Tasmanian coast that their hopes were washed out as they lay in near calm off Freycinet Peninsula while the three New Zealand One-

above: *Graham Walker's* Indulgence, *the best of a mediocre British team in 1983.*

Admiral's Cup and was all out to make it a double in 1971. Bob Watson's 41-foot S&S *Cervantes IV* won the first race, a 180-miler, from *Ragamuffin,* but the Kiwis announced their intention of a fight with *Wai-Aniwa* and *Pathfinder* fourth and fifth. Their three One-Tonners gave greater notice in the next race, a 30-miler, when *Pathfinder* won by 12 seconds from *Ragamuffin,* and *Wai-Aniwa* and *Runaway* were third and fourth. In the third race, *Wai-Aniwa* survived the protest to win by 6 seconds from *Prospect of Whitby,* while *Runaway* was third. Kiwi hopes were somewhat dashed when *Pathfinder* had to start her engine to get off a reef where she had grounded, close to

Tonners ran up to them in a freshening northwesterly breeze. Once with the wind up their tails, the Kiwis used all their skills to compound their luck, and the final result of *Pathfinder* first, *Runaway* second, and *Wai-Aniwa* third does indeed endorse their efforts. Naturally enough, with points counting triple for the long race, the Kiwis took the Southern Cross Cup.

The three One-Tonners took the shine off the front-runners race. Huey Long's *Ondine,* Jim Kilroy's *Kialoa,* and Ted Turner's *American Eagle* were the American team and with Tom Clark's *Buccaneer* were having a great race. *Kialoa* got the drop on the others and finished

2 hours, 45 minutes ahead of *Buccaneer. Ondine* was 5 minutes behind her and *American Eagle* finished 17 minutes behind her.

The following year's race was all Ted Turner's and *American Eagle's.* The Atlantan had left the boat for a year in Sydney and ordered her to be sold. Failing the sale, he ordered her commissioning for the Sydney–Hobart Race. Turner was at his best, taking a wager for a crew dinner with Alan Bond on corrected time placings of *American Eagle* and *Apollo II.* At the time, *Apollo II* and her sister ship *Ginkgo,* owned by Gary Bogard, were cleaning up the trophies inshore and offshore. The two Miller designs were benefiting from their closeness to tune to a greater level than had been possible for 46-footers before, so that Turner's bet had a great deal of braggadocio about it.

It was decided that the race should start an hour later than the usual eleven o'clock because the adoption of daylight-saving time had altered the time of the onset of the sea breeze. Turner reveled in the crowded conditions of the start. Once again, seventy-nine boats answered the gun, and Turner had no compunction in going in among the spectator craft which crowded the harbor on his way out to the Heads.

Everyone had expected that the race would be one between *Ginkgo* and *Apollo,* with *Ragamuffin* waiting for either, or both, to make a mistake. They had made their calculations without taking into consideration the age allowance, later criticized by some of the new boat owners, which the CYCA had introduced that year. That year, *American Eagle* and the second-place *Caprice of Huon* both benefited from this allowance.

The fleet had a spinnaker reach down to Twofold Bay when the wind went southerly and freshened with a shift to the southwest. It gave a fast reach down the Tasmanian coast until the wind backed and blew up to 50 knots. That lasted for some time, but as the leaders headed up the Derwent, they were faced with the on-off situation which is so familiar there. Turner called for seven sail changes in 25 minutes as *American Eagle* neared the line. She claimed line honors, and Turner sat back to wait. Could he hold out and win the double, which had so far gone only to the original race winner *Rani*? Meantime, his wager was being settled. *American Eagle* had finished at a quarter to five in the afternoon; *Ginkgo* and *Apollo II* were in the river eight hours later and fought out a toe-to-toe battle all the way to the line, where *Ginkgo* was just 47 seconds ahead after 630 miles of racing.

The old Wrest Point Hotel will never forget the night that Turner collected his bet from Bond. Some of the *American Eagle* crew had invited a few of their friends "as Bondy's paying" just to swell the numbers. It looked as though all the finishers were there, but the yachties' party was on one side of the room while the regular Saturday evening dinner dance went on at the other – at least for a while until Billy Adams lifted a champagne bottle, shook it vigorously, and sprayed everyone in the room – on both sides. Then everybody had to join in or leave. Most joined in.

There were more joining in the next Sydney–Hobart Race in 1973, another year of the Southern Cross Cup; ninety-two made it to the line. It was a year marked by an all-out attempt on

The Frumious Bandersnatch – *one of the highly competitive Hong Kong team.*

the Cup by the Kiwis in boats of Admiral's Cup size. New Zealand had announced that it would challenge in Britain in 1975, and this was regarded as a major step in that direction, particularly as Britain had sent a powerful team.

It was a year, too, which saw the appearance of two more Miller sister ships, this time One-Tonners *Ceil III* and *Rampage.* They were very much like smaller versions of *Ginkgo* and *Apollo II. Ceil III* brought with her a team from Hong Kong for the Cup which chartered *Apollo* and an S&S 34, *Aquila.*

The New Zealanders were there early and out at practice each day under their team manager, Alan Sefton. It was practice that was to reap dividends, and they were followed by the British team as soon as they realized what was afoot. The Kiwis had three S&S designs: Brin Wilson's *Quicksilver,* a 41-footer; Evan Julian's 45-foot *Inca;* and Doug Johnstone's 42-foot

Sail plan and general deck arrangement drawing of the Ron Holland-designed 78-foot maxi-rating yacht Sassy.

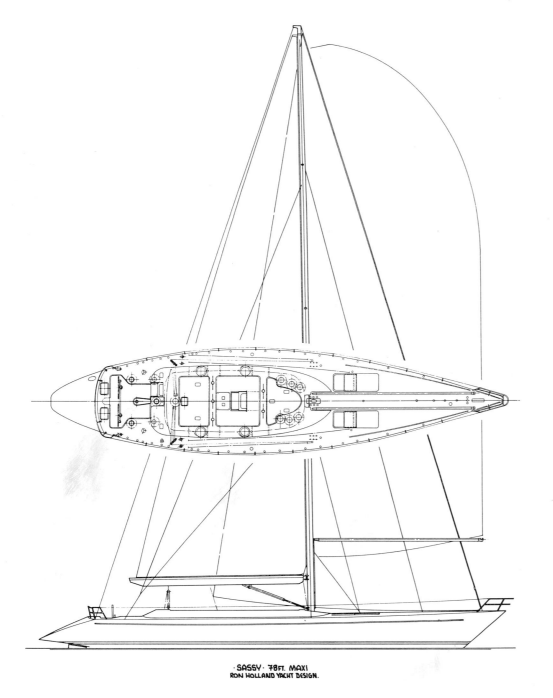

·SASSY· 78 FT. MAXI
RON HOLLAND YACHT DESIGN.

Barnacle Bill. On board were Bouzaid and a wealth of other Kiwi talent.

A first, third, and fifth in the first 27-miler gave the Kiwis a great start, and the British suffered because *Prospect of Whitby* was over the line early and failed to answer her recall. *Apollo* won the 180-miler, breaking her own course record in the process, but the New Zealand boats were second, third, and fifth. The third race of the series was held in a failing wind. The last of the finishers of this 27-miler crossed the line at 1:27 the following morning! *Apollo* won again, but the Kiwis still had the lead. Their 274 points compared with Britain's 217 and Hong Kong's 215.

There was a tragic setback to New Zealand's hopes when a young crew member of *Inca,* twenty-year-old John Sarney, died on the first night of the Sydney–Hobart Race. He had joined *Inca's* crew only as a replacement for another who had injured his knee, and he collapsed when called from his bunk for a sail change. The incident had a depressing effect on the whole New Zealand team, but there was never an excuse offered for being beaten. The British trio got lucky when it was most needed; *Prospect of Whitby* second, *Superstar of Hamble* seventh, and *Quailo III* tenth saw them through to a Southern Cross Cup win.

The race went to *Ceil III,* 2 hours ahead of *"Prospect"* on corrected time, with *Rampage* half an hour behind the British boat in third place in a race which had easterly moderate breezes which backed toward the end of the race and blew up to 45 knots. Yet there were no retirements in 1973.

In a non-Cup year, the fleet was down to sixty-three for 1974, the first time that Peter Kurt's *Love and War* won the race. It was one of moderate easterlies followed on the fourth day by strong northwesterlies: a real test of strength. In the line-honors fight, the latest of Huey Long's *Ondines* beat Jack Rooklyn's *Ballyhoo* by 3 hours, but could not match the record set the previous year by Tony Fisher's 72-foot Joe Adams-designed *Helsal,* a ferro-cement flyer known as the "floating footpath."

Jim Kilroy's S&S 79-foot *Kialoa* was only one of nine boats to better *Helsal's* record in 1975, yet was fifty-fifth on handicap. The weather pattern could not have been more perfect for a fast ride, with southeasterlies giving way to northeasterlies for most of the race, while the tail-enders brought a southerly across Storm Bay and into the finish.

Kialoa's time of 2 days, 14 hours, 36 minutes, 56 seconds stands in 1984, and it will need a very fast boat and a repeat of the ideal conditions for anyone to beat the record. *Kialoa* averaged just over 10 knots for the 630 miles.

Peter Packer's *Rampage,* third two years earlier, took all the advantage of the later stages

of the race to win on corrected time from the diminutive *Fair Dinkum* of Jim Robson-Scott from a fleet of 102.

Ballyhoo got her line-honors win the following year when John Pickles' Farr-designed *Piccolo* took the handicap prize, but *Kialoa* was back again in 1977 to become the third boat to take line honors and handicap prizes. That year, she had a fine tussle with *Windward Passage,* the last they were to have as ketches, in winds which brought about 59 retirements from the record 129-strong fleet.

The following year, *Love and War* did it again, from a fleet of ninety-seven, with *Apollo* taking line honors. In 1979, as the New South Wales team were winning the Southern Cross Cup, the Ron Holland-designed Half-Tonner *Screw Loose* led a rash of tiny boats in the handicap lists. That year, John Kahlbetzer's 77-foot Frers-designed *Bumblebee 4* took line honors from Bob Bell's *Condor of Bermuda,* the

then Fastnet Race record holder. The small-boat benefit was due to light head winds in the latter stages for most of the fleet, while the tail-enders came in with freshening favorable winds. It was much the same two years later when New South Wales retained the Southern Cross Cup, and Bernard Lewis' *Vengeance* took line honors. Then it was *Zeus II* and a bunch of small boats finishing fast that took the top prizes.

The in-between year was one of easterlies in the early stages of the race. They freshened, and it was not until the third night that they and the hopes of a new record faded. Peter Blake with the 68-foot Farr-designed *Ceramco New Zealand* (with the 'Ceramco' missing because of the racing rule preventing advertising) led all the way and became the fourth of the line-honors and handicap winners of the race.

In 1982, it was Ray Johnston's *Scallywag* which took top place in a race that was a fast slide for a couple of days and then went light with

Panda, *the Hugh Welbourn-designed 44-footer, owned by Peter Whipp, which was disqualified in the 1983 Hobart race following a port and starboard incident inside the Heads.*

head winds and then more wind followed by variables. It brought with this changeable weather the closest ever line-honors battle with just 17 seconds separating *Condor of Bermuda* and *Apollo,* otherwise known as "The Green Gherkin."

No one ever expected to see a finish like that again, but 1983's came close to it. Had *Condor* not run aground, the difference between her and Marvin Green's *Nirvana* might have been just as close.

That year of 1983, however, was a Kiwi year. The New Zealand team annihilated all the opposition in the Southern Cross Cup. Once again, the Kiwis fronted with three One-Tonners, this time identical Farr 40-footers to the new One-Ton 30.5-foot rating. It was almost as devastating a performance as they had produced in 1971. Geoff Stagg and Peter Walker jointly skippered Del Hogg's *Pacific Sundance,* and

leader in the big race; Lou Abrahams' *Challenge,* a 46-foot five-year-old Sparkman & Stephens was fifth. *Challenge* "lucked out" across Storm Bay and up the Derwent, carrying her wind all the way to the finish. For the boats astern of her there was no mercy; the fickle breezes returned to glaze the waters and try the patience of the crews. What they also did was put *Challenge* in an unchallengeable first place on corrected time.

Ahead of them, however, the 80-foot *Condor* had rounded Tasman Island 4 minutes ahead of the 81-foot *Nirvana* in a light northeasterly. The gap between them narrowed just after they had rounded the Iron Pot, the lighthouse which marks the entrance to the Derwent. The breeze, too, had begun to fade in a partial announcement of the coming south-easterly thermal wind. Both yachts went well to the east into Opossum Bay, clawing their way up

Pacific Sundance rounding the southernmost cliffs of Tasman Island. At this point she was a clear handicap leader over the fleet but ran into calms in the Derwent.

their results were almost perfect. In the three inshore races, they had a first, a third, and a fourth among the twenty-seven boats in the Southern Cross series. They capped that with a first in the 180-miler and were top boat of the Cup fleet in the Hobart race to take the individual prize for the series.

Some 40 miles from home, as she rounded Tasman Island, *Pacific Sundance* was the overall

the shore to cheat the ebb tide. *Nirvana,* 6 lengths behind *Condor,* went closer to the shore and failed to get the heading puff which the leader suffered. *Nirvana* slipped past inside, and the lead changed hands. Four miles farther on, approaching White Rock, *Condor* handed her genoa for a very light one and picked up speed. Ted Turner at the wheel steered to go between *Nirvana* and the shore. Steve Colgate at the

wheel of *Nirvana* tried to shut the gap but was too late. The cry for water came from *Condor* just before she hit the submerged rocks, and there she stayed for 7 minutes. *Nirvana* sailed away, but again *Condor* came back at her and was only 2 minutes, 16 seconds behind on the line. There was, however, a protest flag on *Condor's* backstay, and at the hearing the next day, *Nirvana* was disqualified. It was the first time the line-honors winner had been disqualified, but the protest committee found from the facts presented to them that *Condor* had made her move to go to windward of *Nirvana* when there was adequate water for her to do so and that *Nirvana* had not responded to the hail in time for *Condor* to avoid grounding. There were those in Hobart who thought the decision could have easily gone the other way.

The incident that slightly marred the great front-runners race of 1983 occurred when Condor *went inside* Nirvana *only to run aground just five miles from the finish.*

China Sea Race

Chris Ostenfeld's La
Pantera, *a Peterson
42-footer, winner of the
1980 China Seas Race.*

A group of expatriate yachtsmen, anywhere in the world, will sooner or later organize racing for themselves. Generally they will not be satisfied with keeping it to themselves or racing against each other all the time, but will arrange a regatta to encourage visitors from elsewhere. From such philosophy originated the China Sea Race and the series it begat. It is also true that there is something compelling about the distance of 600 miles; the Fastnet, Bermuda, and Hobart races are all around that distance, and so is the race from Hong Kong to Manila. The China Sea Race has aspects that other races lack, and has become a serious attraction for yachtsmen from all over the world. The original intention to get competition for the Crown Colony's sailors is working and the number of starters has risen from five in the first race of 1962 to fifty for the 1982 event.

It all began when Sim Baldwin took his 40-foot S&S centerboard yawl *Morasum* to Manila in December 1959 through the heavy seasonal weather. He had tired of the confines of Hong Kong's cruising grounds and wished to prove the seaworthiness of his boat. His cruise a success, he returned with the germ of an idea to race over the same course. His enthusiasm was infectious, and a small committee was formed to organize it. The first China Sea Race was held in April 1962.

It attracted five entries, three of them designed by S&S. As in all expatriate sporting events, the entry list was impressively international with five nations represented. Naturally enough, Sim Baldwin was there with *Morasum,* representing the United States, while *Reverie,* another 40-foot S&S yawl, but with a fixed keel, represented Sweden for her owner Chris von Sydow. Her sister ship, *Griffin,* was owned by Charlie Morton from the Manila Yacht Club, which had also been involved in the organization of the race. Subsequently Commodore of that Club, Paul Caderara, of Switzerland, entered his Robb-designed 37-foot *Tolo* and the fleet was completed by Shintaro Ishihara, a Japanese film producer, with the 37-foot *Contessa II.*

That first race was notable only for the five yachts being becalmed in fog throughout the first night off Waglan. When the breeze came, it took the fleet five days to reach Corregidor Island, but once in Manila the partying began in style. The foundations of the race were well and truly laid and the wise decision was made to hold it every two years.

Reverie won that first race; Hector Ross navigated her to a 1½-hour win over *Morasum.* It seemed as though *Reverie* was going to do it again in 1964. She was first to cross the line, the pre-race line-honors favorite having retired with a broken mast, but David Westerhout's 39-foot *West Wind II* scraped home with enough to spare for a 65-second win on corrected time, the smallest margin in the history of the race. Twelve yachts started that race and only the 62-foot *Aquaries* retired. It is a feature of the race that there are very few retirements; of the 263 boats which have started over the years only twenty-three have retired and there has been but one disqualification.

West Wind II proved that her win was no fluke by winning the next race in 1966; this time *Reverie* was down to third of the thirteen starters. The only retirement that year was the Japanese *Fuji,* which ran out of drinking water 200 miles from Manila. Line honors went to Kees Bruynzeel with *Stormvogel;* a combination that collected ocean races like some people collect stamps.

The 60-foot *Green Beret* established a record in 1968 by being first to finish in the slowest race ever. She took 4 days, 14 hours, 26 minutes for the course, while the race was won by the 35-foot *Snow Goose II* of Chris Moller and Eric Holm. Holm took this boat again in 1970 and

finished sixth of the nineteen starters, all of whom completed the course. Two Japanese boats, the 40-foot *Chita III* and *Epicurean II,* dominated this race with first and second places; *Chita III* managed the line honors and handicap double, and if this were not enough smashed the course record into the bargain.

The record went again in 1972, by 10 hours, 50 minutes. Ron McAulay's Nicholson 55 *Mamamouchi,* with the imported talent of Don Parr and Steve Allinson from *Quailo III* on board, completed the double despite light winds for much of the race. She was more than 8 hours ahead of Bill Turnbull's Swan 36 *Ceil II* on corrected time. She was also first home in 1974, but this time was placed no better than sixth in a very slow race, which Alan Briddon's *Norlin 34* took on corrected time, at the same time winning Class II.

There was another close finish, on corrected time, in 1976. This time the winner's margin was 92 seconds. Jack Rooklyn's 73-foot *Ballyhoo* claimed both line honors and handicap wins in a race that was delayed for 28 hours because of Typhoon Marie. The green-hulled *Ballyhoo* was able to sail through the resultant hole in the wind left by the typhoon and make Manila in time, just in time, to beat John Ma's *White Rabbit II.*

The fuzzy-haired David Bongers could be seen leading the celebrations at the end of the 1978 race. It was little wonder. The South African sailor had been one of Hector Ross' crew of *Uin-na-Mara III,* which had won. It had been a tough race to win, too, with thirty-five starters, including the two American maxis *Kialoa* and *Windward Passage.* Jim Kilroy's 79-foot S&S ketch was first in, breaking the course

record by 2 hours, 52 minutes, but the 42-foot Farr-designed Two-Tonner *Uin-na-Mara III* was an easy winner on corrected time, by nearly 3 hours from Bill Jeffery's *Pak Ling,* a Heritage One-Tonner.

Many of the Hong Kong crews of the 1979 Admiral's Cup and the gale-strewn Fastnet took part in the 1980 race, which was won by Chris Ostenfeld's *La Pantera* from John Ma's *Mile High* in a fleet of thirty-four. *Mile High,* a Peterson 52, was first to finish in a time only 50 minutes longer than that which *Kialoa* had taken in the previous race in 1978; she took 3 days, 12 hours, 35 minutes.

There were fifty starters in 1982, and it was to be the year of the small boats' success. The course record was again shattered, this time by the 65-foot Frers-designed *Mamamouchi II* of Ron McAulay. She knocked 3 hours, 33 minutes off *Kialoa's* best to be home in 3 days, 8 hours, 12 minutes, for a course that had been extended 10 miles farther into Manila Bay. The race went to Rolly Schmitt's Ron Holland-designed One-Tonner *Red Baron,* which was nearly three quarters of an hour ahead of the Holland Two-Tonner *Jelik,* for which Tony Castro had produced altered lines at the end of 1981. Schmitt shipped with him a real hot-shot crew, which included Peter Jolly, who had won aboard *La Pantera* two years before, Kiwi Graeme Woodroffe, and as navigator Don "Motormouth" Tracey, who has drawn the lines across the charts of many winning boats around the world. *Red Baron* was, however, only second in the five-race series that ran in conjunction with the race. Top honors in that series went to the Ed Dubois-designed One-Tonner *Bimblegumbie* of Keith Jacobs.

A spinnaker peel aboard
Highland Fling.

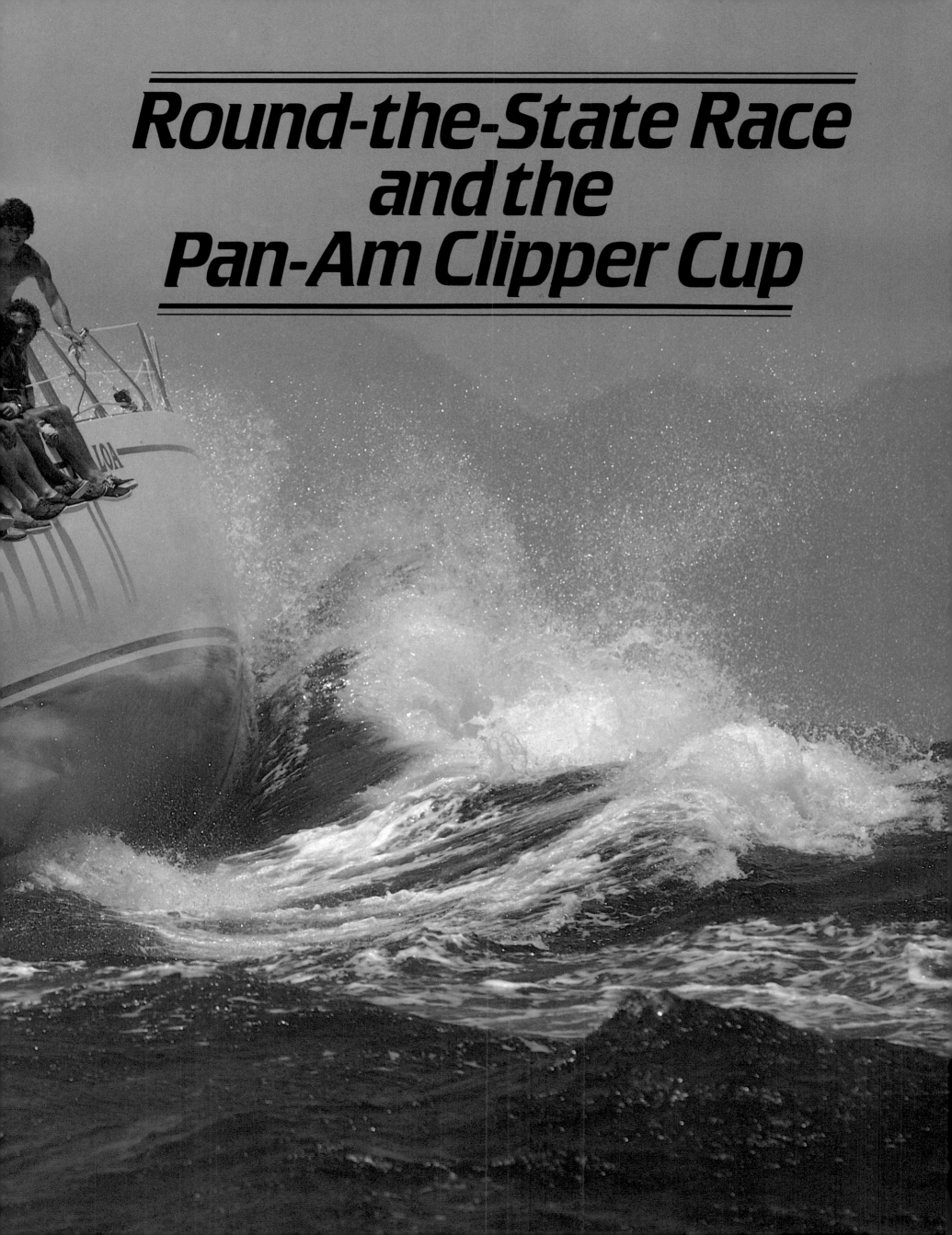

Round-the-State Race and the Pan-Am Clipper Cup

previous page: Kialoa, *the fourth to carry the name for Jim Kilroy, an 80-foot Ron Holland design which broke the Round-the-State Race record in 1982.*

The world's ocean-racing yachtsmen have a great deal for which to thank Dick Gooch. It was he who forced life into the Pan-Am Clipper Cup. Having first encouraged overseas sailors to take part in the Round-the-State Race, he so developed it that he created for them a five-race series which has no equal. Gooch, who lives in Honolulu, persuaded Pan American Airways to become the major sponsor of the event while managing to round up other commercial sponsorships for the series. He did not stop there; he became chairman of the management committee and traveled the world promoting the event and obtaining entries.

Not, of course, that anyone who has sailed the Hawaii series would ever consider allowing anything to prevent him from returning and doing it again and again. Nowhere else in the world are yachts raced in more ideal conditions. The steady and warm northeast trade winds provide the motive power for exciting racing, and they are almost guaranteed to blow in August. But Hawaii is famous for other things, the leis and the "alohas" among them, and there is not a red-blooded "yachtie" who is not amused by the antics of residents of the Stop Light bar.

It is surprising, therefore, that it was 200 years after Captain James Cook had discovered the Hawaiian Islands and the Polynesians for the Western world, before the Clipper Cup series began. Immediately, it promised to become the mecca for yachtsmen in the Pacific. With Gooch's drive and enthusiasm, it will continue to attract entries from all over the world. It is a series designed to test all the skills, with three 30-mile Olympic-course races, a short offshore race, and the 775-mile race around all the islands that form the fiftieth state of the Union. Like all American IOR series, the time-on-distance system of handicapping is used (everywhere else in the world, the time-on-time system prevails),

opposite page: Phantom— *holder of the Round-the-State Race record until 1982.*

below: Kialoa (*Jim Kilroy*) – *the 79-foot Sparkman & Stephens design under her ketch rig.*

which does favor the larger yachts taking part. But since this series has yet to fall into line with the other major series, which form the Champagne Mumm World Cup, and limit the rating band of those competing to 30- to 40-feet IOR rating, it does a lot to encourage the owners of bigger yachts to take part.

If Gooch required any further encouragement to seduce sailors to the Clipper Cup, he need only remind them of the action of one of the crew members of Tom Stephenson's *Magic Pudding* at the inaugural series in 1978. Enthusiastically lightening the boat for the long race, he left all the crew's foul-weather gear ashore. It was not really needed.

The first series, in 1978, drew team entries from Australia (two), New Zealand (two), Japan, and the United States (two). But this series, unlike the Admiral's Cup, is raced with nonteam boats taking part, and there were other visitors, from Tahiti and from the Taipeh Yacht Club in Taiwan. The latter was a Farr Half-Tonner, *Don Quixote,* which won the 100-mile-around-Oahu race. She was owned and skippered by ex-patriate Foo Lim, who had been the manager of the Taiwan team which had been refused entry at the Kingston Olympics in 1976. Foo Lim now lives in Honolulu and campaigns from there.

The series turned out to be dominated by the Antipodeans, with the Australia A team winning from the two New Zealand teams. It was a powerful team led by Syd Fischer's *Ragamuffin,* a Frers-designed 47-footer. *Magic Pudding* was owned by John Karrasch, skippered by Tom Stephenson, and designed by Doug Peterson. A One-Tonner, she was previously known as *B 195.* The third member of the team was Marshall Phillips' *Big Schott,* a Peterson-designed Two-Tonner. Spreading its rating band widely, the Australia A team had the capability to be consistent in all conditions.

The owners of the boats had also gone to some lengths to see that they would be sailed to their maximum potential. *Ragamuffin* had had an only moderate season in Sydney before the Clipper Cup, but in this series, she was well sailed in every race with some highly praised crew work. Star-class gold-medal crew John Anderson was one of those who strengthened *Ragamuffin*'s crew, together with Americans Ben Mitchell and Burke Sawyer. Drawing the lines across the charts on *"Rags"* was Richard "Sightie" Hammond, who had two previous Round-the-State races under his belt, and was probably the most respected ocean-racing navigator in the Southern Hemisphere.

Tom Stephenson had done much to boost the chances of *Magic Pudding.* She was a centerboard One-Tonner in the contemporary fashion. Stephenson had consulted with Doug Peterson about her centerboard, and Peterson had drawn a new, shorter, and squatter board

with a high-lift section for this series, in which heavier winds were expected than those in which *Magic Pudding* normally sailed. Bill Tripp, from the Peterson design office, was one of her crew. So was Ross Guiniven, an Auckland sailmaker, whose fractional-rig knowledge greatly enhanced the rig tune of the boat.

Big Schott, which Marshall Phillips had bought to fill a gap before he had a new boat, was generally reckoned to be a light-weather performer. In the heavy winds which prevailed for the series, however, she hung in with good enough results to support her two teammates to victory and claim third place in her class.

A restructuring of the two New Zealand teams would have seen the Kiwis winning. In the New Zealand A team was the top-scoring boat of the series, Jim Dowell's *Monique,* while the next best Kiwi boat was Evan Julian's *Inca,* fifth overall individually, in the B team. The 1975 Admiral's Cupper, *Gerontius,* a cruising design by Farr that went so fast she had to be chosen,

Sweet Caroline *(Marshall Phillips), the Laurie Davidson-designed Two-Tonner which had won the Sydney – Suva Race prior to being on the winning Australian team in the 1980 Clipper Cup.*

and Clyde Colson's *Country Boy,* a Farr fixed-keel One-Tonner, completed the A team. A similar boat, Jack Lloyd's and Keith Andrews' *Lovelace,* together with the Ben Lexcen-designed 50-foot *Anticipation,* owned by Don St. Clair Brown, completed the B team.

Monique was the undoubted star of the show. A Farr-designed Two-Tonner, she was a sister ship of the Hong Kong Admiral's Cup reserve *Uin-na-Mara,* and was built in molds taken from the Hong Kong winner of the China Sea Race. Dowell had ensured that her glass-reinforced plastic structure had been kept light, but *Monique* was by no means a stripped-out

racing-only boat. She was laid out for family cruising with plenty of creature comforts.

Dowell gathered around him a powerful team. It included sailmaker Mike Spanhake and the evergreen Don Pollock, whose ability aboard Kiwi ocean racers is almost legendary. He had also invited America's Cup skipper Jock Sturrock from Australia, as Sturrock was having a similar boat built at the time. *Monique*'s own class record was enviable, with four firsts in the first four races and a second in the Round-the-State Race. In the overall fleet, her placings became 6, 4, 1, 2, and 4, giving her a five-point win over *Ragamuffin.*

The line-honors battle in the series was between the two American maxis: *Kialoa,* in the United States Blue team, and *Ondine,* in the Red. *Ondine* followed the lead of *Kialoa* and had been converted from a ketch to a sloop. She also sported a new high-lift keel. Both these modifications had been under the direction of MIT professor Jerome Milgram. He had moved the mast 7 feet farther aft than before and added 11 feet to its height above the deck. *Ondine* improved as the series went on. She beat Jim Kilroy's *Kialoa* by 6 seconds at the end of the 100-mile race, and there was another close finish at the end of the second Olympic-course 30-

miler, when *Kialoa* crossed the line 16 seconds ahead. *Ondine* came into her own the very next day with a devastating 6 minute, 40 second win in a 22-knot breeze which gave a true test of sailing. In the lee of the island of Hawaii, *Ondine* overtook *Kialoa* by tacking to the south in a rain squall and reaching a new southeasterly breeze before her rival. It gave her a 20-mile break, which developed into a 3-hour win in the Round-the-State Race.

The Class-A battle appeared to be a walk-over for Syd Fischer's 47-foot *Ragamuffin.* She won every race in the class to score a maximum number of points, while her fleet placings

Anticipation *(Don St. Clair Brown), the New Zealand Class A winner of the first two races in 1982, chases* Checkmate *of the United States.*

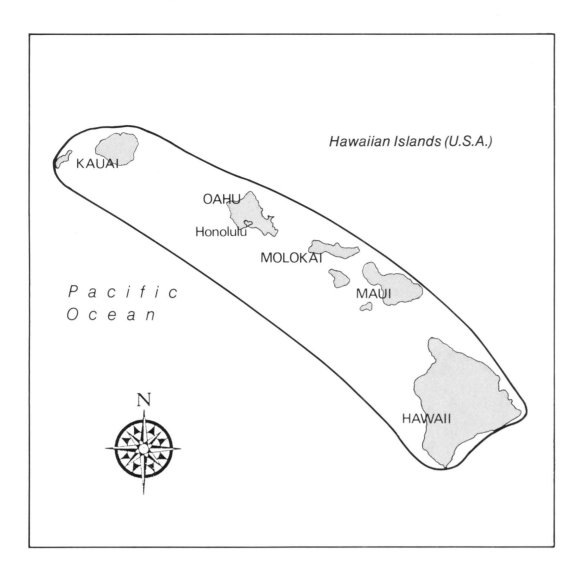

Hawaiian Islands (U.S.A.)

KAUAI

OAHU

Honolulu

MOLOKAI

MAUI

Pacific Ocean

HAWAII

N

The course around the Hawaiian Islands for the Round-the-State Race.

Impetuous (Graeme Lambert), a Holland Two-Tonner in pursuit of Tomahawk.

worked out as 11, 3, 2, 1, and 3. *Anticipation,* reveling in the strong breezes, had her best-ever series to be placed second in the class. Among her crew was the 1956 Olympic gold medalist from the 12-Square-Metre Sharpie class, Peter Mander. Monte Livingstone's *Checkmate,* a Peterson 50-footer built by Carl Eichenlaub, was third. *Checkmate* was designed with long, downwind races like the Transpac in mind and has a wide beam with an undistorted run aft for power reaching which takes little notice of the IOR benefits of stern distortions; she displaces only 23,000 pounds. Her rating was unnecessarily high for the series.

The 100-miler was dominated by the little boats; the Farr One-Tonner *Carrie Ann V* in the United States Red team was second to *Don Quixote* after passing *Magic Pudding* in the lee of the Waianae Mountains where the Kiwi boat was becalmed. *Carrie Ann V* went on to win the first of the Olympic-course races from her sister ship *Lovelace. Monique* won the next and *Ragamuffin* the third of these 30-milers, all of which were held in 18- to 25-knot breezes.

It was only in the Round-the-State Race that the breeze fell off, much to the disappointment of the competitors. They started in the trade winds and had a good leg to Kauai after a beat

around Makapuu Point; but then the winds faded, and most of the leg from Nihau to Ka Lee, the South Cape of Hawaii, was hard on the wind in fluky airs. *Magic Pudding* held higher than most on this leg and sailed into a southeasterly sea breeze off Oahu, from where she was able to lay Ka Lee on starboard tack. This gave her a huge advantage and an overall win in the Round-the-State Race which helped her team, Australia A, to an overall win in the series.

By 1980, the word had gotten around about how good the Pan-Am Clipper Cup series was, and as a result there were eleven teams entered. Three of them came from Australia, one formed the day before the series began; three from the United States; two from New Zealand; and one each from Japan, Hawaii, and Canada. This time, it was a real cleanup for Syd Fischer and the Australian No. 1 team led by his *Ragamuffin*.

This boat was the fourth ocean racer to bear the name *Ragamuffin,* a 45-foot Peterson design which had been part of Australia's 1979 Admiral's Cup winning team, a yacht whose selection for that event had caused more than a little controversy. Syd had "Sightie" Hammond with him once again to navigate *"Rags,"* and his experience was to be granted, pre-race, to the other Australians for the Round-the-State Race

strategic discussion. There was further strength in the boat from another direction. Also on board, as tactician, was Lowell North, the head of the international firm of sailmakers.

Joining *Ragamuffin* in the No. 1 team were Lou Abrahams' 46-foot S&S-designed *Challenge* and Marshall Phillips' Davidson Two-Tonner *Sweet Caroline. Challenge,* with a fractional rig, opened the series in great style with a win in the 100-mile Oahu race and followed it with a second in the first of the Olympic-course 30-milers. She came unstuck, however, in the next race, when her forestay parted as she was in a winning position, and she dropped to seventeenth in fleet. *Sweet Caroline,* also fractionally rigged, had been launched for the previous Australian season and had won the Sydney–Suva Race on her way to Hawaii. In her crew were Norm Hyett and sailmaker Hugh Treharne. The Australians were coming properly armed for the series, and no team was able to match this trio, which amassed a huge points lead to win.

There were three maxis to fight out the line-honors battle this time. Frank Johnson's Gurney-designed *Windward Passage* had been rerigged as a sloop and taken a new lease on life with John Rumsey skippering. Bill Whitehouse-Vaux had bought *Ballyhoo* from Jack Rooklyn

The 1980 fleet at the Waikiki Yacht Club marina.

and renamed the Lexcen-designed 71-footer *Mistress Quickly,* while Rolly Tasker's self-designed *Siska* completed the front-runners. These three took the first three places on corrected time in the opening race, with *Mistress Quickly* taking the honors after *Siska* had beaten the course record. *Windward Passage* was then the fleet winner of the first 30-miler.

The 50-foot *Anticipation* took Class A in both these races and was second in fleet in the Olympic-course race, with *Challenge* third. *Windward Passage* won the next race, with the three maxis claiming the first three places in a 22-knot breeze with the time-on-distance handicap system working overtime on the bigger boats' behalf. *Ragamuffin* was fourth in fleet, and with *Sweet Caroline* eighth, the Australian No. 1 team was well clear in the overall points despite the failure of *Challenge*'s forestay and the loss of places it caused.

It was the fourth race that was to provide the surprise of the series. The Japanese 40-foot *Unchu* took the "wrong" side of the first beat to gain a huge benefit which she never released. *Unchu* was designed by Ichiro Yokoyama and became the first Japanese-designed and -built IOR yacht to win a major offshore race outside her own country. Her win stopped *Windward Passage,* which was second, from making a hat trick of the Olympic-course races.

The smaller boats did not have a very successful time, in fleet at least, but the performance of one of the Class-D One-Tonners is worthy of note. *Gold Coast Express* was built for a syndicate of sixty members of the Southport Yacht Club in Queensland, each of whom put $1,000 into the project. They then raised $20,000 more in a raffle to ship the boat to Hawaii for the series and were co-opted into the Australian No. 3 team. *Gold Coast Express* won each of its races in class but could do no better than a fifteenth in one race in fleet — she wound up fourteenth overall.

It was the final 775-miler around all the Hawaiian Islands that was to settle the series and the class places. There was a big scrap for first place between *Ragamuffin* and the Kiwi second team's *Shockwave,* a 46-foot Davidson fractional rigger owned by Neville Crighton, with the maxi *Windward Passage* having the slight advantage after four races.

There was a 15- to 18-knot blow of trade wind for the start of the Round-the-State Race, but as in the previous race, it was to fade on the first night out. It took the leader, *Windward Passage,* 71 hours to get to Ka Lee, where she again emerged from the lee of the volcanic peak, some 14,000 feet high, into the northeast trade winds. She tacked up the southeast shore of the Big Island, under a number-three genoa and double-reefed mainsail, and it was not until five hours had elapsed that *Mistress Quickly* rounded the South Cape to chase her. Then came the 52-foot *Zamazaan,* a Farr-designed and New Zealand-built United States Blue team boat which looked like the handicap winner, just half an hour behind the blue-hulled *"Mistress."*

Ragamuffin and *Shockwave* came next, and the race to the finish was a cliff-hanger. *Ragamuffin* beat up the shore toward the northeast cape, after having been "parked" earlier, and set off northwesterly keeping close to the rhumb line, with the lower-rated *Shockwave* still within handicap distance astern. *"Rags"* then stayed offshore of the rhumb line to avoid the flat spot where the wind lifts over the island of Oahu, and by doing so, closed the gap on *Zamazaan. Ragamuffin* finished after 124 hours of racing and did enough to beat *Zamazaan* into second place with *Shockwave* third. *Windward Passage* had been first to finish, but dropped to twelfth in fleet for the race and to third behind *Ragamuffin* and *Shockwave* in the overall standings. *Sweet Caroline* was fourth and

Challenge ninth to give the Australia No. 1 team a runaway victory in the series.

Of course, they said, it could not continue – near perfect racing conditions. But it did for the third series, and the winds blew harder to make it more difficult. Three tropical storms influenced the winds, and masts tumbled, sails ripped, and there was a fair amount of damage to the boats. The one black cloud that did hang over the series concerned the rating of the overall winner.

There were again eleven teams: three from the United States—Red, White, and Blue; Australia and two state teams, from Queensland and Victoria; three from Japan; and two from New Zealand. Australia's winning sequence was to be broken by the United States Blue team of the 80-feet Holland-designed *Kialoa,* owned by Jim Kilroy, the Peterson 55-foot *Bull Frog* of Dave Fenix, and Clay Bernard's 50-foot Davidson-designed *Great Fun.*

The top individual yacht in the series, and the one which caused the rating protest, was the 39-foot *Tobiume,* a fractionally rigged design by

opposite page, above: *Part of the 1980 fleet beating off Oahu.*

opposite page, below: Challenge, *the 46-foot S&S fractionally rigged design which Lou Abrahams took to the Clipper Cup with success in 1980 and 1982.*

below: Great Fun, *Clay Bernard's Davidson 50-footer, in ideal Hawaiian conditions.*

opposite page: *Clipper Cup fun for the sailors is spinnakers, sunshine, and surfing.*

left: Scarlett O'Hara *snatches the inside berth at the gybe mark.*

below: *The 73-foot Alan Gurney-designed* Windward Passage *thrashes her way to windward with a reef tucked in.*

Osamu Takai, who had been best known previously for his Quarter-Ton designs. She was built using a great deal of carbonfiber in her lay-up over a Klegecell core, both the hull and the deck. Displacing 11,500 pounds, *Tobiume* carried 2,000 pounds of this as internal ballast. She sported a moderate rig, ideal in the fresh conditions, and rated 29.4 feet. The gripe about her, which brought a protest from one New Zealand boat and two Australian, was that there were hollows in her hull, varying from 3 to 5 millimeters, which were disallowed by the IOR rule. *Tobiume* was hauled out for measurement, but the jury dismissed the protest on the grounds that there was no evidence that the rating of the boat was materially changed by these hollows.

The maxis were there in force. In addition to *Kialoa,* Bob Bell had her near-sister *Condor* as well as his Sharp-designed 79-foot *Condor of Bermuda.* Jack Rooklyn's Lexcen 72-foot *Apollo* was the smallest maxi, and the oldest was *Windward Passage,* fourteen years after her launch, now sporting an even higher rig than the previous year, with a new keel designed by Doug Peterson and a new $25,000 titanium rudder. The crowd's favorite, she lost her series lead in the Round-the-State Race when a spreader collapsed and her mast came tumbling down shortly after she had rounded Niihau. *Kialoa* went on to win that race overall and broke the course record with a time of 3 days, 23 hours, 49 minutes, 46 seconds. But for the mast failure, it

could so easily have gone to *"Passage."*

The shape of the series was changed to put two of the Olympic-course races first, then a new 143-miler around the island of Molokai. The third Olympic-course race preceded the Round-the-State Race. *Condor* won the first race, with the Tom Blackaller-steered *Bull Frog* in second place. *Margaret Rintoul III,* a Frers 51 skippered by Graeme Freeman, won the next, and again *Bull Frog* was second. But the high-tech, aluminum-built *Bull Frog* was having continual problems with her mast, a small section triple-spreader affair from Stearn. It had an internal spinnaker boom track which also served as a stiffening member, and it came adrift regularly; its fastenings, however bolstered, were never strong enough for the job. Conservatively sailed in the Molokai race to save the spar, *Bull Frog* was again second in the Olympic-course race.

Great Fun was the winner of the Molokai race, sailed in winds of 30 to 40 knots after a 24-hour delay. The fourth race, sailed in the lightest winds of the series, around 20 to 30 knots, was won by *Kialoa.* Her Round-the-State win was one of total domination. *Condor* was second, but 4 hours, 45 minutes behind. With the US Blue team's *Kialoa* fourth overall behind *Tobiume,* the 46-foot Frers *Bravura,* and *Condor,* which shared second place, and with the Blue team's *Great Fun* fifth and *Bull Frog* eleventh, the United States Blue team were comfortable winners.

previous page: *The start of the 1981 Transpac.*

I t was the summer of 1906, the year of the great San Francisco earthquake and also the year of the first yacht race across the Pacific. At noon on June 11, three yachts started from the end of the San Pedro breakwater in a stiff southwesterly breeze bound for Honolulu. Although only three in number, they were as diverse a group of boats as has ever been assembled for a race. There would have been seven but for the disaster in San Francisco earlier, however those that did start varied in size from 48 feet 6 inches overall to 115 feet 5 inches.

The smallest was a schooner, *La Paloma,* owned by Clarence Macfarlane of Honolulu, while the largest was an auxiliary steam ketch named *Anemone,* owned by Charles L. Tutt and in the charge of one Captain Linderberger, who had recently sailed her from New York around Cape Horn. Between them in size was *Lurline,* a schooner 85 feet 10 inches overall, and skippered by her owner, H. H. Sinclair, the Commodore of the South Coast Yacht Club.

Lurline began to leave the fleet behind her after only 5 minutes and was to lead all the way to Honolulu, where she arrived after 12 days, 5 hours, the clear winner of a race which was held without handicap. She had had a largely downwind passage with plenty of fresh wind for the 2,200 miles, and she had achieved one day's run, to noon on June 13, of 265 miles. *Anemone* was 41 hours behind *Lurline,* and *La Paloma* another 60 hours after *Anemone.* After the race, the people of Honolulu began to build a yacht with which to try to win the race.

The boat turned out to be a 70-foot schooner. She was named *Hawaii,* and the race she took part in, in 1908, was started on July 4 by President Theodore Roosevelt, who pressed an electric button to set the yachts on their way.

There were four starters: the 68-foot San Diegan yawl *Lady Maud;* the 50-foot yawl *Gwendolyn II* from Seattle; *Hawaii,* which had a squaresail yard on the foremast; and *Lurline* again. *Lurline* was the scratch boat, since handicaps had been introduced, and she did enough to save her time, finishing in 13 days,

right: *The finish of every Transpac is party time.*

opposite page: Windward Passage, *still a ketch in 1977, was one of the great Transpac competitors.*

130

Merlin, *the ULDB which was first to finish in 1977.*

21½ hours. The hopes of the Hawaiians were destroyed. *Hawaii* was last to finish and last on handicap, 30 hours behind the leader.

After two more races, in 1910 and 1912, there was a long gap to 1923, when the schooner *Mariner* established a course record of 13 days, 13 hours. Three races later, in 1930, as four American J-Class yachts were seeking selection to defend the America's Cup from Sir Thomas Lipton's *Shamrock V,* four other boats set out again from San Pedro, on the now traditional July 4, for Honolulu. The race was won by Morgan Adams' 136-foot schooner *Enchantress,* which took 1 day, 1 hour, 46 minutes less than *Mariner.* In the first three days, she covered 779 miles, including one noon-to-noon run of 280 miles, and was over a third of the way to Honolulu.

There were only two boats for the ninth race, in 1932, when the 44-foot ketch, *Fayth,* which had been built in China, was the winner. Her opponent was the 56-foot yawl *Mollilou,* which finished 18 hours behind the leader. For relatively small boats, the time of 14 days, 9 hours was fast, and while neither managed more

than 188 miles in a day (*Mollilou*), *Fayth* only once dropped, by 2 miles, below 150.

The entries were up to twelve, in three classes, for the 1934 race, won for the first time by a Hawaiian vessel, the 61-foot schooner *Manuiwa,* but the first to finish had been the 60-foot ketch *Vileehi* in a few minutes under 12 days. Last to finish, and smallest of the fleet, was the 28-foot sloop *Common Sense.* Six days out, she lost her mast 12 feet above the deck and thus had to make the rest of the passage under jury rig. Her cockpit was not self-baling, so her helmsman was often up to his knees in water and had to be constantly lashed in. She finished within 15 minutes of the 34-foot *Naitambe* in 16 days.

The fleet was twenty-one strong two years later, and the two leading boats were no more than 1½ miles apart. The double Fastnet winner *Dorade,* a 51-foot yawl designed by Olin and Rod Stephens for themselves and now owned by James Flood, was the first to finish and first on corrected time – a great double of which the owner claimed: "We won because we didn't dare to lose."

In 1941, Rad Pratsch, the skipper of *White Cloud,* a 31-foot gaff yawl, the smallest boat in the race, described his navigation as "following the trail of beer cans I left in 1939, and in 1939 I followed the trail I left in 1936!"

Walter Elliot's *Escapade,* a California 32, the nearest thing to a stock boat prewar, was third to finish but took first place on handicap from the seven starters. The happenings at Pearl Harbor put an end to transpacific races until 1947.

Thirty-four boats went on the first postwar race in 1947, when Frank Morgan's Alden-designed 70-foot schooner *Dolphin II* took overall honors. The start of the race had been moved to Los Angeles, and the course was 22 miles shorter. Two years later, there were only twenty-four boats, but the course record, which had stood for twenty-three years, was broken. The 98-foot schooner *Morning Star* was home in 10 days, 10 hours to knock over 40 hours from the previous record. Fred Lyon's 46-foot *Kitten* won overall, while *Morning Star* dropped to twelfth.

The story of the 1951 race was that of Ted Sierks, who fell overboard from the yacht *L'Apache.* She radioed on the seventh day of the race, when 880 miles from Hawaii, that Sierks had gone overboard and had not been recovered. He had fallen over at dusk, and they had not been able to find him. The miracle came thirty hours later when two off-watch sailors on the U.S.S. *Douglas A. Munro,* a destroyer sent to search the area, spotted Sierks in the water. One of the things which had kept him going for so long was that he had seen a flare dropped from a B-17, which told him that a search was on.

The race went to the smallest boat in the twenty-seven-strong fleet, the gaff ketch *Sea*

Witch, while *Morning Star* came within 6 hours of her record.

No race with a 161-foot schooner taking part is ordinary, but despite her size, Ralph Larrabee's *Goodwill* could not break the course record in the light winds that made the 1953 race ordinary in other respects.

The winner of that race, Ira Fulmor's 39-foot ketch *Staghound*, won again the following year from a record fleet of fifty-three yachts. This was the fastest race on record, with three boats bettering the previous record for the course. And the fastest of them was Richard Rheem's *Morning Star,* rerigged as a ketch, which finished in 9 days, 15 hours, 15 minutes.

If that one was fast, the next was equally slow. The leader, *Barlovento,* took 2 days longer than *Morning Star* had done.

Nalu II won in 1959 when *Goodwill* this time came closer to the record, with 10 days, 12¼ hours. *Ticonderoga* and *Sirius II* had the line-honors battle, 37 minutes separating them at the finish after 10 days, 10½ hours. The 1961 race went to the 66-foot *Nam Sang* of Arthur

Robbs. A field of thirty-two boats was headed by the 40-foot sloop *Islander* in 1963, in a race that was to pall into insignificance beside that of two years later. There were fifty-five entries, and the race to be first to finish between *Ticonderoga* and *Stormvogel* was a classic. As they came into the Molokai Channel, both boats showed the signs of being hard driven and damaged. There was no more than 100 yards between them, but *Ticonderoga* was forging ahead because Cornelius Bruynzeel's *Stormvogel* had lost her main boom early in the race and was using a genoa instead of a mainsail. Bob Johnson's *Ticonderoga* was also damaged, her boom hanging limp at the gooseneck, which was broken. Yet she beat the course record by more than an hour in 9 days, 13 hours, 51 minutes.

The race was dominated, on corrected time, by stock Cal 40s. Don Salisbury's *Psyche* was first. Other Cal 40s were second and third.

The Cal 40s were at it again in 1967; Skip Allan and a very young crew taking first place with *Holiday Too.* *Stormvogel* was first to finish this time, but without the competition from

Drifter, *the great rival of* Merlin, *with the huge stern "planting board" extension.*

In 1983 Irving Loube's Bravura *was the handicap winner.*

minutes was 18 minutes faster even than her time two years earlier. Her performance also gave her first on corrected time and brought a big smile to the skipper, Mark Johnson. Andron had to be content with first in Class C and tenth overall. The 35-foot *Chutzpah* took Class D and the overall race, while the line honors went to the syndicate-owned *Ragtime,* a 62-foot Spencer-designed lightweight plywood downhill sled. Despite her lightness, she was more than a day outside the record. *Chutzpah* gave Stuart Cowan another win in 1975, and *Ragtime* was first to finish in a mirror image at the front of the twenty-eighth race. They were paving the way for the Ultra-Light Displacement Boats (ULDBs) in the future.

There could not have been a more lightweight 67-footer than Bill Lee's *Merlin,* which in 1977 completely shattered the course record with a time of 8 days, 11 hours, 1 minute, 45 seconds – knocking 22 hours, 5 minutes off *Windward Passage's* record. *Merlin* just beat the 70-foot *Drifter* by 17 minutes; but on handicap, neither could challenge the "conventional" maxi *Kialoa,* which was beaten home by *Windward Passage* but had done more than enough to take overall honors by 4 hours. The separation of the ULDBs and the IOR boats marked an interesting concept for future races.

"Drifter" was the word of 1979; it described the race and named the first to finish. The winner of the IOR division was Dennis Choate's 48-foot *Arriba,* while *Drifter,* due to her huge rating, was down to twelfth of the eighty starters.

Two years after that it was the turn of the smallest entry, the Farr-designed *Sweet Okole* of Dean Treadway, to take the overall honors. *Merlin* was the front runner after *Drifter* withdrew with a damaged skeg, and she piled on the pressure, making 297 miles in a day. She failed to beat her own record by 46 seconds.

The year 1983 saw *Merlin* fit a 32-inch prop and a 2½-ton diesel in an effort to reduce her rating to the 70-foot maximum for the race. There was a double challenge to her line-honors superiority from the 68-foot Nelson & Marek-designed *Saga* and the Ron Holland-designed *Charley.* There were good breezes, and a new record was always on the cards. *Merlin* still had the short speed bursts, with one surge recorded at 29 knots, but *Charley* recorded several days of over 300 miles. With 48 hours to go, *Charley* led by a mere 3 miles. She was, however, the faster on the dead run to the finish and was there in 9 days and just under 2 hours—15 hours off *Merlin's* record. Nolan Bushnell's *Charley* was a veritable electronics mine, but her navigator, Stan Honey, had designed a fine program for the on-board computer to help her win. Irv Loube's 46-foot Frers-designed *Bravura* took Class C and the overall prize in the fastest, and many say the best, Transpac of all time.

Ticonderoga she was slower. Bob Johnson was to break his own record the following year with *Windward Passage,* the Alan Gurney-designed 72-foot ketch, but lost it when penalized 2 hours for an infringement at the start. She had sailed the course in 9 days, 9 hours, 25 minutes; the penalty gave the new record to Ken de Meuse's *Blackfin* in 9 days, 10 hours, 21 minutes. Once again, the race went to a Cal 40: Jon Andron's *Argonaut.*

"*Passage,*" however, was able to even the score in 1971 when her time of 9 days, 9 hours, 6

Charley, *with the menacing artwork on her spinnaker, was first home in 1977.*

Sardinia Cup

Glamor surrounds the Sardinia Cup — it has to. The venue, Porto Cervo, is a multi-million-dollar (everything in Italy is multi-million lire) development of the Costa Smeralda by a syndicate headed by Prince Karim, the Aga Khan. He aimed to make Porto Cervo one of the great meeting places of international yachting and to do so invested huge sums to turn a small fishing harbor into a holiday paradise for yachtsmen, with a 450-boat marina complex blasted out of a rocky sea bed and carved from the neighboring hillside.

The Aga Khan, one of the world's richest men and spiritual leader of the world's Ismailis, has a villa which overlooks the harbor. Four years after the harbor had been constructed, its promoter realized that it was grossly underused. The success of the One-Ton Cup, held there in 1973, put the development in front of

yachtsmen, and the prince decided that Porto Cervo needed a regular international regatta of some standing to popularize the facilities. After all, by 1978 there were but ninety fully paid members of the Yacht Club Costa Smeralda, and this is one of the world's most stylish yacht clubs. It maintains a cool oasis atmosphere, even at the height of an international regatta, with its Moorish architecture and roof-top swimming pool; it is a haven for the "seriously" rich. To enhance its stature and encourage further membership, Prince Karim planned an Italian equivalent of the Admiral's Cup, with the same IOR 30- to 40-feet rating band. The Admiral's Cup had begun modestly with just two teams entered, but such was the enthusiasm and energy pumped into the Sardinia Cup that the inaugural event, in 1978, had twelve. That many of these competed was due to lavish inducements.

Acadia, skipperedbyBurt Keenan, shortly after the start of the long race in 1978.

138

Freight charges for the boats of the American and British teams, for example, were paid by the organizers of the series; so were those of the German boats. Members of the Australian team had their air tickets presented to them from the same source. The result was that the event was "up and running" before it had been born. And with the Costa Smeralda's climate providing sun and wind, it is not surprising that from its very beginnings, the Sardinia Cup was popular with the competitors.

The twelve teams were not all that they might seem. Further encouragement was given to other nations to make up their teams with yachts from Italy that were not selected for the home side. In this way, the Belgian team was boosted to be a far stronger team than it had been at the Admiral's Cup the previous year, and then there was the Costa Rican team. . .

It was apparent from the outset that the race was going to be between the Italians and the Americans, with the Germans making their presence felt. The British team, despite the inducements offered, was definitely second division. The American team was not. Burt Keenan brought the 51-foot *Acadia*, a Frers design that had already won at the SORC and at the Onion Patch, while Seymour Sinett brought the highly successful 46-foot Peterson-designed *Williwaw*. To complete the team, Pat Malloy bought the 44-foot Holland-designed *Mandrake* from Giorgio Carriero, a sister ship to Chris Dunning's *Marionette*. Carriero sailed with Malloy in the first of the Sardinia Cup races, the 150-mile Asinara race, in which his local knowledge was found to be invaluable.

The American influence was everywhere, nowhere more so than in the Italian team. Two of

Seymour Sinett's Williwaw *going upwind in the first inshore race.*

the boats were identical Two-Tonners from the
design board of Californian Doug Peterson. They
were the stars of the series, with more American
help in the form of Ron Love of Sparcraft from
California as sailing master of *Dida V,* and *Jena* in
the hands of Dennis Durgan and Jim Pugh, the
latter from the Peterson office. It was the sort of
influence which was bound to produce the very
best from the twin Two-Tonners. Tom Blackaller

flew in from San Francisco, carrying his golf
clubs, to skipper the third Italian yacht, *Vanina
II,* which had been designed by Australian expatriate Scott Kaufman in New York. An Italian-
American bond was forged.

The series was one of four races, a 30-mile
coastal race following the Asinara short offshore.
Then came the long race, through the Straits of
Bonifacio between Sardinia and Corsica and

northwest to the Iles des Porqueroles, off the French mainland at Hyères, and back the same way to Porto Cervo. Another 30-miler concluded the series. No one was prepared for the setback to the first race, however; the wind blew at 50 knots through the Straits of Bonifacio, and there were memories of the One-Tonner that had been lost with all hands and without trace in the Mediterranean the previous year. So the noon start was postponed for 5½ hours. The wind moderated and shifted to the north.

It was a beat all the way to Asinara; first with the odd reef in evidence and then, as the wind faded overnight, with full sail to the outer turning mark. On the way home, as the daylight cleared the skies of the night's bright stars, the wind began again, backing to the west-northwest. It was a hair-raising run home, with sails blown out all over the place. On *Mandrake,* the new watch queried the amount of sail set and was told by the skipper that no one felt brave enough to take any of them down; they were all busy keeping their weight aft in order that the boat did not bury her bow! God had to take a hand to help, and shortly afterward, *Mandrake* broached wildly and the blooper was ripped off as it dragged in the sea. As *Mandrake* came upright, shaking sea water from her sails like a recently landed dog, all that was left of the blooper was half the tack pennant at the bow, the clew patch on the end of the sheet, and the head patch waving from the masthead at the end of its halyard.

Others were not so lucky; the German Two-Tonner, *Champagne,* racing for Austria, lost her mast, and *Williwaw* broke her rudder but still hobbled home to take fifth place. *Dida* loved the fresh downwind leg and won the race on corrected time from *Acadia,* with Giorgio Falck's *Guia IV* in third place.

the breeze returned from its more regular northwesterly direction to give the yachts a fast run home, allowing them to cover the course in a couple of days. *Dida* and *Jena* were outstanding; they finished first and second on corrected time. Belgium's *Black Swan,* the first of the Nautor Swan Holland 39 Imp clones, was third with a similar design, custom-built in aluminum. *Chigoe,* for Switzerland, was fourth. The American team was still hanging in with *Williwaw* and *Acadia,* benefiting from the time-on-distance handicapping working in its favor and taking the next two places. But even so, the Italian lead was really too big for the Americans to have a chance. *Acadia* and *Williwaw* were first and second in the final race, but with *Vanina* third and *Jena* fifth, the Cup was Italy's.

Not unsurprisingly, two years later, the

Fast takedowns at the leeward mark were essential in the stiff competition of the second Sardinia Cup.

It was the turn of two former German Admiral's Cuppers to shine in the first of the short races; *Saudade,* an S&S 45, winning from *Rubin,* with *Dida* third and *Acadia* fourth. The start of the long race was delayed for the exact opposite reason that had postponed the Asinara; this time, there was no wind. When it did fill in, from the east, it gave a spinnaker reach to the Straits, and the fleet carried their kites all the way to the Baie d'Hyères, where the breeze was light and fluky. Once clear of the Iles des Porqueroles,

entry had increased to fifteen teams. The number of races had been increased too, to five, and the structuring altered to cope with this. In addition, the organizers had found a way to anchor turning marks in the deep water and thereby to hold two of the races, the first and the third, around a 25-mile Olympic course set off the mouth of Porto Cervo harbor. The middle-distance and long-distance races were as before, with the series concluding with a 28-mile coastal race. It marked also the first visit to Porto Cervo of

143

former British Prime Minister Edward Heath, as captain of the British team, with his Ron Holland-designed *Morning Cloud.*

It was not, perhaps, the best team that the British could have mustered. *Morning Cloud* had begun to show some of the potential in her second season that she was to realize in the next. There was no doubt that Dave Johnston's *Casse Tête V* was going faster than she had done in the Admiral's Cup trials the previous year, but she was still not as fast as Chris Dunning's former *Marionette,* from which she was the Swan 441 copy, now racing as *Formidable* for Holland. The baby of the team was the Ed Dubois-designed *Panda,* a 39-footer owned by Peter Whipp, who was inexperienced in the ways of international offshore racing. Dubois was her helmsman.

Britain had lost its star performer in the Admiral's Cup, the 39-foot *Eclipse,* by charter to Ireland. This Peterson design, built as a prototype of the Contessa 39, was a great loss for the British but a gain for the Irish. *Regardless,* the Holland 40 which had been the top points scorer in the Admiral's Cup before the wind-blasted Fastnet, and the Holland 44 *Silver Apple of the Moon* completed the team from the Emerald Isle on the Costa Smeralda.

Somehow the defense plans of the Italians went awry. The selection procedure was technically valueless. The choice of the team was haphazard. A new *Yena,* not chosen by the selection trials, was included in the team after *Dida* had dropped out. *Yena* was again a Doug Peterson design, a 44-footer built in aluminum for Sergio Doni. After the Admiral's Cup, in which she was tenth boat individually, *Yena* had some keel alterations and her stability reduced; her rating came down to 33.1 feet. Doni gathered around him a formidable crew which included Gary Weiseman and Ian Macdonald-Smith from North Sails and the redoubtable Jim Pugh from Peterson's office. No one doubted the seriousness of this effort, but the choice of the other two boats left something to be desired.

Viola, a near minimum rater designed by Peterson, and *Blu Show,* a compromise cruiser/racer Two-Tonner from Vallicelli, were preferred to *Brava* and *Guia 2000.* Vallicelli himself preferred *Brava,* a 46-footer built in aluminum by Minnefords, because she was a flat-out racing boat. Chartered by the Canadian team, *Brava* wound up fourth on points, beating *Guia 2000,* a Frers design in high-tech plastics on charter to the Argentinians, by one place. An Italian team of these two boats together with *Yena* would have proved unbeatable.

Having come close to success in 1978, the Americans put in a determined effort to win. Their team was led by Burt Keenan's SORC-winning *Acadia,* a custom-production Serendipity 43 of Peterson design from New Orleans Marine. She rated a fraction over the

Two-Ton limit and came with John Kolius and a complete wardrobe of Ulmer sails which he had supervised. *Acadia* was joined by two Frers designs. Bob Hutton's *Tatoosh,* a 46-footer, was steered by Lowell North, and there are no prizes for guessing who made her sails. Jack King's *Merrythought,* a 45-footer of slightly lighter displacement, was the visually outstanding boat of the series. She carried a Kevlar/Mylar mainsail whose fabric had been dyed black to protect it from the ultraviolet rays of the sun and which led to speculation that it might be of carbonfiber.

The German team had two Peterson designs very akin to *Yena* in *Pinta* and *Container,* while their third boat was a Britton Chance minimum rater, *Vineta.* Argentina's team was very patriotic in having all three boats to German Frers's designs. He steered *Guia 2000* and was joined by similarly sized *Red Rock* and Two-Tonner *Sur.*

Racing began in 15 knots of breeze, with the biggest boat in the fleet, the 51-foot Holland-designed *Midnight Sun,* scoring a win for Sweden. At her wheel was spar builder Tim Stearn. *Tatoosh* was second, and *Bla Carat,* the *Acadia* of the previous Cup, was third for Sweden with *Yena,* the only one of the smaller boats to figure highly because of the dying breeze, fourth.

The Asinara race was a triumph for the Italians, although it was the German Two-Tonner *Suca,* sailing for Switzerland, that was the overall winner. The Italian team of *Blu Show, Viola,* and *Yena* occupied the next three places in conditions that were ideal for the lower-rated boats, a light easterly breeze throughout.

In the second of the Olympic-course races, there was a goodly breeze to start with, some 18 to 20 knots; but during the course of the race, it tailed away to end in a near calm. *Tatoosh* and *Midnight Sun* reversed the positions they had had in the first race, the fading breeze and the time-on-distance handicap system working in the big boats' favor. *Acadia* was third.

The long race was a test of men and boats. It began in light winds which held until dark, when they fell away to nothing. On the next day came the mistral, the northwesterly Mediterranean wind, blowing at 40 to 50 knots. And the mistral held until the majority of the fleet had finished; then it died as quickly as it had come, leaving the smaller boats to finish in near calm. The race was a great one for the two Dubois designs, the 39-foot *Panda* and the 46-foot *Dynamo* of Canadian Gerry Moog; they finished first and second. Everybody in that race has his own personal memories; perhaps one of the best is that of Mike Jamieson, a crewman on *Panda.* "We were running back from the Porqueroles, four hours after rounding with Ed Dubois on the tiller and the genoa poled out instead of a spinnaker. The wind had dropped from 50 to just over 40 knots when Ed shouted to the owner, Peter Whipp,

Light airs marred the third Sardinia Cup. Here Brian and Pam Saffery Cooper's Dragon *chases* Magic Maestro *around the leeward mark.*

opposite page, above: *A full sail beat to windward in the second inshore race.*

opposite page, below: *The gybe mark in an Olympic-course race.*

145

opposite page: Midnight Sun, *the 50-foot Holland design, leads the fleet in the short offshore race.*

who was below: 'Pass up the spinnaker, Peter.' Back came the reply: 'I don't know, but it's going to be bloody good fun.' " It was around five in the morning and to quote Jamieson again: "It was pomping" – blowing hard. The spinnaker went up, and *Panda* averaged more than 10 knots for the leg home, the bow wave back to the mast and the underwater part of the speedo aerating so much that the clock often registered zero. She had rounded the outer mark 45 minutes astern of *Morning Cloud,* but Ed Dubois' "bloody good fun" saw her only 8 minutes behind at the finish and an easy winner on corrected time.

1981 Admiral's Cup beset by faint and fickle breezes, the competitors went to Porto Cervo the following year in the hopes of regular winds. But it was not to be. It was so bad that only four of the scheduled five races were held, and boats failed to finish the long race within the 95-hour time limit – one that gave them an average of 4 knots to beat. It was a regatta that many would like to forget, not least of them the race committee of the Yacht Club Porto Cervo. For to some extent, they compounded the felonies of the conditions by setting bad starting lines and more than indifferent courses, where the skill of

Thunderbolt, *one of the United States team, rounds the gybe mark just ahead of* Guia V.

Midnight Sun had been first home, but she was well down the lists on corrected time when twenty boats finished within two hours. *Yena* took third place ahead of *Merrythought, Brava, Container, Guia 2000, Acadia, Morning Cloud,* and *Tatoosh.* The other two Italian boats were among those that lost out in the final calm. *Tatoosh* won the last race, the 28-mile coastal event, but *Yena's* sixth was good enough to give her the Star Point Trophy for the best individual performance. The Sardinia Cup, however, was America's, with Italy second and Germany third.

The honeymoon had to finish sometime; the statistics were against Mediterranean weather being good every time the Sardinia Cup was held. In 1982, the pattern broke. After a

yacht racing was overshadowed by the luck.

There was little doubt that the front-runners of the nineteen teams were expected to be the defenders, the Americans, and the home team. The Italians have a reputation for light-weather sailing; with the huge anticyclone, which ensured the faint breezes for two weeks, in control, the conditions were made for them.

One thing was certain: Chuck Kirsch's 45-foot Frers-designed *Scaramouche* was bound to have a close tussle with her near sister ship, Robin Aisher's *Yeoman XXIII. Scaramouche* was joined in the American team by Bill Powers' Holland 44, *High Roller,* and the Nelson and Marek near minimum rater, *Thunderbolt.* Italy favored two Peterson designs in *Almagores* and

On one of the days when there was any breeze in 1982, Espada *made a good showing.*

Mandrake, with the Vallicelli-designed *Brava;* it was the team which had been at the Admiral's Cup, but now they were without their three California skippers. Two of the British boats were from the three which had won the Admiral's Cup: *Dragon,* Brian and Pamela Saffery Cooper's Dubois 39-footer, and *Yeoman XXIII.* The other was a 41-foot Holland design, *Woolly Jumper,* owned by John Hogan, with a largely South African crew led by David Bongers.

One might be forgiven for thinking that the race committee, with a general recall and a postponement, might have gotten the starting line somewhere near square for the first race, but it did not. Even then, the race might not have been all bad had the committee not set the leeward mark so close to the shore that it was in the area badly affected by the hills along the shore. It sat in a totally flat patch. The three maximum 40-foot raters had shown what might have been with a battle royal among *Midnight Sun,* a Holland 50-footer racing for Papua-New Guinea; Victor Forss' Frers 51, *Carat* (ex-SORC-winner *Retaliation*); and Dennis Doyle's beautifully varnished Frers 51, *Moonduster,* a boat of slightly earlier vintage than the other

Big Foot and the Ridder *Sabina,* were third and fourth. The bigger boats were nowhere, not even the well-sailed ones.

The 145-mile Asinara race took the first boat more than 27 hours to finish; it was a stop-go race, with the wind switching on and off throughout. *Big Foot,* penalized for a premature start from the previous race, got this one right – at times sailing level with *Moonduster,* rating 10 feet above her – to win from *Almagores.* Then came three Frers 45s led by *Bribon IV,* sailed by Star world champion Antonio Gorostegui for Spain, *Scaramouche,* and *Yeoman XXIII.*

The light winds put an end to any inshore racing before the long race, which was a windless marathon with *Almagores* first home after 88 hours, 12 minutes. Only forty boats

two. All three came to a grinding halt as they ran toward this vacuum at the end of the third leg of the Olympic course. The pileup around the buoy was such that carefully planned strategies earlier in the race which had produced good positions were evaporated with the breeze, and the outcome was no more than a lottery. Out of the ruck came the Dubois minimum-rater *Highland Fling* (formerly *Vanguard*), steered by Eddie Warden Owen for Hong Kong, to take the corrected-time win from *Espada,* a 30-foot rating Judel & Vrolijk design racing for Austria. Two other minimum-raters, the Norlin-designed

finished within the time limit, and there were those like Jean-Louis Fabry of France who turned around and sailed home before the final outcome of the series was known. There was only time to sail one more inshore race with a depleted fleet. The Italians won the series, with the United States second and Belgium third. Everyone left Porto Cervo hoping that this was very much a one-off set of conditions and wondering whether the effort had been worthwhile. But the conditions will be forgotten before the next Sardinia Cup. Porto Cervo has too much to recommend it.

Moonduster *leads* Midnight Sun *and* Carat *as the three 40-foot racers lead in the first inshore race in 1982.*

Middle Sea Race

The Middle Sea Race falls somewhere between eulogies and politics. Those who have competed in the race find it has its own charm, one not found even in other Mediterranean races, yet its development has been retarded by the Maltese government.

When it began in the late 1960s, that decade of riotous development when tomorrow was ignored if it promised any problems, the race had everything going for it. There was talk of marinas, of concessionary rates for boats and their maintenance, and of possibilities of other races to encourage even further the overwintering of northern European boats in Malta.

The race was the brainchild of two young men, then sailors in Malta. One was Alan Green, later to become the Secretary of the Royal Ocean Racing Club but at the time working for the government. "When Jimmy White and I started it," he said, "we did it because we believed that there should be just such a race. We believed that the weather in October and November was conducive to holding a 600-mile race and so we

set about organizing it." Green and White were both members of the Royal Malta Yacht Club and used that club to help to organize the race, but at the same time they both realized the international implications of the event, and also approached the RORC for support. That support was forthcoming and has continued.

Among the field of twelve yachts that lined up for the first race in 1969, six different nationalities were represented. Any fleet of that time that could include Kees Bruynzeel's van de Stadt-designed ketch *Stormvogel* could claim to be a quality fleet. That famous yacht was not to be the winner, however. That honor went to the Guy Thompson-designed and Italian-owned *Surprise* of Nicola Puccinelli and Mario Violati. John Ripard's Swan 37, *Tikka,* was second, while in third place was a young lieutenant in the Royal Navy, Leslie Williams, with the 53-foot *Spirit of Cutty Sark,* the boat in which he had finished fourth in the previous year's OSTAR.

Williams has happy memories of the three Middle Sea Races he has taken part in. "Green

Waiting for the gun — Sebastien *(France),* Levantedes *(Italy), and* Gemini, *partly hidden, 1983. The start was very slow due to the sheltered harbor.*

previous page: *The imaginary starting line, with the Valletta Bastion in the background.*

Bill McAteer's Immigrant *(Canada) participated in 1981.*

Start of Class I, 1981.

was right," he said. "It is a super course. It has its disadvantages however. The wind never seems to hold throughout; there is always a period of calm." Others who have competed at other times agree. "It's sailing through the Aeolian Islands in the moonlight that I remember best, and the chance of a puff of smoke from either Etna or Stromboli," added Williams.

The course from Valletta goes first to Lampedusa to the southwest, then northwest to Pantelleria and around the north side of Sicily to Stromboli, down through the Straits of Messina and back to Valletta. The famous whirlpools of mythology, Scylla and Charybdis, add to the current problems in the Straits of Messina, while the circular course, with its grand scenery, promises virtually every wind direction.

Williams was perhaps not so happy soon after the blowy start of the second race when all the headsails, or almost all, of the 71-foot *Ocean Spirit* had the luff wires pull out. "Not only that," he said, "it was one of those races in which the prizes are given out in reverse order of ratings." The time-on-time handicap system of the RORC was perhaps not right for this stop-go race.

John Rippard won that race, while Alan Green skippered *Ismaele* to a Class-I win. A year later, Eric Tabarly entered *Pen Duick III,* but failed to win either overall or in class; Cino Ricci won the race with one of the smallest boats — another reverse order of ratings type of race.

In 1973, when Wally Stenhouse was busy accumulating points for his World Offshore Championship win, he took *Aura* to the Mediterranean and won the race, and for many years lived in the record books as the fastest around the course. Warren Brown and his crew on *War Baby* will continue to dispute that. *Aura* won her class, and Ted Turner won his in *Lightnin'.* There were thirty-two boats in the race and the event appeared to have established itself firmly on the map.

All that did not take account of the changes

that were to be made in Malta. When Dom Mintoff came to power, the development of yachting took a back seat. The number of starters began to fall off, even when Martini International became sponsors of the race. Giorgio Carriero won the 1974 race with his S&S *Mandrake* and Enrico Masini did it again for Italy with *Valentina* the following year.

"Ziggy" Kahlbetzer had won Class II with *Bumblebee II* in 1973, and he did the same thing with *Bumblebee III* in 1976. He considered his efforts in this race with an Australian boat to be more than just worthwhile, but he still did not get the overall win that he sought; that went to the One-Tonner *Sumbra IV,* which was nearly an

hour ahead of *Bumblebee III* on corrected time.

Benbow, a 65-foot Dick Carter design, won Class I that year, and did it again in 1977 when she was first home and won the race on corrected time. The following year Bill Whitehouse-Vaux entered *Mistress Quickly* in the race and went around the course in record time when the wind held generally well. He could not emulate *Benbow's* performance, however, and was beaten by the Italian *Nita IV* by 1½ hours on corrected time. The twenty-five starters that year came from ten nations.

There were only fifteen starters when *Nita* did it again the following year. She did it again in 1980, when once more "Ziggy" Kahlbetzer

turned up to win his class (this time Class I) with the latest *Bumblebee* (this one was number IV), and on this occasion he did win line honors.

The number of starters was down to thirteen by 1981 when the French *Antares,* a mini-maxi that had won the Seahorse Maxi series in Britain, brought off the line honors and handicap double in a light-airs race.

There was still some magic for the big boats in 1982 when Marvin Green took the Bermuda Race record holder *Nirvana* to Valletta for the race. *Nirvana* obliged by giving her owner line honors, but there was no way that the Pedrick-designed 81-footer could hold her time on handicap to beat Giuseppe Diano's *Levantedes.*

Fantasque *(France) chases* Manfredo *(Italy) and (top left-hand side)* Gemini *(Italy) and* Saudade *(Germany).*

155

Observer
Single-Handed
Transatlantic Race

Only a man as courageous and adventurous as Blondie Hasler would have given second thoughts to a single-handed race across the Atlantic in the late 1950s. Hasler, to be precise, Lieutenant-Colonel H. G. Hasler, Royal Marines (Retired), was the instigator and leader of the famous "Cockleshell Heroes" raid to St. Nazaire in the Second World War and had taken to ocean racing, with considerable success, with the "converted" 30-Square-Metre, *Tre Sang*. It was the sort of boat which gave Hasler an additional challenge. Totally unsuited, as everybody agreed, for offshore sailing, *Tre Sang* had been designed under the International rule of her class as a day racer for inshore waters – in fact, a large class of them flourished for many years on the Swiss lakes.

Hasler was an innovator. He had experimented for many years with different rigs in an effort to make sailing less demanding on the energies of the skipper. He was certain that there should be ways of steering a boat without needing someone constantly at the helm. He was aware of the self-steering for model yachts and felt that this type of control could be adapted to full-sized yachts. From his early experiments with the twin mainsail Lungstrom rig, Hasler went on to develop, on his 25-foot Folkboat, a Chinese lugsail rig on an unstayed cantilevered mast. This, he believed, was capable of taking him across the Atlantic with a minimum of discomfort, since the sail could be trimmed, reefed, and unreefed without him having to go out on deck.

For a race to take place, however, there was a need for another competitor. Hasler found one in another highly individualistic man, whose early years had been spent as a solo aviator over very long distances – Francis Chichester. His navigational skills were unquestioned, and

Eric Tabarly's 73-foot Pen Duick VI *almost dwarfed by the 236-foot four-master* Club Méditerranée *of Alain Colas at the start in 1976.*

previous page: *Nick Keig's* Three Legs of Mann III *at the start of the OSTAR 1980.*

Chichester had begun to derive great personal satisfaction from sailing alone. He and Hasler met, and the germ of an idea grew. Chichester went as far as saying that if no one would organize the race, he would take Hasler on for a wager of half a crown. Several yacht clubs did turn down the race; single-handed sailing across oceans was considered foolhardy.

All credit, therefore, must go to the Flag Officers and Committee of the Royal Western Yacht Club for agreeing to organize the race from Plymouth to New York, and similarly to the editor and directors of *The Observer* for accepting the sponsorship. These two organizations pumped breath into the embryo, formulating the rules and disseminating the information. More than fifty inquiries about entering the race were received from places as far apart as Germany and the United States, and by the time entries closed, there were eight

signed up. Only five started, and one was late.

Francis Chichester had by far the largest boat, the 39-foot Robert Clark-designed *Gipsy Moth III* (she was named after the famous de Havilland aircraft Chichester had flown). Hasler's junk-rigged Folkboat, at 25 feet, was not the smallest boat, and in Val Howell's *Eira,* she had a conventionally rigged sistership to afford comparison. One of the Laurent Giles-designed Vertue class, *Cardinal Vertue,* was sailed by Dr. David Lewis, while the late starter was Frenchman Jean Lacombe, with the tiny 21-foot *Cape Horn.* It was an assorted collection.

On June 11, 1960, four yachts left Plymouth at ten o'clock in the morning on what can hardly be described as a race. The extra size of Chichester's boat soon saw him leading, although Hasler's *Jester* had been first across the line. Each of the skippers had preconceived ideas about how to tackle this Atlantic crossing. The bearded Welshman, Howells, and later Lacombe, had decided to take the Trade Wind route, going south to warmer climes and fairer winds. It was a longer way to go than the Great Circle route, but it had the advantage of greater comfort and less demand on the boat and its rig. Chichester, the navigator, and Lewis opted for the shortest distance, taking the Great Circle, but Hasler, always the inquisitive adventurer, went farther to the north to get on the top side of the low pressure Atlantic depressions in order to find easterly winds.

It was not long before they were into gales, although the first major damage came after only 3½ hours, when *Cardinal Vertue's* mast broke and Lewis had to head back for repairs. He returned to the race two days later. The gales hit on the second night out and gave even Chichester something to note in his log: "The noise these seas make is terrific. So much that I several times started getting out of my berth thinking the yacht had been struck by a steamer or that the mast had gone overboard."

When Chichester was halfway across, and had just endured a storm during which he estimated that the wind reached 100 mph, the fleet was widely spread. Lewis, after his restart, was nearly 400 miles behind on the same track, while Hasler, on his northerly route, was driving through a gale with only a fragment of sail hoisted and bemoaning the fact that he was not cruising, when he would have been comfortably hove to. For one at least, the difference between racing and cruising was all too readily apparent.

Chichester passed the Ambrose Light at the entrance to New York, which was the finish of the race, after 40 days, wondering if anyone had made it earlier. He need not have worried. His longer boat had seen to the necessary extra speed, but Hasler's opportunism did give him considerable gains in the more favorable winds, so that the much smaller *Jester* was only 8 days behind the winner. It was another 8 days before Lewis came home third.

Val Howells had all sorts of problems; battery acid over his food and clothes, coupled with the loss of his chronometer and thereby any means of establishing longitude, forced him to sail into Bermuda (he could still discern his latitude and sailed down that of Bermuda). He stayed there for a week before taking up the challenge again to finish after 63 days, with the Frenchman still at sea for another 11 days.

What the race had proved was that it was possible, that self-steering devices worked, and that for all competitors it was a worthwhile exercise they would like to do again.

They did – four years later when the race was next held. That race, however, was very different from the first. Analysis of the 1960 race had been made by several people in several different areas. In France, Eric Tabarly, a thirty-two-year-old lieutenant in the French navy, had decided to build a boat to try to win the race. In Britain, the features editors of newspapers had also seen the potential of the adventurous nature of the race and signed up several of the competitors for regular daily radioed reports, despite *The Observer's* sponsorship and its regular weekly coverage. All over the world, sailors contemplated the answers to the numerous problems of single-handed racing, and, in consequence, the entry list trebled.

Tabarly was then unknown in the ocean-racing world. He calculated, however, that he could handle a 44-foot yacht of moderately light displacement, believing that the largest boat stood the best chance of winning. His thinking was well reasoned and logical—a much older man, Chichester (fifty-eight years old in 1960), had been able to cope with a 39-foot boat which everyone had thought beyond him, and had come through to win. Tabarly himself was only interested in winning, and to keep some of his plans in proportion, he chose a ketch rig with its proportionally smaller headsails. Even so, at the time, it was considered a formidable project.

There was no real answer to Tabarly and his *Pen Duick II*. Two years earlier, Chichester had done a 33-day crossing, but the Frenchman was to knock nearly a week off that time in the race. He maintained radio silence, which tended to drive his fellow competitors, and the press, wild – Tabarly's answer was that he did not like the radio. It was Chichester who feared him most, and in one of his radio reports to *The Guardian* he expressed this, saying: "Tabarly is the dark horse in this race and I think I can hear him galloping through the night. If my senses tell me right I can make him out about 120 miles to the north." Chichester must have been psychic. The winner of the first race was, nevertheless, making much better time than before.

When Tabarly was at last sighted, by a Royal

Canadian Air Force plane, he was 350 miles from Newport, Rhode Island, where the race was due to finish; it was estimated that on his average of 100 miles a day, he would complete the course in 27 days, two thirds of the time Chichester had taken four years earlier. He was just under 4 hours over that time, but it was only then that it became known that his self-steering had packed up when 1,000 miles out from Plymouth, and from then, he had never had more than 1½ hours

of sleep at any one time and that rarely.

Tabarly was a hero. All Frenchmen took him to their hearts; he had won a victory, one against perfidious Albion. President Charles de Gaulle reflected that esteem by making Tabarly a Chevalier of the Légion d'Honneur.

Without the interference of Tabarly, Chichester's time of 3 minutes short of 30 days (his aim in 1960) would have been impressive. So, too, would that of third-placed Val Howells in

the 35-foot *Akka,* 1½ days behind Chichester, as he had been damaged at the start and forced to return to Plymouth to make repairs. In turn, he was 4 days faster than a man who was to make a greater name for himself and his boat later, Alec Rose with *Lively Lady.*

That year, 1964, the first three multihulls were entered, and, although their performance was inauspicious, attracted Tabarly's notice.

Four years later, he was back with a

Walter Greene with his own designed and built trimaran, Chaussettes Olympia.

trimaran, 70 feet long, which was finished only just in time for him to make the start; and he was not alone. Of the thirty-five entries, thirteen were multihulls, including the winner of the 1966 Round Britain Race, the 35-foot Kelsall-designed *Toria*, renamed for this race *Gancia Girl*, as Martin Minter-Kemp was one of those to secure sponsorship (from the company making the Italian sparkling wine Gancia). Booze was the name of the game in most of the sponsorships; Les Williams had his from Cutty Sark whisky, Bill Howell from Courage's brewery, and Colin Forbes from Watneys. The name of one of the world's most famous yachtsmen was given to a British boat as a tribute to his commercial empire, which survives him. *Sir Thomas Lipton* was the 57-foot Robert Clark-designed monohull ketch of Geoffrey Williams; a contrast in beverages from alcohol to Lipton's tea.

The big boats took most of the prerace publicity – after all, it had been the biggest boat which had won the previous two races – but considerable attention was also given to the delicate form of the 30-foot proa *Cheers*. When Tom Follett had first made application to the Royal Western Yacht Club for entry to the race and had submitted drawings of the boat, which Dick Newick had designed and Jim Morris had financed in an effort to win the race, his entry was refused. When he turned up in Britain, having sailed *Cheers* all the way from St. Croix in the American Virgin Islands, the organizers had second thoughts. Follett had proved himself; that year so did everybody else, the race committee having decided that it was essential for everyone to have done at least 500 miles alone in his boat. It was also the manner in which Follett had sailed to the start which attracted members of the specialist press, many of whom were to put an each-way bet on *Cheers* at good odds.

Les Williams, with the 53-foot *Spirit of Cutty Sark*, was one of the favorites, as was the smaller 49-foot *Voortrekker* of South African Bruce Dalling, a design by van der Stadt then rigged as a ketch. The experts pointed to Geoffrey Williams, the quiet Cornishman with the well-tried 57-foot ketch *Sir Thomas Lipton*.

What they were not to know about Geoffrey Williams was that he had managed to arrange his own special weather predictions from a weather center in London. He was to be informed by radio of the correct course to take from computer predictions of the weather patterns. It was to prove, for him, to be a race-winning element of prerace planning. Ten days after the start, the gales associated with a deep depression made their mark on the fleet. Up to then, Bruce Dalling had been leading, with the two Williamses just ahead of Bill Howell. The storm was so severe that most lay ahull in the 60-knot winds. Geoffrey Williams, however, had been advised of this coming storm and recommended

Peter Phillips, the Exeter policeman, who raised funds for children's charities as he sailed the trimaran Livery Dole II. *Unfortunately, one hull broke away and Phillips was forced to abandon the yacht.*

163

Jester, *the modified Folkboat with a Chinese junk rig, the boat with which Blondie Hasler started it all.* Jester *sailed in the 1960 and 1964 races with Hasler and subsequently every other race with Michael Richey.*

to head north before it arrived and thus avoid the worst. He was, therefore, making miles toward Newport while the rest were "parked" and made between 200 and 300 miles on his rivals, a jump that was to prove unrecoverable by the rest.

Soon after the start, Tabarly bumped into a freighter. He had narrowly missed an earlier one and was down below when he crashed into the anchored vessel at 15 knots. He returned to Plymouth 36 hours after the start and was back in the hunt another 36 hours later; but all was not well, and he pulled out a day later when he found the steering gear being shaken to pieces.

There were other breakages. Masts and rudders failed, and there were leaks which sent others home. Another boat sank when in tow after being dismasted, and then the problems of Joan de Kat and his trimaran *Yaksha* became known. He had repaired his mast in Alderney, and a week later sent out a Mayday call when he had lost mast and a rudder, and one of his outer hulls had come adrift. Ships and aircraft of six nations helped in the search, which concluded with an RAF Shackleton aircraft guiding a Norwegian freighter to pick up the Frenchman.

There were other problems for the race leader. Because of a jammed halyard, he had sailed a long way to the north near the Nova Scotia coast and was heading to the north of the Nantucket Light. He was advised that the course had been amended to take the fleet south of this but replied that his instructions, as received from the Royal Western Yacht Club, had not been amended. Jack Odling-Smee of the RWYC had little time to make a decision but agreed that under the circumstances, *Sir Thomas Lipton* should be allowed to continue her intended course. It is highly unlikely that a decision going

the other way would have altered the result.

Sir Thomas Lipton crossed the line at the Brenton Reef Tower 4 hours under 26 days – 31½ hours faster than Tabarly in 1960. *Voortrekker* was some 17 hours later in second place, while *Cheers,* coming from the Azores southerly route, was a further 6½ hours behind, thoroughly vindicating the Follett-Newick-Morris partnership's faith in their vessel. There were to be only nineteen finishers out of the thirty-five who started, and the race committee was going to look harder at the boats and the sailors in the future. At the tail end of the fleet, 57 days after the start, *Jester,* under her new owner, Michael Richey, crossed the finish line. One of the race's originals, she was last to make Newport. Four years later, Richey took almost a day longer to get there in *Jester!*

For the first race, Chichester's *Gipsy Moth* had been considered, at 39 feet, to be too big for one man to handle. Twelve years later, in 1972, Jean-Yves Terlain had a boat more than three times as long, the three-masted 128-foot *Vendredi Treize.* Designed by Dick Carter, this monster had a relatively simple and easily handled sail plan of three boomed staysails, to which Terlain had added three light weather headsails for the flat patches he had experienced in the previous race when just off the American coast. So far, it had always been the biggest boat to finish that had won, but was it possible for Terlain to handle efficiently a boat this big?

Alain Colas had taken over Tabarly's trimaran and had sailed it many thousands of miles, making alterations that made it faster and more sailable. He was the favorite to beat his countryman. Another well fancied was a third Frenchman, Jean-Marie Vidal, with the trimaran *Cap 33.* If it blew hard, there was no doubt that *British Steel,* the boat which Chay Blyth sailed single-handed non-stop around the world in a westerly direction, would be in the running. She was skippered by Brian Cooke, who had been sixth the previous time with the 32-foot *Opus.* There was also Follett to consider, this time with the 46-foot trimaran *Three Cheers,* as well as the unusual 65-foot monohull *Strongbow* of Martin Minter-Kemp.

Chichester was there too, but Sir Francis' tale in this race was one of woe. He was seventy years old and frail; his craft, *Gipsy Moth V,* was 57 feet and demanding. It was doubtful if he was a match for his boat. At the prerace dinner, he had to be helped to his feet to speak. A week after the start, he was on his way back to Plymouth; through some communication confusion, a French weather ship had gone too close to *Gipsy Moth V* and had damaged her mizzen mast. Then a Royal Navy frigate took Giles Chichester, Sir Francis' son, and transferred him to the boat, together with two friends, to aid the ailing skipper back to port. There is one other sad

Paul Ricard, *Eric Tabarly's hydrofoil trimaran in which Marc Pajot was an unofficial entrant in 1980.*

consequence to this; the French weather ship later collided with an American yacht on its way to help Chichester, sinking it with the loss of seven lives. Chichester sailed no more; he died later that year.

There were fifty-four starters from twelve countries and a reduction in the proportion of multihulls for this race; there were just eight, two of which were catamarans. By general consensus, the race was a breeze, except for a gale on the fifteenth day. It took the masts out of Gerard Djikstra's *Second Life* and Bob Miller's *Mersea Pearl*. Murray Sayle lost his mast sometime later from his catamaran *Lady of Fleet,* but was towed into Newport by the coast guard. Bill Howell was lucky to survive a collision in the fog with a Russian trawler close to the American coast but had to retire from the race.

Halfway across the Atlantic, there was the most amazing coincidence. Colas in *Pen Duick IV* and Terlain in *Vendredi Treize* passed within hailing distance of each other, Colas coming from behind to take the lead, one he never relinquished. He smashed the course record by over 5 days and was 16 hours ahead of Terlain and his huge boat. Vidal, going south with *Cap 33*, was third, while Cooke was not far behind. In all, forty finished, and three others limped in after the 60-day time limit had run out.

In 1976, there was a change of heart by the first two to finish four years before; Colas abandoned the multihulls in favor of a gigantic monohull, while Terlain dropped his idea for a catamaran. Colas' 236-foot four-masted schooner was one of the biggest yachts ever built.

The challenge for Colas was even greater than might be readily apparent from looking at the boat he intended to sail. He had, only

Millbay Dock, Plymouth, prior to the 1980 start.

fourteen months before the start, suffered a serious leg injury, and only his insistence saved the limb from being amputated. The race committee was not keen, in the light of previous experience, to allow Colas to race unless he was perfectly fit, and he had some difficulty in persuading it that he was. He did all that was required of him to qualify both himself and the boat, but in hindsight he must have regretted that he had not had more time at sea to discover the problems associated with a vessel of this size. Undersized halyards were to prove his downfall.

Terlain, however, went for a boat that was tried and tested. With Kriter sponsorship, he took over the 70-foot catamaran *British Oxygen,* with which two years previously, Robin Knox-Johnston had won the Round Britain Race. Terlain, however, made some alterations to the hulls with which neither the builder nor the designer agreed, and, it is believed, these were his downfall. In a gale-beset race, *Kriter III* began to take water through the new hatches in her hulls, and with Terlain unable to pump the water out fast enough, the added strains on the boat

Streamer on the way across to Plymouth.

Tragedy struck before the race started. Lizzie McMullen was electrocuted while working on her husband Mike's trimaran *Three Cheers* just three days before the race was due to get under way. Despite the huge psychological shock, McMullen decided that he would compete. Fellow competitors, as a memorial to his wife, presented the Lizzie McMullen Trophy for the first multihull to finish. Mike McMullen was never to know who won. He was last sighted three hours after the race began; from then, there was nothing more heard or seen of him until four years later, when a small piece of *Three Cheers* turned up in a fisherman's net off Iceland.

In the excitement surrounding the giants prior to the start (the 128-foot *Vendredi Treize* was back, skippered by Yvon Fauconnier and renamed *ITT Oceanic*), one man was generally overlooked. Eric Tabarly had entered the 73-foot *Pen Duick VI,* the boat he had sailed in the Whitbread Round-the-World Race fully crewed. It did not appear that he had made many concessions to single-handed sailing, apart from fitting self-steering, and for that reason alone, most people were prepared to write off his chances. But Tabarly is one man you cannot afford to write off.

This time, four women were in the race. One was the petite Clare Francis, with a boat as big as it was once thought possible for a man to sail alone across the Atlantic—the 38-foot *Robertson's Golly.* Clare pushed herself and her boat hard; she had tight broadcasting and newspaper-reporting schedules to meet, as well as having to sail her boat. In addition, she shot some of the most dramatic and honest footage of the race for a BBC television documentary. Despite these extra pressures, she was able to finish thirteenth of the 124 who started and establish a women's record of just over 29 days.

This was a very impressive performance in light of the weather which the competitors faced that year. Seven full gales blocked the path of those taking the shortest route, and times generally were slow. Casualties were high—fifty-one failed to finish, although five of those did reach Newport after the 50-day time limit had run out. There were many dismastings, five sinkings, and a further tragedy with the disappearance of Mike Flanagan from the 38-foot *Galloping Gael.* The boat was found in mid-Atlantic with no one on board, and it is presumed that Flanagan must have fallen overboard.

The gales nearly wiped out Tabarly. A third of the way across, his self-steering was damaged beyond repair, and he turned back. After a day's thought, however, he decided that perhaps he could carry on, which makes his performance all the more remarkable. He arrived in Newport unannounced early one morning and gilled up and down the harbor until help was at hand. It

caused the crossbeams to fail. Before *Kriter III* sank, Terlain was rescued by a Russian vessel.

It was the year of the American bicentennial, and the entries from the United States were higher than ever before; two of them were possible winners. Mike Kane had the appropriately named (for the year) *Spirit of America,* while Tom Grossman had bought *Cap 33* after the last race and spent a lot of his time learning to sail her offshore. One of the top boats from the United States did not make the start — Phil Weld had capsized the 60-foot trimaran *Gulf*

was 7 hours before the next boat arrived. Tabarly had won the race again but in the most exhausting way, without self-steering for 2,000 miles and with a boat that was not prepared for short-handed racing, one which drove him to the limits of his stamina in conditions that were the worst the race has ever known.

Colas was next home with the 236-foot *Club Méditerranée*, but he had had to put in to St. John's, Newfoundland, to renew broken halyards and had received extra assistance there beyond what the race committee felt was allowed. Colas was penalized 58 hours. Mike Birch sprang the real surprise of the race when he was next home with the 31-foot trimaran *The Third Turtle*. It gained him three major prizes: the Jester Trophy for the small class, the Lizzie McMullen Trophy, and the multihull handicap prize. Just 3 hours after Birch came the Pole Kazimierz Jaworski with the 38-foot monohull *Spaniel*. After him came the more expected front-runner Tom Grossman and Jean-Claude Parisis with *Petrouchka*, closely followed by the first of the British competitors, David Palmer with the pink-hulled trimaran *FT*.

The race organizers reacted strongly to the way boats were being developed for the race; they felt, justifiably, that there was a chance of more huge boats being built and that these were detracting from the original concept of the race, which was "to defeat the ocean." Their restraints were therefore hard. For safety's sake, they limited the fleet to 110 competitors, stipulating also that none should be more than 56 feet overall. The latter limit sent the French sailors into high dudgeon, complaining that this move was solely to curb possible French domination of the event. The decision was made early enough, in January 1977, for all competitors to arrange for suitable boats in time for the 1980 race.

The complaints were forgotten as the race approached and a rash of new boats began to appear. The intervening Round Britain Race had seen Chay Blyth win with the maximum-sized *Great Britain IV,* followed by Nick Keig with *Three Legs of Mann II*. However, Blyth withdrew from the race with sponsor difficulties, and Keig sold his boat and built another. Tabarly entered his foil-borne trimaran *Paul Ricard,* while Phil Weld, who had been third in the Round Britain Race with the 60-foot *Rogue Wave,* built a new boat to the maximum dimensions, *Moxie.*

Grossman obtained sponsorship for another maximum-sized trimaran from Kriter, designed by Dick Newick, who also modified the drawings of *Three Cheers* for an Olympus-sponsored boat for Mike Birch. The United States challenge was formidable; Walter Greene and Phil Steggall in identical Greene designs, both entered in the moderate-sized Gipsy Moth class, and a triple-pronged attack possible with Gerry Cartright in the Jester class with the monohull *Le First.*

Once again, there were four women, led by Dame Naomi James. She had another race on her hands — with her husband, Rob, who was to sail the 31-foot trimaran *Boatfile.* Naomi was sailing the boat in which she had become the first woman to sail round the world single-handed, renamed *Kriter Lady.* This boat first sailed in the OSTAR in 1968 as *Spirit of Cutty Sark,* when it was considered more than a handful for Leslie Williams. Florence Arthàud just failed to make the starting line with her 49-foot *Miss Dubonnet;* a rigging screw gave way as she was sailing to the line, and the mast folded neatly over the side. Judy Lawson had her mast crumple in mid-Atlantic, and her *Serta Perfectsleeper* was taken aboard a passing freighter. The fourth woman, Joan Connors, never got to Plymouth. Naomi, however, put in a new record time for women of 25 days, 19 hours, more than 4 days faster than Les Williams in the same boat in 1968! She was twenty-fourth, but lost her race with Rob, who was 3 days ahead and sixteenth.

For this race, each of the boats was fitted with an Argos system transponder. The signals from these passed via a satellite to a ground station, and a regular accurate check was kept on the position of every boat throughout the race. It was a complex communications package which benefited the competitors because the weather information the Argos transponders automatically transmitted was able to allow the Meteorological Office at Bracknell in Berkshire to provide more accurate forecasts for the fleet. These were broadcast each day over the BBC's World Service program at 0300 GMT. The accurate positioning of the boats also made for greater safety; each of the transponders was fitted with a "panic button."

Prior to the start, the bookmakers' favorite was Tom Grossman, but he had the bad luck to be hit by a fellow competitor just before the start. He had to turn back into Plymouth and lost 26 hours before he could restart. It was too much for Grossman to catch up to the leaders, but he was eventually tenth despite the late start and a time penalty for being late for the scrutineering.

Tabarly was forced to withdraw because of an old skiing injury, but his sponsors asked if Marc Pajot could replace him. The race committee decided that Pajot had not completed the qualifying cruise but allowed a transponder to be fitted to the boat and Pajot to be an unofficial entrant not eligible for any prizes. The same indulgence was granted to Jean-Yves Terlain and the catamaran *Gautier I;* he was a late entry and only admitted because he had competed in the previous three races, but he, too, could not take any prizes this time. Not that he would have; he was forced to retire.

The early part of the race was very fast with northerly winds blowing, so that all the yachts were on a point of sailing that they liked. There

were ninety-two of them, with *Paul Ricard* setting the pace. Behind Pajot were Weld, Loizeau (with the trimaran *Gauloises IV*), Birch, Steggall, and Keig, with Rob James not far astern of the leaders. Paul Rigudel, with the trimaran *VSD,* was another of the front-runners, and after the first week he was right up with Weld, chasing Pajot. The French press, to a man, had declared that if Pajot were first into Newport, official entrant or not, for them he would be the winner.

It was a fast week, but it took its toll. Loizeau's boat split a hull in the pounding and headed home. Birch's tri lost some of the underside of the bridge deck, and he had to slow to effect repairs. He told the race committee that he now could not really be considered a competitor but was heading for Newport. Luckily, he was not taken at his word.

Eight days out, Weld dipped slightly to the south to avoid some bad weather, which slowed the Frenchmen to the north of him and allowed Weld to take up the front running. It was a strategic move that was to pay handsome dividends. By this stage, what was going on was not quite clear, as some of the Argos transponders had failed; their casings cracked and let in water which discharged the batteries.

Weld pressed on, while Pajot had to go to Newfoundland to repair the genoa furler. The rest of the entries were trailing astern of *Moxie;* Rigudel's *VSD* had lost a lot of her crossbeam fairing; Greene and Keig were hanging in; Steggall's position was unknown.

The fogs and calms of the Newfoundland Banks continued to Cape Sable and on to Nantucket; it was frustrating for the sailors and delayed the leaders by more than a day. It was early in the morning when *Moxie* crossed the line at the Brenton Tower 48 minutes under 18 days from the start. The huge spectator fleet, expecting an American win, got their fill. The horns screeched, and the cheering was loud for the oldest competitor in the race and the most popular, particularly with the home crowd – the man who had spent ten years preparing himself through a succession of boats for just this moment. A year earlier, writing in *Sail* magazine, Weld had made the prophecy: "On Wednesday 25 June 1980, a trimaran will win *The Observer* Single-Handed Transatlantic Race." He added: "He'll be followed within 24 hours by six other boats, any of whom might have won had they had his luck." It was June 25, 1980, and five boats did cross the finish line within 24 hours of Weld. Seven hours after the winner came Nick Keig, followed 40 minutes later by Steggall, with Mike Birch (retired? – far from it) another half hour behind. Pajot came in 6½ hours behind Birch, and then came Greene.

The American flag flew proudly over Newport. Weld's win, together with Steggall's first in the Gipsy Moth class, might have been made perfect had Gerry Cartright completed his declaration to show that he had taken stores from a fishing boat. As it was, he lost his Jester class first place by disqualification.

Three Cheers, *the Dick Newick trimaran in which Mike McMullen disappeared during the 1976 race.*

Observer
Europe 1 Two-Handed
Transatlantic Race

previous page: Elf
Aquitaine *and* Sea Falcon
*moored at Goat Island,
Newport, at the finish of
the 1982 Race.*

below and opposite page:
*Rob James and Chay Blyth
and their 66-foot
Shuttleworth-designed
trimaran* Brittany Ferries
GB, *winners of the 1980
Two-Handed Trans-
atlantic Race.*

The limitations of the size of boat and the
number in the fleet of the 1980 OSTAR
led to consideration by the organizers
and sponsors that there should perhaps be
another race into which those who were
disappointed for one reason or another should
be accommodated. The success of the 1979
Transat en Double pointed the way to a two-
handed race, and the course from Plymouth to
Newport, Rhode Island, was classic.

The race, which started on June 6, 1981, had
103 cross the line at Plymouth. It was to prove
tough yet fast and popular with all the
competitors. It was also to prove firmly the total
superiority of multihulls in this type of ocean
racing–it will be a long time before circumstances and conditions are such that a monohull
will win one of these events outright. In assessing
the opposition before the start Rob James hardly
bothered to give the monohulls a second glance,
except, that is, for the 70-foot *Kriter Lady II,* the
Freedom 70 which his wife, Dame Naomi, was
scheduled to sail with Ron Holland's wife, Laurel.

"I really didn't think they would have a
chance. I had, for a long time, felt that the
modern trimaran could, if properly rigged and
sailed, go as fast, if not faster, to windward as a
monohull," said James before the race.
Afterward, he was more convinced than ever
that he was right, and the results bore him out.

James was racing with Chay Blyth on the
65-foot John Shuttleworth *Brittany Ferries GB,* a
boat which had been built specially for the race.
It was as big as Blyth and James felt that the two
of them could handle. They had had the
experience of sailing the 54-foot *Great Britain
IV* together and knew that they could handle a
slightly bigger rig, but the hull size would
depend on its weight; that weight which their
maximum efficiency would drive effectively.
They had time to sail the boat, assess its potential,
and make some alterations before starting this
race, rather more time than they ever had had
before. They needed it because the advances in
multihull design in the previous twelve months
had been enormous.

Two of the bigger boats, James was prepared to dismiss; one, as it happened, quite erroneously. The 80-foot *Jacques Ribourel* was old fashioned both in hull form and with ketch rig. Strong winds crippled her, bending her mizzen mast after a week and forcing her skipper, Olivier de Kersauson, to retire. The other was Robin Knox-Johnston's 70-foot catamaran *Sea Falcon*. The wide-staying base of her mast precluded her from pointing efficiently, but her skipper's choice of course kept her very competitive. *Sea Falcon*, a modification of the British Oxygen design, was a heavy boat.

The 63-foot *Elf Aquitaine* of Marc Pajot was quite a different kettle of fish. Pajot had entered

Charles Heidsieck, *Alain Gabbay's 66-foot Vaton design, at the finish.*

this sport from the top level of dinghy racing, winning a silver medal at the 1972 Olympics with his brother Yves in the Flying Dutchman class. He was aware, therefore, of the need to have a thoroughly efficient rig, with low drag characteristics, on fast hull configuration. She was narrower than *Sea Falcon* in her hulls, which had less freeboard. Her rig, too, was clean, fractionally rigged, and efficient. The trimaran *Royale*, a 60-footer, had been as fast as *Elf Aquitaine* on her first outing, and her skipper, Loic Caradec, had fitted her with retractable hydrofoils since then in order to gain stability.

Mike Birch and Walter Greene together in one of the latter's creations was a formidable partnership. Their 53-foot *Tele-7-Jours* had a sistership in the Italian Paolo Martinoni's *Star Point.* A trimaran of similar size was Rigudel's *Lesieur Tournesol,* formerly *VSD,* the winner of the Transat en Double. There were also two 55-foot proas, like two-thirds of a trimaran: *Sudinox,* skippered by Guy Delage, and *Eterna Royal Quartz,* with Jean-Marie Vidal. One day, if race organizers allow proas to race much longer, someone was going to master the proa configuration, and they will be a serious threat to

the more "conventional" multihulls. Neither of the two mentioned, however, survived more than five days of the race, while a third proa that was entered was lost on its way to the start.

In slightly smaller, but no less potent, boats were Phil Steggall and Eric Loizeau. Steggall had finished third in the previous OSTAR, but his 45-foot *Bonifacio,* designed by Dick Newick, was generally felt to be too small to win this race. By the same token, so was *Brittany Ferries FR,* the former *Olympus Photo* in which Birch had finished right behind Steggall in the OSTAR. Loizeau, on the other hand, was known to be a tough sailor, and though his boat had retired from the single-handed race with structural damage, this Newick 44-footer was fast.

Two of the big monohulls had been designed specifically for short-handed racing; *Kriter VIII* and *Monsieur Meuble* (ex-*Kriter V*) were 75 and 69 feet long, respectively. Michel Malinovsky skippered *Kriter VIII,* while *Monsieur Meuble* was in the hands of Florence Arthaud. The other two big monohulls were both IOR boats designed for the forthcoming Whitbread Round-the-World Race: *Charles Heidsieck III* for Alain Gabbay and *Faram-*

KRITER LADY

Serenissima for Bruno Bacilieri. They were to put in remarkably good performances, but the largely windward conditions of the early part of the race must have helped them.

Four days before the start, Dame Naomi James was taken ill and into the hospital, where an ovarian cyst was removed. With it went her chances of competing, and her place with Laurel Holland was taken by 12-Metre skipper John Oakeley aboard *Kriter Lady II.* They were forced to retire in the later stages of the race when the step of one of the three masts came adrift, and there was danger of the mast going through the bottom of the boat.

The start was in a brisk southwesterly which saw all the boats with shortened sail. Within 2 hours of the start, *Brittany Ferries GB,* with a double-reefed main, well-rolled jib, and small staysail, was in the lead. Blyth had her hard on the wind in excess of 10 knots. *Royale* had led her away, but after 3½ hours, she was out of the race with a broken mast. The visibility was bad, but from *Brittany Ferries,* James saw *Sea Falcon* and *Jacques Ribourel* heading below them on a freer course but in a more northwesterly direction than their own westerly port tack was taking

them. It was an easier course for the others, and they would make many more miles; but Blyth and James had decided to follow the rhumb line to Newport in much the same way that Phil Weld had done in the single-handed race of the previous year. Knox-Johnston, on the other hand, had declared before the start that he would be taking the shorter, Great Circle route, which is why when the Argos reports were computed after a couple of days, *Sea Falcon* was level with *Brittany Ferries GB* for the lead.

The southwesterlies continued, backing a little to allow the leaders to crack sheets slightly and make even better progress. By midday on the fourth day out, Blyth and James had pushed *Brittany Ferries GB* 936 miles toward Newport at an average speed of 9¾ knots. Then, for them, the wind went into the southeast, and they set a spinnaker and began to fly along, touching 20 knots at times. The wind increased to the point where the spinnaker had to come down, yet with full main, jib, and staysail set and the wind beginning to veer, the speed was still there, until it came all the way around and the boat was close hauled with some deep reefs and down to 9 knots.

Kriter Lady II, *the Freedom 70 which Dame Naomi James was to have sailed with Laurel Holland. Her place, when she fell ill, was taken by John Oakeley.*

175

It continued to blow all the next day, and by morning it had reached 50 knots from the west. *Brittany Ferries GB* was 50 miles ahead and 240 miles south of *Sea Falcon*. Blyth got a change of wind to the south on the sixth day out and ran 250 miles. The lead went up to 90 miles, and Mike Birch in *Tele-7-Jours* was level with *Sea Falcon*. By then, Tabarly was out of the race – his *Paul Ricard* was leaking in the main hull. Phil Steggall's *Bonifacio* had capsized when both crewmen were down below. She had gone over in moderating weather. Both were picked up by a Royal Navy vessel.

The seventh night at sea was described by James as "one of the most unpleasant that I have ever spent at sea." The 65-foot tri was pounding into enormous waves and 60 knots of wind. Trying to steer facing forward was like standing in the way of a fire hose at full bore. It was not until they tried the autopilot, standing in the shelter of the hatch controlling the autopilot when the wind changed, that either of them had any relief. By noon seven days after the start, *Brittany Ferries GB* was 1,500 miles down the track with a lead of 55 miles. *Elf Aquitaine* was lying ninth at this stage, but she was the biggest threat to the two men on the leading boat, as she had more relative sail area and should deal better with the lighter winds on the west side of the Atlantic.

The ninth day gave the leader her best run: 320 miles of largely spinnaker reaching with the autopilot doing the work. The lead was 130 miles, and there were 1,000 miles to go. *Tele-7-Jours* and *Elf Aquitaine* were now the two nearest boats, and although *Sea Falcon* had lost ground, she had begun to gain places again and was eighth. Two days later, and the leaders faced a tactical decision. They were then near the southernmost tip of the Newfoundland Banks. Either they could stay north in the shallow water off Nova Scotia and then head southwest over the Georges Bank to Nantucket, thereby avoiding the adverse Gulf Stream, or they could sail south of the rhumb line to meet the southwesterly wind in a better place. The decision had to take account of the fact that *Elf Aquitaine* was 80 miles to the south and *Tele-7-Jours* 40 miles farther south on the same line as *Gauloises IV*. Blyth and James chose to stay clear of the Gulf Stream, and spent the next day wondering whether they had made the right decision as they plugged through head winds, making good only 150 miles from 225 sailed.

By noon on the thirteenth day, there were only 310 miles to go for *Brittany Ferries GB*. Birch and Greene had run into trouble with *Tele-7-Jours*. The port forward crossbeam was damaged, and she could be sailed only on starboard tack. Even then, the inventive pair tried sailing her backward in an effort to go where they wanted, but finally they were forced

to go for Liverpool, Nova Scotia. A day's run of 175 miles left *Brittany Ferries GB* with 135 miles to go after a fortnight at sea. She averaged 11 knots to the finish with Blyth and James failing to get there before dark, but they were ensured a warm reception and a large spectator fleet.

A time of 14 days, 14 hours meant an average of 8.5 knots for the course. It was a new east-west sailing record and gave the winners a 16-hour lead over *Elf Aquitaine*. Blyth said afterward that he thought they had won because they had sailed so close to the rhumb line and had made good most of the miles they had sailed. "Wastage gets you nowhere," he declared. Reliability had also helped; very little had gone wrong with the boat or its gear to stop it for very long. They did once have a spinnaker halyard snap shackle open and the boat sail over the kite so that they had to drop the mainsail to slow the

boat in order to retrieve the sail. Just a few hours out from Plymouth, the mainsail outhaul slug had pulled out of the boom, putting a lot of strain on the outhaul wire, which had broken, forcing them to lash the clew of the sail to the boom and lose its adjustment. Apart from those mishaps, a slightly torn mainsail which had had to be repaired, and a sticking genoa furler, the gear on *Brittany Ferries* had been trouble free.

That Loizeau's *Gauloises IV* finished so close to Pajot was a remarkable performance. She is only 44 feet long, and her placing was due to the determination of Loizeau and his crew, Halvard Mabire, and their choice of a southerly course. Robin Knox-Johnston, finishing fourth, believed he had the fastest boat in the race but had made a mistake by going north in the early stages, on the Great Circle route, rather than taking the rhumb line. The latter had proved

right for Weld a year earlier, and this time was definitely the right way to go.

Faram-Serenissima was the first of the monohulls to finish, 36 hours behind the leader and 2½ hours ahead of *Monsieur Meuble*. Philip and Frances Walwyn from St. Kitts were the first of the husband and wife teams to finish, with their 45-foot cruising catamaran *Skyjack;* they were fifteenth. The only monohull to take a prize was *Philips Radio Ocean,* crewed by Patrick Elies and Dominique Hardy; she took Class V. One of the outstanding performances of the race was that of Mark Gatehouse and Michael Holmes with the spidery 30-foot trimaran *Mark One Tool Hire* – they hired the right tool for the job and finished twenty-fourth of the seventy-six finishers in 22 days, 8½ hours, a day faster than Tabarly's winning time in the single-handed race with the 73-foot *Pen Duick VI* in 1976.

The 53-foot trimaran Tele-7-Jours.

Round-the-World Races

Ramon Carlin returns to a triumphant welcome at Portsmouth on Easter Day, 1974. His Sayula II *was the handicap winner.*

Burton Cutter, *Les Williams' 80-foot ketch, which suffered hull problems shortly after leaving Cape Town.*

The idea of a race around the world had been in the minds of yachtsmen for many years. It was proposed as long ago as 1924 when Conor O'Brien sailed around the world in *Saiorse.* The idea became a reality in 1967 with *The Sunday Times* Golden Globe trophy for the first man to sail solo non-stop around the world. Even then, this was not strictly a race, since there was no single starting time or place. In 1969, Anthony Churchill and Guy Pearse, both well versed in ocean racing and its organization, produced a brochure at Cowes Week with details of a race which largely followed the old clipper-ship routes and had stops at Cape Town, Sydney, and Rio de Janeiro. Churchill and Pearse were enthusiastic; but the race was expensive to arrange, and they had trouble finding sponsors. They already had many inquiries by early 1972.

The Royal Navy had proposals for adventure training, and the race seemed likely to form part of its plans; but the navy needed the race to be confirmed. At the same time, the Royal Naval Sailing Association interested Whitbread's brewery in sponsoring a glamorous yacht race. Churchill and Pearse agreed that if they could not find a suitable sponsor by April 1972, they would hand their files over to the RNSA. The hand-over took place on May 8, and the date for the start was fixed shortly afterward – for Saturday, September 8, 1973.

The initial response was huge, but only seventeen boats made the start to the race, which was for fully crewed yachts rated between 33 and 70 feet IOR Mark III.

It is generally agreed that there were several attitudes among those who took part in this race. Most viewed it as an adventure; many, with some trepidation. They were setting forth into the unknown. Those sailors who had gone around the world had done so with no other purpose than satisfying themselves that it could be done; none of them had faced the challenge of doing it against the clock, let alone against a competitor close at hand. The race posed new problems for most of those taking part – the close proximity of only a few fellow beings for a relatively long period was just one of them. Few knew whether it was possible to *race* in the southern oceans, whose Roaring Forties and Screaming Fifties were something that the majority knew only from books. Certainly there were those who saw the race as nothing more or less than a cruise, in company propitiously forced upon them by the

organizers of the event. The comparison between this attitude and that of the early single-handed transatlantic races was all too obvious.

The starters varied from the technically highly prepared *Pen Duick VI* of Eric Tabarly and *Great Britain II* of Chay Blyth at the top end of the range to the aging Polish boat *Otago* and the German *Pieter von Danzig* at the other extreme. In between was a motley collection whose owners ranged from millionaires like Mexican Ramón Carlin to dreamers like Roddie Ainslie, who arranged the charter of *Second Life* and had his crew pay £3,000 ($4,500) for the pleasure of competing in the race. There were the two service entries of *Adventure* from the Royal Navy and *British Soldier* from the army; blue-water sailor Les Williams teamed with businessman Alan Smith to build a maximum-sized boat, while

Frenchmen André Viant and Jack Grout put together similarly sized projects. The media experts predicted all sorts of things for every boat in the race, but none knew just how it would work out. It was, after all, a departure into the unknown.

There may have been more than a year to prepare for the race, but in Vernon Creek at Portsmouth, with a week to go to the start, it appeared as though hardly anyone had taken full advantage of it. The two service boats were by far the best organized, together with Eric Tabarly's *Pen Duick VI*. At the other end of the scale, Leslie Williams and Alan Smith had their crew finishing the building of the 80-foot *Burton Cutter*. A holdup due to the financial instability of the builders had put them way behind in their program – for the crew it was a case of "if you

Giorgio Falck's Guia *nearing the finish.*

Sayula II *being nursed up the Solent to the finish — her fore-stay was stranding and could have broken at any time.*

want a bunk, build it!" She left the dock an hour before the noon start off Southsea Castle, and hoisted her sails only 30 minutes before Sir Alec Rose fired the 100-year-old cannon which sent the seventeen yachts away. More than 3,000 spectator craft were in the Eastern Solent to watch the departure.

The English Channel gave the crews an early taste of the race, with thunderstorms at night and a dying wind followed by fog. The two big ketches, *Great Britain II* and *Pen Duick VI,* led the fleet to Bembridge Ledge, the only mark of the course between the start and Cape Town. In the early stages, the handicap leader, as computed from the radioed reports, was *Adventure,* the Royal Navy's well-prepared Nicholson 55.

In the third week, the doldrums were entered, and this was where judgment played a great part. *Adventure* had opted to go farthest east of any. She was aiming for the windward route around the South Atlantic High, and was through the windless belt in 3 days. *Pen Duick VI* and *Sayula II* were at the western extreme and took 2 days longer to get into the trade winds. They were planning to skirt to westward of the high in fairer winds, but sailing a longer distance. The off-wind sailing would suit the ketches with the extra free sail that they could hoist, yet Leslie Williams chose to go the windward route with

182

Burton Cutter. Williams, a former naval officer, ensured that traditional customs were observed on board when "Crossing the Line," while *Adventure* signaled Race Control that she had been "boarded, greeted, and granted free passage by King Neptune in 15 degrees W at 1600, 30 September" – 22 days out.

By the Canaries, Tabarly was a day ahead of Blyth. The French yacht with its spent-uranium keel was creaming along in the trade winds until midnight on October 3. Then when sailing under number three jib, heavy genoas, staysail, and main, she was dismasted. She was 1,200 miles from Rio and 2,200 from Cape Town on longitude 23 degrees W. There was little option but to head to Rio and radio France for a spare mast to be airfreighted out. For Tabarly, the race was effectively over, but the honor of France was at stake. He had to get back in as soon as possible and show, on the other legs at least, what might have been.

When 250 miles from Cape Town, *Adventure* was becalmed. Two days before, she had seen *Burton Cutter* just 4 miles ahead. The windward course was paying. The wind filled in from the south. *Adventure* knew how close she was to *Burton Cutter* and that *Great Britain II* was also in the offing. It was Leslie Williams and the big white ketch that was first across the line at Cape Town, early on the Saturday afternoon of

October 20 – 6 weeks after leaving Portsmouth. *Adventure* was just over 24 hours behind and easily took the handicap honors, the real first place on the leg. Three hours after her came Blyth, and then there was a whole day before *Sayula II* and another day before *33 Export*. *Adventure*'s lead was a phenomenal 77 hours over *Sayula II,* with *33 Export* another 5 hours adrift.

There were some crew changes in Cape Town. Paul Waterhouse, who was scheduled to do only the first leg on *British Soldier,* found himself a berth for the second leg on the Italian Swan 55 *Tauranga*. When asked how he felt about this while at a party at Stellenbosch, he said: "I'm overboard about it." The remark was to prove desperately prophetic.

When the race restarted, four yachts – *Great Britain II, Sayula II, Pen Duick VI,* and *Kriter* – escaped to the stronger breezes, leaving the rest becalmed in the shadow of Table Mountain for a night. Tabarly had made it from Rio only 2 days earlier, but turned around fast, despite some sail repairs. The boats were soon into stronger winds, and 2 days of pounding to windward took its toll on *Burton Cutter*. The crew found themselves badly trimmed by the bow, but conditions were so bad that they could not open the forehatch and look into the forward watertight compartment for another day. When

Kriter II (formerly Burton Cutter) and Great Britain II at the start of the 1975 Financial Times Clipper Race in the Thames Estuary on a gray September day.

they did, they found that it was full of water. Plates and stringers of the aluminum hull had sprung, and *Burton Cutter* was leaking badly. Williams and his crew shored up the plates and headed north for Port Elizabeth to effect repairs. There, regrettably, the repairs were not approved by the South African Bureau of Standards and had to be redone twice, by which time all hopes of getting to Sydney in time for the restart were over; the yacht then made her way to Rio de Janeiro for the fourth leg.

Once into the westerly winds that blow undisturbed by land masses at the bottom of the world, passage across the Southern Ocean was rapid if somewhat hazardous. The dangers became all too apparent on November 19, when during a strong southwesterly with winds gusting well over 50 knots, Paul Waterhouse was lost overboard from *Tauranga.* A 4-hour search was made for him, but to no avail.

In the same gale, Eddie Hope broke his arm aboard *Great Britain II.* Blyth contacted Dr. Robin Leach aboard *Second Life* for instructions on how to set the limb in a cast of glassfiber. Unfortunately, too much hardener in the resin resulted in burning Hope's arm, but his great reserves of strength allowed him to hold out without using too many pain-killing drugs until they reached Sydney. But Blyth's troubles did not stop there. They had already blown out a spinnaker and broken a spinnaker boom when, as Hope's arm was being fixed, the mizzen broke just above the deck. There was nothing to do but ditch it and carry on under sloop rig.

Four days later, Dominique Guillet went overboard in another gale. When changing a headsail, Guillet was washed out of the boat by a huge wave. He was not found. Death had struck the race twice in a short time.

Halfway between Cape Town and Sydney, *Sayula II* capsized. According to Butch Dalrymple-Smith, the chaos below was unbelievable. Almost everything emptied out of lockers, and two ruptured water tanks spilled 140 gallons into the bilges as the craft righted herself. In Dalrymple-Smith's mind, the next two hours of bucket-chain bailing, before they assured themselves that they were not going to sink, were the worst. It took a day to get the boat back into some order when they could start sailing again, but it was nearly a week before *Sayula II* was really racing again.

Adventure had her share of problems: first a boom broke, and then it was discovered that the rudder stock was moving inside the blade. Her

184

crew steered her for much of the rest of the leg using only the trim tab.

Tabarly was first into Sydney, just 29 days, 8 hours after leaving Cape Town. *Great Britain II* was next, 10 hours behind *Pen Duick VI.* Another 16 hours later came *Second Life,* just ahead of *Kriter* and *Sayula II.* It was the Mexican boat's leg on handicap, despite her capsize.

Christmas made life difficult for the crews, with urgent repair jobs and the start scheduled for December 29. All the boats were ready, and *Pen Duick VI* led the fleet out of the Heads, into a period of flat calm. All but *Second Life* headed to go south of the South Island of New Zealand. Roddy Ainslie, having read *Ocean Passages for the World* with the phrase "the passage through the Cook Strait may be taken with advantage,

above: Adventure, *the joint services entry in 1977, approaching Auckland.*

right: *Naked as nature intended, Bill Porter – Lord of the Horn – takes a sun sight aboard* King's Legend.

especially from October to February," went that way. He was to regret it later.

Some 200 miles out of Sydney, *Pen Duick*'s mast fell down again. This time the help from France was minimal, and a new spar was built in Sydney by Alspar before *Pen Duick* was under way again.

It was not long before the fleet hit a southerly "buster" and many sails were blown out as this violent wind change caught several boats unaware. Ten days into the race, tragedy was to strike again. Bernie Hosking was clearing up after a sail change on *Great Britain II* when he overbalanced and fell into the sea. Blyth and his crew searched for 3 hours, but to no avail. Hosking, who had been recovered from going overboard on the first leg, was gone.

The Royal Navy's ice-patrol ship H.M.S. *Endurance* was off Cape Horn to meet the fleet, but passage was slower than had been imagined due to an unusual amount of head winds. Even after being becalmed 2 days out from the Horn, *Great Britain II* was first to round. It was 3 days later that *Sayula II* arrived there, 3 hours ahead

of *Kriter,* with *Grand Louis* just over a day farther astern. Blyth was to write in his log that one rounding each way was enough for a lifetime and concluded: "That's my lot." Of course, it was not to be, and he even now admits that there will probably be another two before he stops to add to the three he has already done.

Great Britain II kept her lead to the finish, but it was *Adventure* that was to take the handicap prize, with *Sayula II* second and the overall leader after three legs.

The final restart was staggered, with the smaller boats going first. *Adventure* had to beat *Sayula II* home by 3½ days to win the race, but the Mexican boat's starting two days behind gave her the advantage in that she could follow *Adventure's* track and not lose contact with her. But Ray Conrady, *Sayula II's* navigator, used the morse weather forecasts to give him a better idea of the weather patterns and as a result took the most easterly passage of any boat in the fleet.

Great Britain II had her best leg of the race and passed all the earlier starters to claim line honors for the second time. In addition, she was

to claim second place for the leg on handicap. *Adventure* was next home, back into her port and the Royal Navy dock at H.M.S. *Vernon,* where the yachts were to be berthed. She was easily the leg winner, even when *33 Export* came in a few hours later. *Burton Cutter* was next, followed by *Grand Louis* a few hours later on the Saturday night. The next day was Easter, and the day that *Sayula II* sailed up the Solent. Her rig was much reduced – five of the nineteen strands of her forestay had parted, and her crew was nursing the Swan 65 to the finish with enough in hand and nothing to lose. The race was hers, a never-to-be-forgotten first.

The success of the Whitbread Race was undisputed and encouraged the *Financial Times* to go ahead with a single-stop race two years later. It had an extra challenge: that of beating the times of the clipper ship *Patriarch,* which in 1869 to 1870 set the amazing record of 69 days on each leg of the Thames–Sydney–Thames passage. The new race came, however, too soon after the Whitbread to gain many entries, and only four boats started on the last day of August 1975.

Great Britain II was back in the fray but without Blyth. For the first leg, she was skippered by Mike Gill and for the second by Roy Mullender, each with a joint services crew. *Burton Cutter,* renamed *Kriter II,* was also racing, this time with Olivier de Kersauson as skipper. The other two starters were the 56-foot welded-steel ketch *The Great Escape,* skippered by Henk Huisman on leg one and Dirk Nauta on leg two, and the 60-foot schooner *CS e RB II* of Doi Malingri. These four were joined for the second leg by the Australian maxi *Anaconda II,* which had been specially built for the race but could not make the start in Britain because of an injury to her owner-skipper Josko Grubic.

For the two bigger boats, it was a neck-and-neck race on the first leg. *Great Britain II* passed through a line due south of Cape Town just 20 hours before *Kriter.* Across the Southern Ocean, they regularly had runs exceeding 240 miles a day. *CS e RB II* put into Recife for some repairs but was back in the race as quickly as possible.

As they headed for the Bass Strait, *Great Britain II* was 150 miles ahead, and there was little doubt that *Patriarch's* record was due to fall. Light winds almost put an end to her chances as she went up the Australian eastern coast, while *Kriter,* farther out to sea, still had good wind and was narrowing the gap. A mile from the finish, *Great Britain II* was becalmed for 2 hours and beat the French yacht home by only 6½ hours. *Patriarch's* record was broken, and the party could begin. It was many days before the other two finished; 24 for *CS e RB II* and another 10 for *The Great Escape.* With a slight handicap allowance, *Kriter* took the handicap prize from *Great Britain II.*

Pierre Fehlmann's Disque d'Or *approaching the finishing line at Cape Town in 1981.*

The restart was inauspicious, but the race at the front was on all over again. Four days out, Christmas Day, in fresh northeasterly winds, *Kriter II* blasted through to take the lead. But not much more than an hour later, her rudder had gone. *Kriter II* was forced to sail back to Sydney, and the sting had gone out of the race for Mullender and his crew. They did still have *Patriarch*'s record to go for, and there was always *Anaconda II,* but it was nothing like the race they had intended to have with Olivier de Kersauson and the French.

Great Britain II was first to the Horn, and for Mullender and Bill Porter it was the second time in two years; both had been on *Adventure* on the third leg of the Whitbread Race. *Great Britain II* was 26 days out of Sydney. She was on schedule to beat the clipper's record. And beat it she did, arriving in Dover half an hour before midnight on February 25 in 66 days, 21½ hours. De Kersauson was sworn to beat that record when he left Sydney with a new rudder. For a time it looked as though he might, but the doldrums ended his challenge, and he was 35½ hours longer. It was *Anaconda II* that was next to Dover, almost 12 days behind the winner, well out of contention on handicap.

The one-stop race had its enthusiasts. But it

has not been repeated, probably because of the success of the Whitbread Race and of the lack of time between Whitbreads to organize boats and crews, to say nothing of the financial support.

There were, in fact, fewer entrants for the second Whitbread Race, in 1977, than there had been for the first. Fifteen boats answered the starter's gun at noon on Saturday, August 27, with *Great Britain II* leading them away on her third race around the globe. This time she was skippered by Rob James; as crew, he had a charter party of sixteen, each of whom had paid £4,000 ($6,000) for the pleasure of competing in the race. James had the problem of teaching many of them to sail as he skippered the boat in the most hazardous race in the world, but he did have the six weeks of the first leg to Cape Town before subjecting them to the Southern Ocean.

Much attention had been afforded to the 79-foot *Heath's Condor,* a John Sharp design jointly skippered by Leslie Williams and Robin Knox-Johnston. She was the biggest boat in the fleet and stepped a carbon fiber mast only a few days before the race began. She was fancied to be first into each port and to do well on handicap. But there was another yacht, more quietly produced, which had the nod of those in the know, the 65-foot aluminum Sparkman &

Stephens-designed *Flyer,* skippered by Cornelis van Rietschoten. What had impressed people who had taken part in other races was that the Dutchman appeared to have done his homework well, leaving no stone unturned in his efforts to have everything working properly. He had the right sort of boat, the right sails, and the right crew; just as important, there was no limit to the boat's budget.

There was one other boat like her—the sloop-rigged Swan 65 *King's Legend,* owned by Nick Ratcliffe. He had combed the ocean-racing centers to get a top crew and had lavished much time and money on the preparation of the boat. She, too, lacked for nothing, but Ratcliffe's budget was getting strained by the time the boats put to sea.

There were two other Swan 65s, both ketch-rigged. Clare Francis had *ADC Accutrac,* while Pierre Fehlmann had *Disque d'Or.* What had been *Pen Duick III* was there in ketch rig as *Gauloises II;* she had been in the last leg of the previous race, the race in which *Adventure* had won three of the legs on corrected time. She was back again, with joint services crews including Sharon Hope from the WRAC.

The early part of the first leg was uneventful, except that *Heath's Condor* had a new radio

transmitter flown out to Tenerife and delivered by helicopter as she made a slight detour. For some of the leaders, the doldrums hardly made any impact—*Flyer* never dropped below 112 miles for a noon-to-noon run, while *King's Legend* was delayed only a day. They were learning fast on *Great Britain II* but lost 100 miles in the doldrums to emerge 100 miles behind *Flyer.*

On September 15, there was a sickening crunch on board *Heath's Condor* as she was going to windward in a fresh southwesterly with two reefs in the main and the yankee and working staysail set. The carbon fiber mast was in three pieces. The decision was made to sail under jury rig to Monrovia, and there effect a repair. The race was over, but there were still the honors that could be taken in legs two, three, and four; Williams and his partner ashore, Knox-Johnston, were determined to salvage something from the race. Knox-Johnston organized a replacement mast to be sent to Monrovia, and within nine days of the dismasting, Williams and his crew were dressing the replacement mast with rigging and getting it back into the boat and themselves back into the race.

Up front, the race was on between *Flyer* and *King's Legend,* with the Dutch boat getting in

Kriter IX, Andre Viant's 62-foot Frers design, approaching Auckland, where she was the handicap leader.

189

exactly 2 hours ahead — a close enough finish between two equally rated boats after 38 days of racing 6,650 miles. They were to retain these positions on handicap as well. It was another 30 hours before the leaders were joined in port by *Great Britain II,* which had spent about that time stationary in the South Atlantic high. *Disque d'Or* followed a day later, and then it was the turn of *Tielsa, Gauloises II,* and *ADC Accutrac.*

Auckland replaced Sydney as the second stopover port, and the leg to there was 7,400 miles. The two leaders into Cape Town were the pacemakers away from it. After two days, *King's Legend* was 50 miles ahead of the rest. *Gauloises II* lost the rudder she had fitted as a replacement in Cape Town in the first gale and headed back to Port Elizabeth, where Eric Loizeau's fiancée arrived by plane from France with a new one.

Once into the stronger winds, the big *Heath's Condor* came into her own and began mopping off the miles at more than 250 per day. On October 30, five days after the restart, she sighted *King's Legend* abeam and left her in the night. By 50 degrees E, at Crozet Island, *Flyer* was the northernmost at 45 degrees S, while *King's Legend* was at 52 degrees S with *Heath's Condor.* Only *Debenhams,* at 55 degrees S, was lower.

At Kerguelen Islands, on 70 degrees E, *King's Legend* and *Heath's Condor* were down to 55 S, with *Flyer* still at 48 S. Deep in the Southern Ocean on November 11, a serious leak was

discovered around *King's Legend's* rudder skeg. It got worse, but her crew had to pump her regularly all the way to Auckland, where the skeg was repaired, together with those of the other Swan 65s in the race. The following day, *Heath's Condor* logged 298 miles. The day after that, Bill Abram was flipped over the side of the 79-footer by a spinnaker sheet. He was back on board in ten minutes, due to the superb seamanship of Peter Blake and Robin Knox-Johnston.

Great Britain II had begun to catch up. She was in second place about 200 miles astern as they crossed the Tasman Sea. The battle between *King's Legend* and *Flyer* was still the tops: they swapped places twice, and they fought it out in lighter winds down the eastern coast of New Zealand. *Heath's Condor* was first home, in 30 days, 9 hours. *Great Britain II* was 31½ hours behind her. There was another 21 hours before *King's Legend* and 1 hour, 12 minutes to *Flyer.* But this was to be a small boat's leg on handicap, with Alain Gabbay's 56-foot *33 Export* winning from Philippe Hanin's 51-foot *Traité de Rome,* entered from the EEC.

The December 26 restart saw Auckland Harbor filled with boats to watch the fleet away. "Difficult to see marks of the course," wrote Alan Green in *Debenhams'* log. Crossing the International Date Line gave the crews two New Year's Eves — one in moderate conditions, and one in a gale that the next day rolled *33 Export* to

The 1978 winner Flyer *was converted from a ketch to a sloop and renamed* Alaska Eagle — *the first American entry in the Whitbread Race.*

above: Flyer, *Cornelis van Rietschoten's line-honors winner of every leg in the third Whitbread Race, a mile from the finish at Portsmouth and on the way to a second overall victory for the Flying Dutchman.*

left: *A two-day calm near the Azores robbed* Charles Heidsieck III *of an almost certain overall win for the French.*

more than 140 degrees. She survived and was back racing almost immediately. *King's Legend* and *Flyer* logged 423 and 425 miles respectively in two days of gales.

Great Britain II was first to Cape Horn, with *Flyer* 137 miles astern. She in turn was battling with *Heath's Condor*. When the Dutch boat rounded, *Heath's Condor* was 12 miles astern of her. *King's Legend* was over a day behind, but for one of her crew, her rounding completed a remarkable record – Bill Porter, known as Lord of the Horn, was racing around the most feared landmark for the third time within four years.

the boat's overall record for a circumnavigation, that by the Service crews of the armed forces in the FT Clipper Race.

It was 32 hours before *Disque d'Or* arrived, the third to finish; behind her *King's Legend* and *Flyer* continued their battle to the bitter end. *King's Legend* won this one, by 1 hour, 17 minutes, but the real honors were *Flyer*'s. She had won the race by 58 hours (the difference of the third leg) from *King's Legend*, with *Traité de Rome* in third place 7½ hours behind. There might have been a different result had *Gauloises II* not had to return to Port Elizabeth on leg two

The young French crew of Charles Heidsieck III trained hard for the race – here is the boat off Nassau competing in the 1981 SORC.

The finish of the leaders in Rio was close. Rob James and his now well-experienced charter party on board *Great Britain II* beat the newer *Heath's Condor* across the line by just 18 minutes. *Flyer* was only 12 hours behind, but nothing could stop the 57-foot *Gauloises* from beating her on handicap with *Traité de Rome* third.

The leg home was uneventful. "Life on board is very pleasant, though a little dull," recorded Gerard Djikstra, the navigator of *Flyer*. She had a difficult crossing of the doldrums, but her greatest rival for the overall honors, *King's Legend*, fared even worse. *Heath's Condor* was first into the strong westerlies after the Azores high and romped home the line-honors winner. It was 15 hours before *Great Britain II* crossed the line, the overall line-honors winner of the race – a fine effort for a young skipper and his "passengers" in a time that was close to breaking

because of her rudder failure. She won the last leg and the third, and was third on the first one. But this race is won by the fast reliable boat.

Four years later, the race had grown and matured. There were twenty-nine starters; at the front of the fleet, there were several highly sophisticated racing machines that had proved their worth in other races, with skippers determined to do well. One of these skippers was the highly experienced Kiwi Peter Blake, who had competed in both the previous Whitbread races and who had this time managed to get the support of the entire nation of New Zealand and the commercial backing of a consortium led by the Ceramco group of companies. His Bruce Farr-designed 68-foot *Ceramco New Zealand* was the result of experience and planning and had to be the boat for everyone to beat.

"Conny" van Rietschoten was back to defend his trophy with a new Frers-designed

77-foot *Flyer.* He said his aim was to be first into each of the stopover ports (this time, Mar del Plata in Argentina replaced Rio de Janeiro) and did not care much about the handicap honors. Well, that is what he said. Nothing had been overlooked to make the new *Flyer* the best ocean-racing boat in the world. It was obvious, therefore, that both the front-runner's battle and the handicap placings would be fought between *Ceramco New Zealand* and *Flyer.* There would be others involved, but in the main, these two had everything going for them.

The other big boats could not quite match *Ceramco New Zealand* and *Flyer;* all had compromise built in. Leslie Williams was going for a third time with the relatively new 80-foot 6-inch *FCF Challenger,* a design by David Alan-Williams and Doug Peterson, which could have been a front-runner had there been a big enough budget for new sails. *Great Britain II* was back, renamed *United Friendly,* with Chay Blyth in nominal control. She had been rerigged as a sloop, but this was a rush job and the sails looked far from perfect.

Charles Heidsieck III, however, lacked nothing and was a strongly prepared potential race winner. Alain Gabbay and his crew had raced the 66-foot Gilles Vaton design all over the world, and French hopes for her were high. So were they for Eric Tabarly and the 73-foot *Euromarche* (formerly *Pen Duick VI*), but the boat was eight years old and outclassed by her modern sisters. One of these was André Viant's *Kriter IX,* a 62-foot Frers design, and another the 58-foot *Disque d'Or,* a Farr design in the style of *Ceramco New Zealand.*

Noon on Saturday, August 29, 1981, and the cannon boomed to send twenty-eight boats on their way – *Vivanapoli*'s departure was delayed for a day to allow the scrutineers to go over her, since she had arrived at Portsmouth only the day before the race. It was a gray day, with a light head breeze for the leg to the Bembridge Ledge buoy. *Flyer* and *"Ceramco"* were the first to get away and set their spinnakers on the back side of the Isle of Wight, making their way down Channel and into the Western Approaches.

The early stages of this leg were uneventful; a high-pressure area in latitude 13 degrees N produced doldrumlike calms which impeded progress. *Flyer* was first to cross the equator, three weeks out from Portsmouth, some 50 miles ahead of *"Ceramco,"* with *FCF Challenger* another 70 miles astern. By then, they were enjoying the southeast trades, clocking up runs of 220 miles per day. Two days later, just after noon on Monday, September 21, the race was over for *"Ceramco,"* at least from the point of view of her having any chance of an overall win. There was a loud bang, a crash, and the boat which had been hammering along to windward under the number four jib and a reef suddenly

came upright. The mast was over the side. An intermediate stay rod had fractured where it went over the spreader end.

It was like a bad dream for skipper Peter Blake. Four years earlier, about 400 miles from the spot where he was now, Blake had seen the mast of *Heath's Condor* topple. This time, he argued that there was no going back to Monrovia. With the crew, he devised a plan to restep as much of the mast as they could, lashing the top 45 feet to the 16-foot stump, cramming on as much sail as they could, and skirting the South Atlantic high to the west and making Cape

Town on the westerlies. It was a daring move, but one which gave time for the new mast to be flown to South Africa and assembled and rigged ready for the boat's arrival. That *"Ceramco"* finished eighteenth and was only 10 days behind her schedule is sufficient testimony to Blake and his crew. That on one day they sailed 232 miles, and in a 3-day period clocked 674, shows how hard they were prepared to work to get to port to repair the rig.

"Conny" and *Flyer* meantime had cracked on and broken the previous record to Cape Town by more than 2½ days. She arrived at the same time as *Rolly-Go* lost her mast (the third one of the leg to go, *La Barca Laboratorio* having lost hers 8 days after *"Ceramco"*) and headed for Recife. *Rolly-Go* was already into the westerlies and continued under a similar jury rig to that of *"Ceramco."*

Second in was *Charles Heidsieck III,* taking

Pen Duick VI, *renamed* Euromarche, *was well off the pace by 1981 – this race has never been kind to her and Eric Tabarly. She broke a mast in 1973 and was disqualified in 1977 because of her spent-uranium keel.*

193

3 hours to sail the last 3 miles in a gale because of rigging problems encountered earlier, which had necessitated using a lower shroud rigging screw for the forestay. Three hours after her came *Kriter IX* to claim the handicap win for the leg. *FCF Challenger* was next, having sailed for more than a week on starboard tack only because her mast had split and the port main shroud was in danger of pulling out.

She was repaired in time for the restart on October 31 and led the fleet away from the shadow of Table Mountain. But after a short time, *Flyer* and *"Ceramco"* made the front running and piled on the miles, logging over 1,700 in the first 8 days, despite only 224 miles in the first 45 hours. There were 30 miles between the two boats as they passed 150 miles to the south of Iles Crozet after 9 days. Two days later came the first casualty; the 58-foot *33 Export* lost her mast and headed for the Kerguelen Islands for repair.

As *"Ceramco"* went south of the Kerguelens, *Flyer* was just 6 miles farther east and 15 miles to the north. The two were match racing. Blake desperately wanted to be first in to his home port, while van Rietschoten had set himself the aim of being first into every one of the stopovers. The nearest boat to them was *Euromarche,* 100 miles behind. For another week they battled neck and neck across the Southern Ocean, and *Flyer* only began to pull away a little as they faced the head winds up the western side of New Zealand. It was there that Blake pulled a fast one on his rival, giving him a bogus position which kept the Dutchman farther to the west and punching into a head wind while *"Ceramco"* freed sheets and went closer to the coast. It worked to some extent, but not quite enough. *Flyer* was first home in 30 days, 9 hours, beating *Heath's Condor*'s record by 4½ hours. It was 06:35 local time when she crossed the line at Orakei Wharf, but there were hundreds of people there to watch her finish. But this crowd was nothing like that of 8 hours, 20 minutes later, when the Kiwi boat came home. Pushing the boat that hard had ensured one win for them at least — *"Ceramco"* was the handicap winner of the leg, the one all her crew had wanted to win.

It was 40 hours before *Euromarche* came in, and another 16 to *Charles Heidsieck III.* Fifth home was *Kriter IX,* to retain her overall handicap lead from *Charles Heidsieck III,* with *Flyer* third at the halfway stage.

A *dismasting on the first leg spoiled* Ceramco New Zealand's *chances of winning the race and her crew had to get her to Cape Town with a jury rig.*

The jury rig was sufficiently efficient to take the 68-foot Farr-designed Ceramco New Zealand *at over 200 miles a day.*

The December 26 restart saw every man out in the Waitemata Harbor. Blake gave them all they wanted, with *"Ceramco"* leading the fleet away to the mark boat 5 miles distant. He chose, in the next 3 days, to head south rather than aim for Cape Horn. It was a ploy which worked and left *Flyer* some 50 miles behind when at last *"Ceramco"* headed east. Closest to her then was *Euromarche* – Tabarly followed *"Ceramco's"* stern for as long as he could see her. On the seventh day, *"Ceramco"* managed a noon-to-noon run of 315 miles, just 1 mile short of her record, while *Flyer* broke all records with 327. Two days later, *"Ceramco"* did 316, but *Flyer* was by then only 20 miles behind.

After 10 days, the Kiwis spotted *Flyer* 3 miles away on the starboard bow, almost within shouting distance after 2,380 miles. By then, *Gauloises* had been dismasted and was heading for Tahiti under jury rig, and *United Friendly* had been into Gisborne for repairs to her mast track. A week later and *Flyer* had doubled her lead, to 6 miles!

Flyer was first to Cape Horn, with *"Ceramco"* 30 minutes behind; but in the Straits de le Maire, the Kiwis got the right side of a wind

shift and went to the front. Another wind shift put *Flyer* back in place again later in the day. She was first in to Mar del Plata in 24 days, 1 hour, with *"Ceramco"* 7 hours, 17 minutes behind her, but this time they were not to figure as highly in the handicap results. That win went to Phillipe Poupon and Eugene Rigudel with *Mor Bihan,* a 48½-footer, with *Disque d'Or* second. *Charles Heidsieck III* had moved up to be the overall leader by 11 hours from *Kriter IX,* with *Flyer* third, 34 hours behind the leader.

The battle of the two leaders continued all through the final leg, with *Flyer* getting home 15 hours ahead of *"Ceramco."* Then *Charles Heidsieck III* had 600 miles to go to Portsmouth, but head winds and light winds delayed her arrival sufficiently for *Flyer* to be the overall handicap winner by 30½ hours. The leg was *"Ceramco's"*; once again, the Whitbread was a race of what might have been. The Kiwi boat was still the third fastest around the world and eleventh of the twenty finishers on handicap, despite having taken 10 extra days because of her broken mast. No one, however, would deny the Dutchman his glory; to win both line honors and on handicap was a marvelous achievement.

195

BOC Around Alone

David White had nurtured the idea of a single-handed race around the world for many months. It gained extra impetus from a discussion held in a bar that is well known to single-handed sailors, the Marina Pub on Goat Island, Newport, Rhode Island, where so many of them meet after OSTARs. Jim Roos, the resident property manager of Goat Island, became involved when he realized how serious White's intentions were. He agreed to help organize the race when White declared that he would build a new boat for it.

The two of them tried hard to get commercial support for their race, which was to start and finish in the United States. Newport, the home of American yachting, would be the terminus while their projected stopovers were Cape Town, Hobart, and Mar del Plata. Their search, however, was unsuccessful.

In Britain, Richard Broadhead tried 800 companies for individual sponsorship for the race without success, but his application to BOC, a worldwide company, did set off a spark of interest; BOC decided to sponsor the event rather than Broadhead.

The BOC Group moved fast, reconstituting the race committee, with Robin Knox-Johnston as chairman. It took over all the promotion and much of the management and changed two of the stopovers – Hobart to Sydney and Mar del Plata to Rio de Janeiro – because of their better standing and BOC's involvement in those cities. By then it was March 1982, and Knox-Johnston made the decision to bring the race forward one month from its planned end-of-September start to August 28 because he believed that the smaller boats would not reach Cape Horn before the "summer window" closed. It was not a popular move among many of the competitors, who already faced a tight deadline to get themselves and their boats ready for the start, but it was generally agreed to be sensible.

There appeared to be thirty-four entries for the race from eleven countries, but by the time of the start, the number had dwindled to seventeen representing eight nations. David White was one of them. He had raced time with a limited budget to prepare his Alan Gurney maximum-sized (56 feet overall) cutter.

Tony Lush was a veteran of OSTAR racing and was head of testing for a Florida firm, Hunter Marine. He had one of their 54-foot production yachts specially adapted with an unstayed cat-ketch rig and was sponsored by Westpoint Pepperell, a textile firm, naming his boat *Lady Pepperell*. His 1,000-mile qualifying cruise was his delivery of the boat from the yard to the start.

Francis Stokes had two OSTARs under his

Credit Agricole *shortly after the start.*

belt and chose a Fast Passage 39, a stock cruiser, for the race in Class 2, for 32- to 44-foot yachts. At fifty-six, he was the oldest competitor in the race. Dan Byrne, at fifty-three, was not much younger. A retired newspaper editor, he did his first single-handed race in his Valiant 40, *Fantasy,* in 1980 in the Transpac. The fifth American was Thomas Lindholm, with the 41-foot *Driftwood.* He was only two days into the race, however, when a succession of problems forced him to retire.

Broadhead, without a sponsor, sought the best boat he could to attempt to win the race within his budget. He bought the 52-foot *Perseverance of Medina,* formerly owned by Sir Max Aikten and built for him in 1973 as an Admiral's Cup trialist to the designs of Britton Chance. Since her original racing days, she had been modified from ketch to sloop rig. Broadhead was resigned to doing the best he could. "I could win with a sponsor," he said, "but without one I will be happy to finish in the first five." He was short of money for sails.

Desmond Hampton took nine months' sabbatical from the firm of real-estate managers of which he is a partner to take in the race. He chartered *Gipsy Moth V,* the last of Sir Francis Chichester's yachts, for the race and had to have 15 inches cut from her stern to get within the maximum-size limit.

Paul Rodgers, the third Briton in the race, had previously made an attempt to be the first man to sail solo twice around the world non-stop with the 55-foot narrow-gutted schooner *Spirit of Pentax,* which had been designed by Mike Dunham for the Parmelia Race. He was forced into Cape Town at the start of his second circuit.

The French have made shorthanded ocean racing their sport, and before the start, the dark horse was Philippe Jeantot, a thirty-year-old diver who had sponsorship sufficient for him to build a boat to the maximum length for the race and to equip it with everything he wanted. A sum of 800,000 francs from the bank Credit Agricole allowed him to build his aluminum-alloy design by Guy Ribadeau Dumas, a boat with ballasting water tanks on opposite sides which could be changed shortly before each tack. Lightweight and cutter-rigged with efficient furling headsails, *Credit Agricole* was right; could Jeantot sail her to her full potential?

One of his countrymen with the experience to do well was Jacques de Roux, with the 41-foot *Skoiern III.* He had a two-handed transatlantic race behind him and many other racing miles afloat, as did the third of the Frenchmen, Guy Bernadin, with *Ratso,* at 38 feet the smallest boat.

"Biltong" Bertie Reed had to start favorite for this race because of his experience sailing alone and the knowledge that his fourteen-year-old yacht, the 49-foot *Voortrekker,* had stood up to heavy weather all over the world. He received sponsorship for the race, and his boat became *Altech Voortrekker.*

Another who knew his boat well was

Australian Neville Gosson, who had sailed the boat since it was built for him, in 1974, in ocean races. He had also sailed *Leda Pier One,* a 53-footer, from Sydney to the start.

Yukoh Tada, a saxaphone playing taxi driver from Tokyo, was one of the colorful characters in this race. His Class-2 boat, the 44-foot *Koden Okera V,* was full of electronic instruments from his sponsors. He had sailed across the Pacific single-handed to prove himself.

There were two Kiwis among the starters: one albeit a trifle late; the other a trifle late to finish. Richard McBride built his 42-foot staysail schooner himself and got support from his home-town: he called it *City of Dunedin.* Greg Coles was late. He and the futuristic 44-foot *Datsun Skyline* set off on a 1,000-mile qualifier as the rest of the fleet started the race. His contact with Rob Koziomkowski in Newport, however, was to prove a lifesaving link later in the race.

Rodgers had predicted that the first three weeks of the race would be the worst, as the course took the fleet down through the Atlantic at the height of the hurricane season. It did not seem like that as the sixteen boats (minus *Datsun Skyline*) left Newport on port tack led by *Nike III.* There was sun and a good breeze.

Spirit of Pentax struck a whale with a "terrible crash." At first it appeared there was no damage, but subsequent examination showed part of the hull planking and a longitudinal stringer had split, causing slight leaking.

Rodgers, together with White and Jeantot, were doing best in the early stages, staying to the west of the rhumb line, while those on the Great Circle course were not getting as good winds. Broadhead, Reed, and Stokes were out on the more accepted route, Reed in fourth place some 400 miles farther from Cape Town than Jeantot. A week later, and Jeantot had begun to show his hand. He was 300 miles ahead of Rodgers and still the same distance ahead of the Great Circlers. They were suffering from light winds, none more so than Desmond Hampton, taking an extreme route to the east. He questioned whether it was better to go extremely slowly in the desired direction with *Gipsy Moth V* or marginally less slowly in another direction.

By the end of the third week, Jeantot was averaging 175 miles a day and was some 900 miles ahead of Rodgers, slogging into the southeast trades. Reed and Broadhead, to the northeast of the Cape Verde Islands, led the rest, with Hampton and Lush 200 miles behind them. Not everything was going Jeantot's way, however; a fractured fresh-water tank left his supplies low, but he devised a method of distilling fresh water from sea water using his pressure cooker and collected rain water.

Then came the frustrations of the doldrums after a week or more of trade-wind sailing. The

The narrow-gutted Spirit of Pentax *was the uncomfortable ride of Paul Rodgers.*

above: Gladiator *was designed by Alan Gurney for David White, the originator of the race.*

constantly changing winds, both in strength and in direction, give one little rest. Jeantot was perhaps better prepared for this than were the others. His computerized navigational instruments were set to trigger an alarm every time they varied beyond limits which Jeantot had decided upon. The rest relied on intuition.

Almost everyone was having problems. Gosson found that he was out of cooking gas and that diesel had leaked into the bilges; Lush had a fracture at the base of his mizzen mast; so did Greg Coles; McBride's homemade self-steering was inefficient; Konkolski sailed into a fleet of moored fishing boats; a spreader split on *Moonshine* to give Stokes a day's work trying to repair it, while Hampton had a broken backstay. At the end of the fifth week, Jeantot was 1,200 miles ahead of the next boat, Bertie Reed in *Altech Voortrekker.*

opposite page: *Desmond Hampton with* Gipsy Moth V, *the last of Sir Francis Chichester's yachts, which was wrecked on Gabo Island.*

201

The leg was Jeantot's. He finished 6½ days ahead of Reed, a lead that was to prove totally impregnable. Broadhead arrived in Cape Town 2 days later and was followed by Hampton, Lush, de Roux, and Rodgers. Then in order came Tada, Stokes, Gosson, Byrne, Konkolski, and Bernadin – the last-named 3 weeks after Jeantot. McBride brought up the rear.

As Rodgers arrived with no food on board, all his stores having run out four days previously, the sponsors decided that they would victual all the competitors' boats before each of the next three legs. In addition, they fitted each boat with an Argos satellite transmitter to record the position of the boats each time a relevant satellite passed over the fleet. With its "panic button" emergency-distress facility, the transmitter was to prove of life-saving capability.

McBride just managed the race against time to be ready for the 6,900-mile leg to Sydney, but

Konkolski was forced by a back injury to stay ashore for four days and was joined by Rodgers with a broken halyard winch. White arrived three hours after the fleet left.

Just before the start, there was a 60-knot southeaster blowing, and most of the boats came to the line reefed right down, even though the wind had died way. Bertie Reed, in front of his home crowd, was soon in the lead from Gosson. The wind returned with a vengeance that night.

No one came through the succession of gales in the first week unscathed, but each of the skippers had known what he was to face on this leg. Self-steering gear suffered badly, and at one time, Broadhead was considering a call to the research community on the Kerguelen Islands to have a part welded. Reed had had to clear five gallons of diesel from his bilge, but it caused an infection in his wrist; for several days Reed could use only one arm.

After 14 days, Jeantot was 70 miles ahead of Hampton as they surged through the seas of the South Pacific, with Reed 30 miles astern. They had had more than their fair share of head winds, but on the fifteenth day, when *Lady Pepperell* was running under bare poles in a storm, she pitchpoled. The masts stayed intact, but the keel reinforcement in the hull became detached and the hull and keel were in danger of parting. It was a long way to Australia, and Lush put out a PAN call and was soon in contact with Stokes, 50 miles ahead of him. Stokes gave him an ultimatum – abandon his boat or go on alone – and Lush did not take long to make up his mind. Stokes hove to and waited for Lush to sail to him. With Argos fixes fed to him, Dave White aboard *Gladiator* in Cape Town co-ordinated the rescue. Stokes spotted *Lady Pepperell* 3 miles off and directed Lush to him over the radio.

Jeantot put in one 7-day run of 1,437 miles, an average of 8.55 knots, a record for a single-handed monohull, and in doing so drew 120 miles ahead of Hampton. Reed was almost another 300 miles astern. Broadhead had found a way to avoid his stop and had effected a repair to his self-steering gear.

The southern oceans were giving the single-handers all they could cope with, winds sometimes going from 50 to 60 to 70 knots. Damage caused Konkolski to divert to Fremantle for repairs and wiped out his chances of winning Class 2. Up front, Jeantot still led Hampton, and 35 days, 9¼ hours after leaving Cape Town, *Credit Agricole* crossed the finish line. Just before this, Hampton had had the misfortune to run *Gipsy Moth V* aground on Gabo Island, 250 miles from the finish. While he had slept, the wind had changed and taken the yacht off course. Within minutes of grounding, *Gipsy Moth V* was stuck in a rock crevice; with the seas pounding her, there was no way out. A famous boat had perished, but Hampton was safe.

Tony Lush opted for twin-cantilevered unstayed masts for the 54-foot Lady Pepperell.

Reed followed Jeantot home by 42 hours, nursing a broken toe; it was another 8 days before Gosson, again out of gas, was the next to finish. He was 4½ hours ahead of Jacques de Roux, the first of the Class-2 finishers, who was 4 days ahead of Broadhead. *"Perseverance"* was in a sorry state, and Broadhead faced a lot of work before the restart just 2 weeks later.

The leg to Rio, 8,250 miles, passes Cape Horn, the sailors' most feared landmark; but after the battering they had suffered on the second leg, the Cape held little fear for the BOC competitors. The pace was hot. In the first week, Jeantot covered more than 1,300 miles. Reed was 90 miles behind him, with de Roux and Broadhead a similar distance astern of him.

Just 13 days out, *Credit Argricole* was knocked flat, her mainsail torn and her rudder damaged. Jeantot contacted her designer by radio, who having heard the extent of the damage, told him that it would be all right if he did not exceed 15 knots! It was all too easy to exceed this in bursts down the faces of waves.

Another 11 days later, during a fierce storm, Jacques de Roux's *Skoiern III* pitchpoled and broke her mast. Before he could cut it free, it had pierced the side of the hull, and the boat began to leak badly. De Roux hit the "panic button."

He was 2,000 miles west of Cape Horn, and although not the nearest to him, Richard Broadhead turned around to sail back nearly 300 miles to rescue the Frenchman. His only aid was a link through a ham radio which gave him the positions of the two boats each time they were updated by a satellite pass over their Argos transmitters. It was 47 hours before Broadhead found him, after having passed within 50 yards of him while he was down below on the radio. Broadhead brought *"Perseverance"* close alongside the sinking French yacht, and de Roux jumped on board. The rescue was only just in time; the wind increased to 35 knots, and within four hours *Skoiern III* sank.

Five days later, Jeantot rounded Cape Horn, setting a new single-handed record from Sydney of 29 days, 23 hours—6 days faster than Alain Colas in the trimaran *Manureva.* He had also broken the 7-day record for a solo sailor again, with a run of 1,552 miles. On the same day, Konkolski set a new single-hander's record for 24 hours of 247 miles. Jeantot was by now untouchable, and he reached Rio 52 seconds under 48 days from Sydney. Reed was next and then Broadhead, who was given 145 hours' allowance for the time lost rescuing de Roux.

Most of the others were able to cope with the problems of the South Atlantic, but Richard McBride found a new problem when he ran aground on the Falkland Islands. Not even a Royal Navy tug could shift him. It took a month and the help of navy divers to place a block offshore for a tackle, and a Chinook helicopter,

but even then, it was with a rowing boat and the yacht's anchor that the refloating took place. McBride reached Rio twelve days after the fleet had restarted. Seven days later, he gave chase.

The final leg was something of a rest. Jeantot was so far ahead when it started that only a dismasting could prevent him from winning. He was pushed hard by Reed, who finished just 24 hours behind him to take second place overall. Konkolski finished next, having beaten Broadhead in a light-air lottery that saw the Englishman finish more than 2 days behind. But Broadhead gained third place overall and a place in history for his rescue of de Roux, a feat which gained him the award of Yachtsman of the Year 1983 in Britain.

Konkolski's late run was not enough to lift him above third in Class 2; his stop in Fremantle had seen to that. The Japanese taxi driver Yukoh Tada won it 36 hours ahead of Francis Stokes.

Koden Okera V was the winner of the small boat class for Japan's Yukoh Tada.

The One-Ton Cup and Other Level-Rating Championships

previous page: *Harold
Cudmore's* Silver
Shamrock III *off Sydney in
the 1977 Half-Ton Cup.*

Racing level, without handicap, is the truest racing of all. It is achieved in dissimilar boats by having them race to a maximum-level rating under the IOR, which allows development of design in a way that racing exactly identical boats would not. Because of this, the Ton Cups are hotbeds of design development where the object of winning might have a secondary purpose. Designers' names have been made, and in some cases ruined, in the races for these international championships.

It all began in 1965 when the Cercle de la Voile de Paris assigned its Coupe Internationale to an offshore series run without handicap and open to all yachts that rated not more than 22 feet under the RORC rule. The cup was originally (1898-1903) used for a French class known as *Un Tonneau,* with 1 ton of ballast, and the English who took part called it the One-Ton Cup. From the One-Ton Cup there spread progressively five other level-rating classes, one of which has recently been dropped after the change in the One-Ton rating to 30.5 feet IOR from 27.5 feet. It was decided that the Two-Ton level was no longer valid.

The level-rating events came under the jurisdiction of the Offshore Racing Council in 1973 when the new rule came into being. The council then recognized these events as world championships, and the competition became stiffer.

In the first of the offshore One-Ton Cups, held at Le Havre, the S&S-designed *Diana III* won the series for Denmark. It must be remembered that the yachts in this series qualified for it somewhat by accident – no one had designed a boat deliberately to fit into the RORC rule at 22-feet rating. It was the year that

Dick Carter's *Rabbit* won the Fastnet, and his office received many requests for designs for the 1966 contest, which was to be held in Denmark. One of those boats, Dick Stettinius' *Tina,* took the Cup that year and led to more design demand on Carter.

One of the requests came from Germany's Hans Bielken, and the resulting steel-built *Optimist* won the Cup at Le Havre in 1967. The Germans, who had the right to nominate where the defense would be held, announced that the 1968 event would be held at Heligoland. Some 13,000 miles away, on the other side of the world, a young New Zealander had set his sights on that trophy. He had already won the Sydney-Hobart Race with his S&S-designed *Rainbow II,* a boat which fitted the One-Ton rule almost precisely. Chris Bouzaid, at twenty-three, was young, brash, and ambitious – ambitious enough to plan a campaign to take his boat to Heligoland to challenge for the One-Ton Cup and clever enough to secure the support of the top yachting administrators at home to help him get the funds to indulge his plan.

Bouzaid failed to win in 1968, and Bielken retained the Cup, but only after a contest in which the Kiwi sailors had proved their worth and the shortcomings of their boat. Bouzaid was in no way disillusioned. He shipped *Rainbow II* back to Auckland to alter her and make another challenge, again at Heligoland, in the following year. It was to be the last year that the Cup would be raced under the RORC rule.

The alterations that Bouzaid made to his boat were in line with the Kiwis' approach to the sport. They were to take all the advantages that they could get from the rules without too much compromise to aesthetics. He hoisted the light-gasoline engine out and replaced it with a diesel,

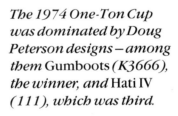

*The 1974 One-Ton Cup
was dominated by Doug
Peterson designs – among
them* Gumboots *(K3666),
the winner, and* Hati IV
(111), which was third.

820 pounds heavier; a steel sheet deck was added to her wooden one (with nails!); and her mast was replaced with a lighter one that was 3 feet 3 inches higher. It meant that *Rainbow II* could now carry more sail under the rule. She was within 10 square feet of *Optimist*'s sail area, and would thus have better light-weather performance.

The revamped *Rainbow II* won the first four races of the One-Ton Cup and took the trophy with a day to spare. The long offshore race, the third one of the series, had been a classic, with *Rainbow II* chasing *Optimist* in the final stages. The final 25-mile leg was a run in light winds, and *Optimist* had a 2½-minute lead to begin it. Bouzaid swapped helmsmen in an effort to get by; then he ordered not only the bilges to be pumped but also the freshwater tanks, to lighten the boat. Bit by bit the Kiwis narrowed the gap, until they began a gybing duel with the Germans. There were eight gybes, and on every one the New Zealand boat gained slightly. Finally, Hans Bielken realized that he was losing and allowed *Rainbow II* to sail unhindered to the finish line, which she crossed 9 minutes ahead. These two boats were a long way ahead of the rest after 285 miles of racing in the North Sea; and far ahead of the rest in their skippers' and crews' appreciation of what made yachts that little faster. It was the start of a new era in yacht racing – Bouzaid and Bielken had shown the way, and to have any hopes of winning, the rest must follow their philosophy.

The two of them dueled again, this time in Sydney in 1972. Bielken had the faster boat, the Carter-designed *Ydra,* but lost the Cup when the forestay rigging screw pulled its threads during the short offshore race. Bouzaid in *Wai-Aniwa* sailed a conservative series and won by the

narrowest of margins, his second win of the magnificent trophy. The party that followed that win, at the prize giving at the Randwick Racecourse, is one that no one who was there will ever forget – and they can answer questions as to why the One-Ton Cup now has a permanent list to port.

Ydra did get her Cup win the following year, but ironically only at the expense of a faster boat making a navigational error. There was no doubt that the Doug Peterson-designed and -skippered *Ganbare* was the fastest boat at the One-Ton Cup in Sardinia, but an error in rounding the outer turning mark the wrong way in the long-distance race saw her disqualified. This gave the Cup to *Ydra,* which was sailed by the Star-class ace Admiral Agostino Straulino.

Peterson did not lose by it commercially, however; he was the man to whom many went in search of their One-Tonner for the following year. They went to him and to Ron Holland, who had won the Quarter-Ton Cup at Weymouth

above: Gumboots, *Jeremy Rogers' One-Ton winner in 1974, rounds the weather mark ahead of* Ciel III.

left: *The David Thomas-designed* Chartreuse *passes astern of the Brazilian* Liho Liho.

America Jane III, *the One-Tonner designed by Scott Kaufman for George Toobey, at the 1976 event.*

with his *Eygthene;* the flair and innovation of the two young Turks made them the busiest men in the business for several years. In 1974, the Peterson *Gumboots* and the Holland *Golden Apple* were the two fastest boats at Torquay. *Gumboots,* sailed by Jeremy Rogers, won the Cup and included in her performance the rescue of six crewmembers of a cruising yacht that had caught fire in the path of the short offshore race course. In third place, with a sister ship to *Gumboots,* was Chris Bouzaid.

The design changes were already well

under way with the Bruce King bilgeboarder *Terrorist* making her appearance at Torquay, where she could easily have taken the Cup. By 1976, the fleet was forty-three strong from fifteen countries, and the weight of designers, builders, sparmakers, and sailmakers that were taking part gave some indication of the importance in which this series was held. The centerboarders in the fleet had things very much their own way. In very light going, the Farr designs from New Zealand cleaned up at Marseilles, but the slightly heavier Britton

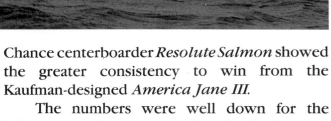

Chance centerboarder *Resolute Salmon* showed the greater consistency to win from the Kaufman-designed *America Jane III*.

The numbers were well down for the following year's Cup, in Auckland; only fourteen boats took part. It was, however, to be a turning point in the Cup's history. The New Zealanders had always dominated the world of centerboard offshore boats, and with the IOR rule favoring this type, there was little point in Europeans and Americans shipping their boats and airlifting their crews to Auckland; there was doubt too as

to how long the IOR would stand center-boarders, and the expense of building new boats for the Cup was considered highly uneconomic. The Kiwis on their home waters in Farr-designed centerboarders proved totally unstoppable.

The other noticeable thing about the boats was that they were all fractionally rigged boats – the Kiwis were keen to exploit the IOR in this respect as well and showed they had the technology to cope with the problems normally associated with retaining efficiency with this type of rig in boats of this size. There were,

The 1976 Three-Quarter Ton Cup was one of contrasts. The Holland-designed Mezzanine *is virtually becalmed to weather of* Too Contentious.

however, deficiencies in the boats. Without some scantling control within the IOR, the boats had become unnecessarily fragile, and this became very obvious in the long offshore race when it blew hard.

In that race, Ray Hasler's *Jenny H* fell off a big wave and cracked her hull forward of the mast. A laminated ring frame had cracked and allowed the longitudinal stringers to break,

In Contention *included in her crew gold medalist Peter Barrett, but a broken mast ended her chances in 1976.*

which in turn imposed unfair pressures on the flat-sided part of the hull forward. A near sister ship, *Hecate*, retired with similar problems, and two of the leading boats when examined after the race were found to be suffering from similar but less serious structural damage.

There was no denying, however, the Farr boats their success. Farr had designed the first three: Stu Brentnall's *Red Lion*, Graeme Woodroffe's *Mr. JumpA*, and Don Lidgard's *Smir-Noff-Agen. Red Lion* opened with a second and a first in the inshore Olympic-course races and then won the short offshore. She slipped to

fourth in the next inshore race and was third in the long race, which was won by *Smir-Noff-Agen*, winner also of the first race. The other race winner was the Doug Peterson centerboarder *B195* from Melbourne. She had been forced to change her name from *Pioneer Sound* because of the rule concerning advertising, yet paradoxically the first three boats in the series were all commercially sponsored, and their names reflected their benefactors. The Offshore Racing Council had a lot on its hands as a result of this regatta.

When the 1978 Cup was held, at Flensburg

in Germany, the entries were back up to thirty-six from thirteen countries. With alterations to the IOR rule, the older Farr boats were no longer competitive; Farr, however, did design a new centerboarder for Stu Brentnall, *Export Lion,* which was leading the series after three races. But the centerboarders were not to dominate this series; that was left to two Ron Holland boats in German hands: *Tilsag,* owned and skippered by Klaus Lange; and *Bremen,* skippered by Berend Bielken, brother of Hans. These two fixed-keel boats proved what Ron Holland had been saying for some time: tuning was as important as design. For a whole season, *Tilsag* and *Bremen* had raced against each other, and both had sails from Bielken, who appeared to have a limitless budget to work with. Both had alterations to their keels, and their mast comparisons were such that when *Tilsag,* with a stiffer Proctor mast, proved faster, the Stearn mast of *Bremen* was suitably stiffened to match that of *Tilsag.*

The series was marred by the loss of the Stephen Jones-designed *Oystercatcher.* Sailed by a British crew, she was only half a mile from the rhumb line of the course in the long offshore

Left to right, Golden Delicious *(GB),* In Contention *(USA), and* Finn Fire *(Finland), the eventual winner of the Three-Quarter-Ton Cup at Plymouth.*

211

Gunboat Rangiriri, *the Farr-designed winner of the 1977 Half-Ton Cup at Sydney chases* Silver Shamrock III, *the boat that would have won had she not lost her mast, and one place, in the short offshore race.*

Skipper Harold Cudmore puts fine trim into the mainsail while John Anderson steers Silver Shamrock III.

race when she grounded. Unable to sail into deeper water, her crew accepted a tow; but the towline parted, and quickly she was blown back onto the sandbank, filled, and began to break up. Her crew was taken off and learned later from the coast guard that the particular sandbank which

had claimed their yacht has been known to move several hundred yards in a day. It was unwise, therefore, of the race committee to have set a course so close to this shifting hazard.

Changes in the IOR rule possibly accounted for only twelve yachts from four countries

attending the 1979 Cup in Newport, Rhode Island. It was not a happy event, except for the performance of John MacLaurin's *Pendragon,* a Laurie Davidson centerboarder that had won the Three-Quarter-Ton Cup the previous year. Davidson had designed the alterations to *Pendragon,* which included a short bowsprit and a taller mast with some extra internal ballast to raise her rating from 24.5 to 27.5 feet. In doing so, Davidson had raised the sail area by 20 percent.

Hurricane David affected the racing, with the second Olympic course not held because of 40 knots of wind and the (unfulfilled) promise of more. There was no provision for extending the regatta, and so the race was lost. When the middle-distance race had to be resailed because of a shifted mark, the third inshore race went too. *Pendragon* won the first race in light winds and fog. Graham Walker's Holland-designed *Indulgence,* with Lowell North, Tim Stearn, and Butch Dalrymple-Smith on board, had led and had no time to get back when the race was shortened. *Pendragon* was subsequently found to have had more than the maximum number of headsails on board; the jury accepted her skipper's reason of an accidental oversight, and she was not penalized. She was also not penalized in the long offshore race for not having had navigation lights alight at night; once again, the jury accepted MacLaurin's excuse that he had had battery failure and let him go free of penalty. In that final race, *Indulgence,* an hour ahead with only 30 of the 245 miles to go, went back to sit on *Pendragon* in order to try to get two boats between them at the finish. It was a move prompted by Lowell North, and it did not work;

it caused a few raised eyebrows too. *Indulgence* won the White Horse Trophy for the long race, although she did not win the Cup.

She was to win that again the following year at Naples when there was a fleet of twenty-seven from twelve nations. It was stop-go racing in Naples Bay for the short offshore race, in which *Indulgence* was leading 20 miles from the finish only to be left behind when the wind died and filled in from a new direction. Her twenty-fourth place in that race eliminated her Cup hopes, despite the attention to detail applied by Harold Cudmore and Phil Crebbin, the two main members of her afterguard.

Indulgence and the other two Holland designs – *Todahesa,* skippered by John Kolius, and *Sharkey,* owned by Mike Swerdlow and with Tim Stearn, Lowell North, and Butch Dalrymple-Smith in her crew—were possibly the fastest boats, but it was the intelligent sailing of Stefano Roberti with the Vallicelli-designed *Filo da Torcere* that took the Cup from Scott Rohrer aboard the Fontana–Maletto–Navone-designed *Buonalena.*

One-Ton Cup interest sagged as the cost of the boats rose. It was impossible for a nonprofessional outfit to keep pace, and there were only a limited number of crews available from the design offices and from sailmakers. The One-Ton Cup appeared to have gotten itself on a carousel of death, and there was little enough other racing for this size of boat, since the rating band of the Admiral's Cup and its derivatives had been set deliberately to exclude the One-Tonners. So for the 1981 Cup, held by the world's oldest yacht club, The Royal Cork (founded 1720), there were only sixteen boats

213

from six countries, and only five of the yachts were really competitive.

Ron Holland, with Ken Rohan, had chartered *Vento,* the former *Todahesa,* in an effort to stimulate some competition with the three-year-old *Indulgence.* For this series, Walker had Crebbin and North together with Kiwi helmsman Andy Ball as tactician. Cudmore had accepted the skipper's job on *Justine III,* Frank Woods' new Tony Castro design. This was the first time that Castro, who used to work for Holland, had faced his old master. The other two top boats were likely to be the Jones-designed

Castro was somewhat unlucky as a designer not to win again with the Hong Kong *Sunstreaker,* which lost a much-disputed protest in the short offshore race, a race which she had won by 5 minutes. With the protest, she lost six places, which might have seen her win the Cup. This went to the Italian 12-Metre skipper Mauro Pellaschier with the Skiomachen-designed *Linda,* which beat the Frers-designed *Califa* from Argentina, with *Sunstreaker* third.

This type of racing was obviously going to have its devotees at other levels. After all, there were many other possible bands where level-

Rakau and the Dubois-designed *Snowball.*

Cudmore did everything that his home club possibly could have desired. The Irishman won each of the five races with *Justine III,* a result unparalleled in the Cup's history. It appeared likely that he had done it on the last occasion that the Cup was to be held in that size of boat when the 1982 One-Ton Cup was canceled. There were not sufficient entries for the Royal Thames Yacht Club to hold the event at Brighton. The ORC decided that the only way to revitalize the Cup was to change the maximum rating to 30.5 feet IOR, but it was a move that could not be taken until 1984, as the Cup was scheduled for 1983 in Brazil and some boats were being built specially for the event.

rating racing was possible. The first offshoot was a smaller rating and was called, with no justification but with some logic, the Half-Ton Cup. Initially raced at 18-feet RORC, the first three events were held at La Rochelle from 1966. For two years, it moved to Sandhamm, where Peter Norlin won on both occasions with his Scampi designs. He proved just how good they were in 1971 when the Half-Ton Cup was held at Portsmouth under the new IOR limit of 21.7 feet by winning with *Scampi III.* It took Paul Elvstrom with *Bes,* the boat he and Jan Kjaerulf had designed, to stop Norlin's winning run.

The Half-Ton Cup grew strongly, with sound designs improving the breed of boats around 30 feet long. By 1976, there were forty boats at

214

Impetuous *leads the pack in the second inshore race in 1979.*

Boats had changed radically when the Half-Ton Cup was next held in Sydney fifteen months later. Almost every designer had been seen offering a centerboarder from his portfolio, and all the front-runners in this event were of that configuration; the first six overall certainly were. The Farr-designed *Gunboat Rangiriri* of Peter Wilcox took the series by one point from twenty-two others, but the win was even closer than the one point indicated. Harold Cudmore would have retained his title with another *Silver Shamrock,* this one a Holland centerboarder of heavier displacement than the Farr designs, had he not lost his mast, and one place, 400 yards from the finish of the short offshore race. The extra one and a half points for that lost place would have given Cudmore the Cup by a mere half a point.

That Half-Ton Cup was preceded by some careful examination of the stability of the new wave of centerboarders. Many were tested with weights while the controversy surrounding their safety continued. Farr had a good series with his *2269,* with John Bertrand on board, taking third place and Ian Gibbs's *Swuzzlebubble* fifth. The fourth place was taken by the Davidson-designed *Waverider,* which could so easily have won the series but for her slump down the lists in the final, long offshore race.

The next year, however, was *Waverider*'s. A record fifty-boat fleet in 1978 at Poole (with more than half the fleet designed by Holland, Berret, or Jones) provided severe competition. The Jones-designed *Indulgence,* skippered by Phil Crebbin, was the early leader, with a second in the opening race and then two firsts, including the short offshore. *Indulgence* was one of the modified "stock" Hustler 32s in the fleet. Larry Marks's *Smokey Bear* was another, and she was scoring regular high placings too, while *Waverider* just kept in contention. At the start of the fourth race, Crebbin played it conservatively, while Helmer Pederson on the tiller of *Waverider* went for everything he could and port tacked the fleet. This early advantage saw *Waverider* finish second, while *Indulgence* was sixteenth. The final 340-miler with four crossings of the English Channel (and two visits to CH 1 off Cherbourg) was a complete test of boats and crews. It was settled in the last 70-mile leg back across the Channel to Poole. At CH 1, *Waverider* was ninth; at the finish, she was first. She had slipped her rivals by superior speed and skill, and no one had seen her going. Marks thought the Cup was his as he crossed the line with *Indulgence* too far back in his sights to beat him on points and was staggered to hear that *Waverider* was not only in, but first.

Waverider did it again at Scheveningen the next year, and again only just. Her opening of a first and second on the Olympic-course races was followed by a twentieth in the short

Trieste when the Ron Holland-designed *Silver Shamrock,* in the hands of Harold Cudmore, took the Cup. Cudmore and Holland had specially prepared this "production" hull for the event, with 500 pounds less in the lay up and a slightly bigger rig. She was undoubtedly the best-prepared boat for the light conditions that existed, but some doubted that she would have been the fastest boat at Trieste if the wind had blown—the Farr-designed *Candu II* showed how fast she was on the only day when the wind held at Force 3. Writing of the series, a Frenchman summed it up well: "The 1976 Half-Ton Cup is a very light claret that may not age too well."

offshore, which ensured that her crew had to work doubly hard in the last two races. They did and brought the modified boat–with more ballast and a different rudder to optimize her performance in the light of the changes in the IOR–to two more wins and the Cup.

It is best that a veil be drawn over the Half-Ton Cup of the following year, 1980. It was full of contentious protests over the second inshore race, and the winner, Gerard Dupuy's *Ar Bigouden,* only triumphed because she survived a protest over a collision which was dismissed for "lack of evidence."

Happiness returned with good racing at Poole in 1981 when sailing's undoubted megastar, Paul Elvstrom, showed his younger rivals the way to tackle championships. He won the first race and then the second and came second in the short offshore. Buried in the pack at the start of the fourth race, he could do no better than seventeenth of the thirty-one starters, proving perhaps that he was human. Then when it really mattered, the king, in the appropriately named Berret design, *King 1,* won the long offshore race and with it the Cup for the second time.

Success in the Quarter-Ton Cup in 1973 secured a place in the international design field for Ron Holland. The smaller class began its championships in 1967 at 15-feet rating RORC and became 18 feet IOR in 1971 (18.5 in 1980). Holland's *Eygthene* did what many had felt was the purpose of ton-cup racing and sailed a consistently good series with no structural breakdowns–a thoroughly reliable boat. There were others at that event in Weymouth that went fast on occasion, but *Eygthene* was an all-around success.

The accent changed in the design parameters, and lighter-displacement boats began to outsail their more conservative sisters. The New Zealanders dominated with Farr and Whiting designs, before the expatriate Kiwi Holland had another taste of the Quarter-Ton Cup in 1977 with *Manzanita.* It was sailed by Rodney Pattisson and Ib Anderson in Helsinki in cold, rainy conditions. The same conditions prevailed for much of the next year's Cup races in Japan, at Sajima. That series also featured strong winds that were to take the masts out of most of the production Manzanitas that were there. It was won by a Japanese-designed boat with two Japanese crew supplemented by a couple of Americans from North Sails.

The Cup history then took a turn for Jacques Fauroux. The next year, 1979, he won the Cup in one of his own designs at San Remo, taking the last race and beating Paul Elvstrom into second place to do so. The same combination of Fauroux and his Bullitt design won again the following year. And in 1981, one of the ingredients was still there, Fauroux's brilliant design. In the

hands of Bruno Trouble and Patrick Haegli, *Lacydon Protis* won the Cup, but it needed determination. Chris Dickson of New Zealand in *Hellaby* won the first race with Trouble second. The Frenchman had the same place in the next race. Both races were sailed in Force 6 to 7 winds. *Lacydon Protis* then won the short offshore in moderate airs. The wind was up to Force 7 to 8 for the fourth race, and down came the mast on *Lacydon Protis,* but that was not the end of Trouble. He stepped a new mast for the long offshore, and after anchoring overnight on the second night out when the wind had reached Force 9 plus, Trouble sailed into Marseilles

The Japanese Koteru-Teru *has a narrow lead over one of the French competitors at Poole.*

217

The spinnaker is about to burst into life and the genoa to come down within seconds of Impetuous *rounding the windward mark.*

second of three to finish to win the Cup.

There was a call for an even smaller class, which made its first appearance in 1978, rating 16 feet IOR (by 1980, 16.5 feet IOR) – the Mini-Ton class. Its popularity has not spread far and wide, since few feel that the type of boat it is developing is strictly suitable for offshore racing, although it has a determined band of followers.

Wahoo won the first two Mini-Ton Cups. The Fontana–Maletto–Navone design won first in the hands of Hubert Raudaschl, and then

Claudio Maletto himself steered to beat John Kolius, sailing a Holland design. The next went to a Kelly design, *Mr. Bill's Dog,* sailed by Kurt Oetking of the United States, who took the series in the blowy last race from Larry Marks in the Jones-designed *Smokey and the Choirboys.* On Lake Constance the next year, Tizanio Nava won with *Gullisara* in a series concluded with a long offshore race of 26 miles. The time had come to take stock.

The bigger classes have always had difficulty

in attracting large numbers, except when held in Europe and particularly in Britain. When *Finn Fire* won the Three-Quarter-Ton Cup at Plymouth in 1976, it was the biggest fleet ever for that size of level-rating boat. The biggest entry for the Two-Ton Cup, now for boats of 32 feet IOR, was when it was held at Poole just prior to the Admiral's Cup in 1979. Then it was won by the superbly sailed *Gitana VII,* a reject from the French Admiral's Cup trials, in the hands of Ghislain Pillet. When there were only sixteen

boats for the Cup at Porto Cervo, a month after the Admiral's Cup was all over, the death knell began to sound for the Two-Ton Cup. The end came when there were insufficient entries in 1983 at Le Havre for the racing to be held, followed later that year by the confirmation of the new rating for the One-Ton Cup, at 30.5 feet IOR. The demise of the Two-Ton Cup is no reflection on level rating, and doubtless there will be those who will want to restore this cup to the lineup of offshore world championships.

Buonalena, *the Fontana-Maletto-Navone design which was skippered by Scott Rohrer to second place in the 1981 One-Ton Cup.*

219

Route du Rhum

previous page: *St. Malo
harbor, with the fleet
gathered for general
viewing before the start of
the 1982 race.*

Mike Birch in Olympus
Photo *crosses the finishing
line 1 hour, 38 minutes
ahead of Michel
Malinovsky in* Kriter V *to
win the 1978 race. After
4,000 miles the lead
changed hands less than a
mile from the finish.*

The Route du Rhum Race was devised by the French, to go from one French port to another. Guadeloupe, while 4,000 miles from St. Malo, is a department of France, and makes an ideal place to finish a race. The course is very different from the OSTAR. The southerly aspect of Pointe-à-Pitre makes the choice of route to take a more difficult one. The Great Circle route, to the north, is the shortest, but by going south it is possible to get into the trade winds and sail faster. The Great Circle route entails meeting head winds. It was regarded as the better route for the monohulls, while the trade wind route would be of benefit to the multihulls. No one could have foreseen the closeness at the finish of the first two boats: a monohull and a multihull, which had sailed the different routes to Pointe-à-Pitre.

There were political reasons for the birth of this race in 1978. In France, shorthanded ocean racing had gained impetus from the successes of French protagonists, and there was considerable commercial support in the form of sponsorship of boats. To gain the most from this sort of sponsorship, the boats had to be big, they had to be the first to finish, and they had to be charismatic. The Royal Western Yacht Club's decision, after the 1976 OSTAR, to restrict the overall length of entries to the 1980 race, met with considerable disapproval in France, particularly from those competitors whose boats were outlawed. There was a need for a race across the Atlantic for those boats, if for no other reason than to keep the sponsors happy. None knew that better than Michel Etevenon – "Mr. Fixit France" – the man who has been mainly responsible for the development of commercial yachting, and it was he who was behind the organization of the race to fill the gap, the Route du Rhum.

There was no shortage of competitors for the race in 1978 and no shortage of drama. The first incident came shortly after the start, when the 75-foot catamaran *Paul Ricard,* sailed by Marc Pajot, was in a collision with a small cruising sailboat. The small boat was in grave danger of sinking before the two boats were parted, and it was also the end of the race for Pajot, whose boat was damaged. It was a great sadness for the Olympic medalist, since the Paul Spronk-designed boat had proved her worth in the trade wind race by beating Phil Weld's 60-foot *Rogue Wave* twice.

There were other moments of anguish at that spectacular start. Eugene Rigudel met his just after dusk. Mike Birch in *Olympus Photo* – the former *A Cappella* of Wally Greene—was slightly ahead, and took an inshore course across one of the bays of the Brittany coast to cheat a foul tide. Rigudel took the Kelsall-designed *VSD* straight across the bay under spinnaker, and became involved in a minor collision with the press boat – the cross-channel ferry *Armorique. VSD* was luckier than *Paul Ricard* and was able to continue, but it must have been a nasty moment for Rigudel.

Not long after this the wind began to blow hard and the self-steering gears of many of the boats began to show weaknesses. Chay Blyth's Kelsall-designed *Great Britain IV,* the boat with which he and Rob James had won the Round Britain Race, was one of the earliest to retire from this cause; the 54-footer turned back with a disappointed skipper. So too did its predecessor, the 80-foot *Great Britain III,* renamed *Disque d'Or* for this event, and skippered by Pierre Fehlmann. She returned to St. Malo after only 15 miles, but was back out again to join the race after making repairs to her vane gear. She averaged 14.7 knots from St. Malo to Ushant, but

pulled out of the race for good when the self-steering petered out again. Single-handed racing had never been a consideration of her design, and very little had been done to improve the prospects for Fehlmann.

The other Kelsall trimarans did not figure well in this race. *VSD* ran aground near Antigua — Rigudel was probably exhausted from trying to steer her manually, while *Seiko,* the former *Three Legs of Mann III,* began to fill her main hull and one float. Kelsall commented at the time that she had never had a chance following major refitting of the boat in the few days before the start. The race rules (designed to keep the boats in St. Malo harbor for the seven days immediately prior to the start as a public spectacle) had prevented any trial sailing after the work on her had been completed.

The two more fancied trimarans, *Rogue Wave* and *Manureva,* were comfortable in the early stages. *Rogue Wave* was skippered by Phil Weld; she was his replacement for *Gulf Streamer,* which had capsized in the Atlantic. His experience with this type of boat was showing, and his early conservatism and excellent preparation began to tell. Alain Colas had sailed thousands of miles in the 70-foot *Manureva,* including a circumnavigation of the world, and had won the OSTAR with the boat that, as *Pen Duick IV,* originally belonged to Tabarly. For Colas, the race should have been just another sail. He was familiar with his boat and its gear. Yet he was to provide the race with its mystery: for Colas and *Manureva* were never heard of again. No one knows how the courageous Frenchman met his death — was it a storm that took him by

The end of Marc Pajot's race with the 75-foot catamaran Paul Ricard *when he ran over a moored spectator boat while hoisting his spinnaker.*

223

surprise or was his trimaran run over by a freighter in mid-ocean? That such an experienced ocean sailor should have disappeared emphasized once again the danger of the sport. Nobody could have been expected to complete the race with more certainty than Colas.

One of the more interesting monohulls in the race was Michel Malinovsky's *Kriter V* (there were three Kriter-sponsored yachts in this race), a light-displacement 70-footer. Malinovsky was determined to take the northern route in the

stronger winds, even though they were head winds. *Kriter V* had a big cutter rig, with her headsails on furling rollers, the type of rig which he could handle well. With him on that route went the schooner-rigged *Wild Rocket,* a similar-sized monohull; both were aimed along the Great Circle route.

Phil Weld took the straight rhumb line route, sailing a constant compass course all the way to Guadeloupe. In contrast, Birch, with *Olympus Photo,* and the schooner-rigged trimaran *Kriter IV,* went on a southerly route, the one which would have been favored by the clipper ships that opened up the original Route du Rhum with following easterlies. Those winds were, however, lighter. There was the interesting prospect therefore of fancied boats contesting the race along through different courses.

Each of the routes had its advantages, and *Kriter V* converged with *Olympus Photo* for the final stage of the race, around the west coast of Guadeloupe and into Pointe-à-Pitre. Then the fight really began. *Olympus Photo* was first to the northwest corner of the island, but down the western side the monohull closed the gap, so that at first light of morning the two yachts were making gentle progress, in sight of each other, in a light westerly breeze. The maneuverability of the monohull was to prove important as the two fought for the advantage as they approached the southern tip of Guadeloupe.

It was there that the wind headed and Malinovsky was able to choose the shifts and use them to his advantage, while Birch took the trimaran farther out to sea. It appeared that Malinovsky had won the day when he got the first of the freshening breeze, leaving Birch behind. But as the leader approached Pointe-à-Pitre, on a close-hauled course, the wind began to free again, and as it did so the perkiness returned to *Olympus Photo*. The yellow trimaran came on apace, closing the gap with the dark-hulled *Kriter V.* Less than a mile from the line, with rival cries of "Go, go, Malino" and "Allez Birch" from the crowd of spectator boats, *Olympus Photo* went past as Malinovsky broke out the staysail in an effort to make more speed. But speed was what the monohull did not have, at least not speed to match the trimaran, and *Olympus Photo* crossed the line 98 seconds ahead, after 4,000 miles of racing. That Phil Weld was third seemed almost irrelevant — after the excitement of the leaders' race, everything else paled by comparison, although it was worthy of note that the first three had each taken a different route from St. Malo to Guadeloupe.

Could there be another race like it? Undoubtedly Michel Etevenon knew how to attract the best entries. Originally the entries had been restricted to fifty, because of the number of "balises Argos," the automatic satellite transmitters, which the Thomson organization was prepared to loan for the race. When a few extra became available, the number of allowed competitors rose to fifty-five to utilize them all. The big names, almost without exception, were lined up in St. Malo in 1982, although it is doubtful that all were ready for a single-handed event. One strange entry most certainly was not.

Whichever way you looked at it there was something odd about *Rosières,* the proa which Guy Delage proposed to sail. Designed by Gilles Ollier and Herve Devaux, it was 60 feet long with 80 feet of beam! It was as complicated a structure as anyone had ever had the nerve to suggest he might sail. Throughout the week prior to the start, it was the center of attention, not only from the hordes of spectators, but also from a small army of helpers that Delage had gathered around him. He is, or was, the guru of proas, and *Rosières* was his flowerchild. Unfortunately, the proa had all the willfulness of such progeny. The thinking behind the boat gave her a windward outrigger, which could be filled with water to counter the heeling moment of the sails, and the whole of her support arm could be pivoted to prevent the leading bow from burying. Just after the start, to be precise 20 minutes after, Delage operated the pivot action of the arm and it went farther than designed. The outrigger hull went right against the main hull, lost its righting effect, and *Rosières* capsized and sank. It seemed that Delage and his

Lestra Sport, *one of the proas which started in 1982.*

designers would have to return to the drawing board and think again.

Meanwhile Marc Pajot, in *Elf Aquitaine,* was just beating Rob James, in *Colt Cars GB,* to the first turning mark and a prize of 10,000 francs. The race was on; there were still forty other multihulls and fourteen monohulls spread out *en route* for Guadeloupe, many of them unprepared. The activity in the dock before the race had been frenetic, only the three British entries and *Elf Aquitaine* being ready, it seemed. But within a very short time all three of the British boats found their preparation of no avail; for one reason or another the skippers discovered they were in trouble.

Chay Blyth had self-steering problems. The link arm to the servo tab on the rudder of the Shuttleworth-designed *Brittany Ferries GB* fractured, and there was no way that Blyth could repair it at sea. By the time that it could have been repaired in the Spanish port where he took refuge, the race leaders would have been too far away for him to chase with any chance of success. Rob James had changed to the second main halyard in his mast. The previous one had seen the 60-foot Holland-designed trimaran win the Round Britain Race; this one had been led the wrong side of the jumper strut inside the mast, chafed on it and broke. The light line "leader," which James had put in the mast when he had removed the old one, had also chafed through and it was impossible for him to reeve another main halyard on the fractionally rigged mast, and he too retired. Robin Knox-Johnston, in the 70-foot Macalpine-Downie-designed catamaran *Sea Falcon,* had battery and charging problems, and had to put in to the Azores for replacements. This took him away from the close chase he was giving to Pajot.

Others, too, succumbed; Daniel Gilard, with the 46-foot Newick-designed *Brittany Ferries* was in and out of port with steering trouble. Florence Arthaud was back in St. Malo for repairs and out again within a day. But these were the lucky ones. There were many others who were forced into St. Malo but found that they were unable to return to the race.

The way was clear for Pajot this time, but then the main crossbeam of *Elf Aquitaine* began to break. The aluminum developed a creeping fracture away from an inspection hatch on its vertical face. Pajot used spare wire halyards to bind the beam together, even using a spoon to stop the wire from biting into the metal of the beam at a corner. The repair was only partially effective, and he had to put into Martinique to get help for a more rational repair. But that failed, too, and the 66-foot *Elf Aquitaine* was back to relying on the Pajot "bandage" to take her to the finish line. Even so, her time was fast. Four years before it had taken Birch 23 days, 6 hours; this time Pajot, even with the stop, was across the

line at Pointe-à-Pitre in 18 days, 1 hour for the 4,000 miles.

In second place was Bruno Peyron with the catamaran *Jaz.* She was designed by Bruno Dubernet, and differed from all the others in having an identical rig on each hull — not the most efficient, but certainly an effective, downwind rig for the single-hander. *Jaz* was 58 feet long and she finished 10 hours behind *Elf Aquitaine.*

Birch this time had to be content with third. Again he had gone for a small boat, or a relatively small one, the 50-foot *Vital.* Unfortunately, he was one of those who was hardly ready for the race; he had had only the delivery trip with *Vital,* from England to St. Malo, to familiarize himself with the boat, and admitted in Pointe-à-Pitre that

he was only beginning to understand in the latter stages of the race how to get the best out of a catamaran. Despite this, Birch was only 2 hours behind Peyron and 12 behind Pajot, a very praiseworthy effort, and he had completed the race in a faster time than that for his exciting race with Malinovsky.

There were many new innovations for this race. Tabarly tried a gaff-type rig on the foiler *Paul Ricard*. It utilized a crane at the masthead and a double halyard system. He was aiming to get greater sail area on, and efficiency from, the rotating wing mast, but the system was perhaps too complex. *Elf Aquitaine* had an even more sophisticated wing mast, and it was the extra loading of this that probably caused the main crossbeam to crack. *Gautier III,* a Langevin-

designed trimaran for Jean-Yves Terlain, sported T-shaped foils, as did *Caddy,* a smaller Langevin trimaran, while Loic Caradec's *Royale* had retractable ones, hydraulically controlled on her outriggers.

One catamaran which generally escaped notice was the Paul Spronk-designed 45-foot *Skyjack* of Philip Walwyn. Essentially a cruising boat, *Skyjack* surprised her more sophisticated sisters by winning the final prime, for the last 50 miles, to take a huge cash prize and put a big smile on her owner's face.

Charles Heidsieck V, *the 60-foot* Shuttleworth *trimaran which Alain Gabbay chartered for 1982. She is better known as* Living Dole III *and became* Travacrest Seaway *for the 1984 OSTAR, skippered by Peter Phillips.*

Transat en Double

Only the French could invent a race which involves crossing the Atlantic twice, by means of rounding a buoy off Bermuda, without a short stop on that delightful coral island. Known as the Transat en Double, the first started from Lorient on May 2, 1979. Like the Route du Rhum a year earlier, it was to put another nail in the coffin of the monohulls.

With 6,000 miles of ocean to cross, however, the pre-race speculation in fact favored the big monohulls, because of the uncertainties surrounding the multis. Eric Tabarly had only recently launched his hydrofoil trimaran *Paul Ricard.* To most people she seemed too complicated, and even Eric and his crew, Marc Pajot, had to admit she was relatively untried.

An early retirement was expected of the smaller trimaran, *VSD.* It was argued that she was too small and that her skipper, Eugene Rigudel, suffered the worst luck of all offshore racers. He was teamed, however, with Gilles Gahinet, whose reputation was for staying the course.

Mike Birch, the Route du Rhum winner, could charter only the relatively heavy *Quest* — renamed *Tele-7-Jours* for the race — and this should not be as good as even his tiny trimaran *Olympus Photo.* He had Jean-Marie Vidal as his partner, though, and they would drag the most from the 51-foot boat. The favorite was Michel Malinovsky with the pencil-slim monohull *Kriter*

V, which Birch had beaten in the sprint to the line in the Route du Rhum. It was expected that the east-to-west crossing would be largely into head winds and that the monohulls would be able to gain sufficient advantage in this direction to hold off the flying trimarans on the way home; *Kriter V,* in particular, should find the race very much to her liking. Malinovsky desperately wanted revenge for that smarting defeat.

Stiff southwesterlies, with two gales in the first week, reduced the forty starters by twelve, and as they had left Lorient it was the monohulls, led by *Kriter V,* which had shown the way. *Paul Ricard* looked awkward with one of her hulls way up in the air, bucking her way to windward and not pointing anywhere near as high as the monohulls. But two days out, Malinovsky saw *Paul Ricard* ahead of him in the driving rain.

The trail of devastation in the wake of the leaders was heavy. One of those to retire was Chay Blyth, with the trimaran *Great Britain IV,* in which he had won the previous year's Round Britain Race. She had broken chain plates. The ketch-rigged *Roger Marthe Video* was dismasted, and the 90-foot trimaran *Charles Heidsieck* simply fell apart. *VSD* had her share of troubles early on; she lost the hydrofoils from her center hull, the fairing of the starboard outrigger arm tore off, and later the boom broke. Rigudel's bad luck had followed him, but he decided that he

VSD, *the 66-foot Kesall-designed catamaran of Nick Keig and Gilles Gahinet which broke her mast seven hours after the start in 1982.*

would press on as well as he possibly could.

At the end of the first week there were two monohulls in the lead, *Kriter V* being ahead of *Kriter IV,* but *Paul Ricard* was in third place. Despite her damage, *VSD* was fifth and *Tele-7-Jours* was seventh, less than 100 miles behind.

During the second week an anticyclone, with its associated calms, spread over the race course. On June 7, Malinovsky and Lenormand, in the big monohull *Kriter V,* sailed less than 50 miles in 24 hours. Tabarly took *Paul Ricard* to the south to skirt the worst of the anticyclone and to avoid the countercurrent of the Gulf Stream, aiming to approach Bermuda from the southeast, as southwesterlies are prevalent in that area. His strategy worked, and 18½ days out *Paul Ricard* rounded the turning mark off Bermuda. Her only damage appeared to be that the fairing of the starboard outrigger had ripped off, and she had torn two of her four spinnakers

Charles Heidsieck III, *the Gilles Vaton-designed 66-footer, sailed by Mario Zimmerman and Joel Picquemal-Baron.*

badly. It was 22 hours before the next boat went around, and Tabarly looked to have the race in the bag. The next boat to Bermuda was the 55-foot *Kriter VI,* the monohull sailed by Olivier de Kersauson and Gerard Djikstra, with Birch and Vidal in *Tele-7-Jours* another 6½ hours behind. *Kriter V's* chances appeared slight when she rounded nearly two whole days behind the leader, and when *VSD* went into St. Georges for repairs, no one would have given her a prayer.

VSD lost 13 more hours as her leaks were stopped and a new fairing put on the outrigger. A new, more efficient, rudder was also fitted as *VSD* was slipped by floodlight. Then she was back in the fray again, sizzling off with sheets freed at 15 knots, but 62 hours, 40 minutes behind Tabarly's silver foiler. For Rigudel and Gahinet there was one target—to make the fastest west-to-east passage. All hopes of catching *Paul Ricard* were out of their minds. However, 2 days later *VSD* had gained enormously. *Paul Ricard* had rounded the Bermuda mark into head winds, while *VSD* had reaching conditions after her repairs. The gap was narrowed to 130 miles.

Tabarly favored the Great Circle route, while Rigudel headed farther to the north in order to get stronger winds. Tabarly and Pajot were handicapped in that their two spinnakers were not right for the conditions. The heavier one was too heavy, while the lighter one would not stand the average breeze. Tabarly and Pajot estimated that in having to use the heavy chute they lost an average of a knot. *VSD* at 4 tons was half the weight of *Paul Ricard* and set much the same amount of sail. She was clearly gaining.

On June 20 and 21, *VSD* logged more than 300 miles each day and overtook *Kriter VI* and *Tele-7-Jours,* leaving only *Kriter V* between her and the leader. The next day *VSD* overtook the monohull, and was just 90 miles astern of *Paul Ricard.* On board the foiler, Tabarly and Pajot listened to the news of the race on French radio stations and put everything they knew into their efforts to stay ahead. Tabarly repaired the heavier medium-weight spinnaker by hand sewing and sticky tape. Meanwhile in search for more speed, the light spinnaker of *VSD* was blown out. By June 24 the gap was 60 miles.

It was the turn then of *Paul Ricard's* crew to try the light spinnaker – it lasted only 12 hours before it blew out. Three days later the gap was down to 40 miles and the next day it was 35, with 250 miles to go.

The following morning, as the wind eased and a mist hung over the sea, Pajot saw *VSD* only 300 yards astern. They were then off Penmarch, 40 miles from the finish. The wind freshened to Force 4, *Paul Ricard* took off under her heavy spinnaker, and *VSD* was lost in the mist. When she reappeared she was a mile to windward, sailing under main and genoa. The two boats converged, and the wind began to lighten as they were no more than 500 yards apart. Gahinet, in hoisting the spinnaker on *VSD,* got a bad wrap as *Paul Ricard* doubled the distance between them. But soon the rainbow spinnaker of *VSD* was drawing in the fading wind and, with more sail area, *VSD* began to close the gap.

A mere 45 minutes from the finish, *VSD* went past. Pajot luffed to try to blanket *Paul Ricard's* sails, but to no avail. Rigudel and Gahinet scored a win by just under 6 minutes, after 34 days of racing. They had gained 62 hours, 5¾ minutes on the leg home, winning not only

opposite page: *The beautiful Florence Arthaud sailed the 60-foot trimaran* Biotherm II *with Patrick Maurel.*

the race but also the prize for the fastest west-to-east crossing. *Tele-7-Jours* was next home 7½ hours behind the leaders, and the first monohull, *Kriter V,* was fourth. Even the monohull supporter, Malinovsky, had to admit that they were now out-classed: "Multihulls are the future; I suppose I shall have to get into them myself." What he did not know then was that the big ketch *Fernande* was going to take only 4 minutes longer than *VSD* for the Bermuda — Lorient passage, albeit in favorable winds.

If that race was considered to be fast, the next one, four years later, must have come as a complete shock. In those years, the standard of multihull design, building, and sailing progressed inordinately. The sponsors had recognized

this fact, which was reflected in the relative numbers of the boats entered: there were forty-five multihulls and just nine monohulls! One of the latter was Malinovsky's 80-foot Mauric-designed *Kriter VIII;* somehow he had forgotten his avowed intention of four years earlier.

The harbor at Lorient was packed with the boats, and all around, the atmosphere in the days leading up to the race was like a circus. The French make their events exciting. The pressure of the sponsors is obvious, and there are spectator days with crowds flocking around.

The maxim "Might is Right" might have been made for this particular race, although the largest boat, the 90-foot Kelsall-designed trimaran *William Saurin,* sailed by Eugene

their 66-foot Kelsall-designed catamaran *VSD* went over the side when they were lying second.

The race was very fast. Rigudel and Le Menec pushed their trimaran to the limit and the times of 1979 were surpassed and became irrelevant. Right on the leader's tail was the 60-foot catamaran *Jet Services,* of Patrick Morvan and Jean le Cam, fighting it out with Daniel Gilard and Halvard Mabire in the 66-foot trimaran *Brittany Ferries* (the "GB" was removed for this race from Chay Blyth's boat for the sponsor). Pierre Follenfant and Jean-Francois Fountaine were not far behind with the 66-foot catamaran *Charente Maritime.*

At Bermuda, without the knowledge of their positions from the Argos satellite plots, the race officials might well have missed the roundings. Four years before it had taken *Paul Ricard* more than 18½ days to get there, but this time *William Saurin* led around the buoy just after ten o'clock in the morning, a little over 13 days from Lorient. Even so, her lead was not all that great. Only 2¾ hours later came *Jet Services,* with *Brittany Ferries* a mere 5 minutes astern of her, and *Charente Maritime* another half an hour behind. Nine boats rounded within 24 hours.

Rigudel did exactly what he had four years earlier, and began his return passage with a distinct northing in his course. He was aiming to get the fair winds that lurk beneath the Atlantic depressions, and within three days was 150 miles to the north of the rhumb line and 60-80 miles north of his nearest rivals. They knew where he was. Everyone was in radio contact with France, many of the competitors being broadcast live on the Europe 1 network, and in any case all were receiving the detailed Argos plots of their rivals.

William Saurin's strategy was less successful this time. She fell into a "hole," one of those relatively windless zones that lie between depressions. *Charente Maritime* headed farther north to avoid it, sailing as much as 55 degrees to the rhumb line to keep up speed in the light winds. Mike Birch in the 50-foot catamaran *Transat TAG Quebec* went south of the rhumb line, and averaged two knots less than the rest—it is not often that Birch makes a mistake like this.

By the time they were closing on the coast of Brittany, Follenfant and Fountaine had taken their catamaran into the lead. They finished in 22 days, 9 hours, averaging 11.35 knots for the 6,100 miles; it was better than 50 percent faster than *VSD* in 1979. There is no doubt that the stimulus of competition had done much to raise the average speed. Rigudel and Le Menec in *William Saurin* were 1 hour, 38 minutes behind, only two hundredths of a knot slower. *Jet Services* and *Brittany Ferries* took the next two places and there wasn't a monohull in the prize lists. The multihull domination was complete. Even Malinovsky acknowledged it, but it remains to be seen if his conversion is now complete.

Rigudel and Jean-Francois Le Menec, did not eventually triumph, although she led for much of the race. The bigger boats showed the way.

The race proved that, despite modern technology, there is nothing to beat good old-fashioned empirical testing for getting things right. It took only 5½ hours for the carbon fiber aerofoil-sectioned wing mast of *Elf Aquitaine* to come down. With it went the hopes of Marc Pajot of the great double; he wanted success in this race to add to the Route du Rhum win the previous year. He would also have dearly loved to revenge the defeat he suffered in the last few miles four years before. Less than 2 hours after Pajot retired, Nick Keig and Gilles Gahinet were out of the race for a similar reason. The mast of

Imp, *Dave Allen's Ron
Holland-designed winner
of the 1977 SORC. Imp was
the first boat to be built by
Kiwi Boats in Florida with
a tubular chassis to take
the rig and keel loads.*

It all began with a race from St. Petersburg to Havana in 1930, and was strengthened with the Miami–Nassau Race in 1934. While Castro's takeover of Cuba put an end to racing between America and that nation, and several other events perished together with the race to Havana, the Miami–Nassau goes on around exactly the same course as it did when it started. It is perhaps the jewel of the SORC, starting from Government Cut and heading across the Gulf Stream to the Great Isaacs Light which marks the northwestern extremity of the Bahama Banks, then east to Great Stirrup Light on the northernmost of the Berry Islands before heading south for Nassau.

Twelve boats started in that first race. Only three boats finished and all of those had ripped sails. The 72-foot *Vamarie* won in 32 hours, 38 minutes, with the second boat, the 45-foot ketch

Musketeer, following 17 hours behind her!

Water Witch, a 50-foot schooner, which was the third boat to finish, won the race two years later, but then there began a winning streak for Robert W. Johnson and the S&S-designed yawl *Stormy Weather.* She won five consecutive Miami–Nassau races from 1937 to 1941, and was to win the series outright in 1948.

On board *Stormy Weather* in her first Miami–Nassau was Rod Stephens, who was in charge. Leading the race to Great Stirrup was the 72-foot Herreshoff-designed *Tioga,* later bought by Johnson and renamed *Ticonderoga.* She however was 12 miles to the north when she had the light abeam; Stephens had it almost aboard, and with the 53-foot yawl beat the bigger boat.

It was not until 1941 that the two organizing clubs adopted the Cruising Club of America's handicapping rules; an adoption made to encourage boats to go south for the late winter races of the Circuit. For 1941 those races were the Lipton Cup, the Miami–Nassau, the Governor's Cup off Nassau, the St. Petersburg–Havana, and a race from Havana to Key West. The series proved to be a tussle between *Stormy Weather,* the 70-foot S&S yawl *Gulf Stream* of Dudley Sharp, and Johnson's 64-foot S&S yawl *Good News. Gulf Stream* and *Stormy Weather* tied, with *Good News* just one point behind.

The Havana Race was held again in 1946 and the circuit was back in business the following year. A Cuban boat, *Ciclon,* won that year with *Stormy Weather* taking the next. Boats which won the long race also took the top place in the circuit for the next nine out of ten years — a St. Petersburg to Miami race being first substituted in 1958, due to the revolution in Cuba.

When the Miami–Nassau was revived, in 1947, it met with a strong blow. *Ticonderoga* led out into the Stream only to be dismasted as the wind increased to 45 knots. On the second night out two men were washed overboard from the 36-foot Cuban cutter *Windy* when she was 25 miles from the finish. One of them grabbed a line, but the other was not recovered. The race was won by Harvey Conover's 45-foot S&S centerboard yawl *Revenoc,* with Rod Stephens among her crew.

The SORC became official in 1952, the year that Carleton Mitchell launched the 57-foot-S&S-designed yawl *Caribee.* With her he won the Miami–Nassau Race, went on to win the Havana Race, and dominated the series. He did it again the following year. Second to her on both occasions was an odd 40-foot yawl, *Hoot Mon,* that bore great resemblance to a blown-up Star. Her three owners, all Star sailors, Worth Brown, Charlie Ulmer, and Lockwood Pirie, sailed her hard, and in 1954 won the series. Mitchell came back with the 39-foot centerboard yawl *Finisterre,* another S&S design, and gave *Hoot Mon* a run for her money, but the 1955 Circuit

Bill Whitehouse-Vaux's Mistress Quickly *finishing the 1980 Miami–Nassau Race. The Ben Lexcen-designed 72-footer was formerly* Ballyhoo.

went to the strange boat for the second time. Mitchell got his revenge the following year and became the first man to win three circuits.

In 1957 it was the turn of a Cuban, Dr. Luis Vidana, with the 67-foot S&S yawl *Criollo.* He won both the Havana Race (the last ever to be held) and the Circuit.

The first race from St. Petersburg in 1958, around the Keys to Miami was a relatively easy one, with the wind veering slowly to give the fleet a reach all the way round. Jake Hershey's *Ca Va* won, and went on to win the SORC as well. In 1960 the direction of that race was reversed because of the demise of the Havana Race and much of the enthusiasm for the SORC disappeared. Only twelve boats took part in what proved to be the only race to go that way, and the next year the St. Petersburg–Fort Lauderdale Race was born. So too was a 40-foot yawl designed by Charlie Morgan and built of glassfiber. She won the Miami–Nassau and the SORC. *Paper Tiger* was to prove the basis of Morgan's boatbuilding fortune; she won the SORC again in 1962.

In 1963 the SORC was won by the 38-foot yawl *Dubloon,* which had a double 360° capsize off Cape Hatteras while on her delivery. The following year was that of the Cal 40 *Conquistador.* Designed by Bill Lapworth, the

Cal 40 had a spade rudder separate from the keel – a decided innovation at that time. Boats have not been the same since! While Bill Snaith won the circuit in 1965 with his 50-foot yawl *Figaro IV,* a young man was placed second in the Lipton Cup. That 25-year-old was Ted Turner.

The next year he was back with a Cal 40, *Vamp X.* He won the Fort Lauderdale Race and the Lipton Cup and did well enough in the other two races to win the SORC.

The following year, 1967, should have been the year of Perry Connelly's *Red Jacket,* a Cuthbertson & Cassian design from Canada. She won the opening Venice Race, was placed second in the St. Petersburg–Fort Lauderdale Race, and won the Lipton Cup. A twenty-third place in the fluky Nassau race took her out of the running and the 48-foot Gurney-designed *Guinevere* took the SORC by half a point from *Figaro. Red Jacket* got her revenge the next year with a win in the Lauderdale race, and a second Lipton Cup win among her winning series.

Jack Powell was back in 1969 with an aluminum 46-foot yawl which he owned with Wally Frank. It was designed by Bob Derecktor and built by him, and although *Salty Tiger* did not win a single race, she was consistently well placed to win overall. *Windward Passage* won two of the races. The 73-foot Gurney-designed

The Frers 45-foot
Scaramouche *of Chuck
Kirsch in the 1981 Lipton
Cup.*

ketch was built on the beach of Grand Bahama Island and was the sensation of the SORC that year, winning the Venice Race and the Nassau Cup and knocking 3 hours, 39 minutes off the Miami–Nassau record, averaging 11 knots.

Turner had *American Eagle* to vie with *Windward Passage* and their duel in 1969 was continued in 1970; these two finished first and second in the series respectively. It is of note that even five years later Geoff Hammond was to write that the introduction of the IOR rule in 1971 would ensure that the 1970 series was the "swansong" for these "two great American ocean

racers." That *Windward Passage* was the overall winner of the Ocean Triangle in 1982 must make Hammond wish he had never written that.

The classic lines of the 61-foot S&S-designed *Running Tide* were well to the fore in 1971. She was the last of the great boats from the Madison Avenue office sailed to the CCA rule, and was helped that year by a considerable amount of windward work in the courses. Another CCA boat won in 1972. Hill Blackett and a bunch of young Chicagoans sailed the four-year-old Cuthbertson & Cassian-designed *Redline*, a 41-footer that was in need of a certain

amount of attention, and took the 120-boat fleet by surprise, in an essentially light-airs series. There was enough wind for Jack Potter's 68-foot Chance-designed *Equation* to better the Lauderdale race record by 45 minutes.

The IOR presence was eventually felt at the SORC in 1973, when the third generation of One-Tonners was being built, including several production boats. Among them was the Mull-designed Ranger 37 *Munequita,* which was deliberately rated at just over 27.5 feet to race in Class D. Her crew included Click Schreck, O.J. Young, and John Dane, all top one-design sailors.

There was also another 37-footer that had been aimed at driving a coach and four through the rule, Jerome Milgram's *Cascade,* a cat ketch that rated only 21 feet. Milgram, an MIT engineering professor, had to cope with an arbitrary 10 percent penalty added by the Offshore Rating Council to his rating, which brought it up to 22.8 feet. *Cascade* also had the misfortune to go the wrong side of a mark off Miami in the St. Petersburg–Fort Lauderdale Race and was penalized a further three hours. This and a poor showing in the Nassau Cup stopped *Casade* from winning the series. She had won the Lucaya Race,

The 73-foot Alan Gurney-designed Windward Passage *was built on a beach on Grand Bahama. Evergreen, she continues to win races fifteen years after her launch.*

241

the Lipton Cup, and the Miami–Nassau, but this was not good enough to stop the consistently sailed *Munequita* from taking the overall honors.

The Venice Race was eliminated in 1974 and replaced with one around Anclote Key, and the Lucaya Race was replaced by the Ocean Triangle; at this time from Miami to Great Isaacs Light, then to the Fort Lauderdale sea buoy, and back to Miami. Doug Peterson had come close to winning the One-Ton Cup with *Ganbare* the previous September in Sardinia, and there were a couple of *Ganbare* clones in *Magic Twanger* and *Country Woman* in the fleet. *Magic Twanger* won the opening Anclote Key Race after *Country Woman* had been penalized for not having two orange smoke flares among her equipment.

The long race started in a light sunny south-

came back with a great win in the Ocean Triangle after a head-to-head tussle with *Charisma* all the way around the course. At that stage she led the SORC, but a northerly breeze made the race to Nassau a small boat benefit and the Frers boat was taken out of the overall ratings, while Ted Hood's fifth was good enough to put him on top of the pile with one race to go.

Robin Too II had a Kevlar mainsail, a daring innovation, which nearly undid Hood's effort when it split on the opening beat of the Nassau Cup, the 30-mile concluding race of the series. The crew reefed the sail above the luff to leech tear and the wind obligingly picked up. But approaching the windward mark, the forestay toggle of *Robin Too II* broke. Luckily the wire luff of the genoa held and *Robin Too II* was borne away around the buoy to take fifth in class and in fleet and the SORC by over 40 points. Hood

Blue skies and sea – Gulf Stream sailing at its best.

easterly which did not allow the fleet to lay the mark at Rebecca Shoals. Ted Turner with *Lightnin'* and Ted Hood with *Robin Too II* were covering each other as though it was a match for most of the way to Rebecca; it was that sort of a race. The Frers-designed 55-foot *Scaramouche* of Chuck Kirsch and the two S&S 56-footers *Yankee Girl* and *Charisma* were in close order, but *Scaramouche* got the best of a lift as she neared Rebecca Shoals. The smaller boats astern of her were able to exploit this even more, among them Hood and Dick Carter with *Rabbit.* When they neared Fowley Rock, south of Miami, however, a dry front went through which gave them a beat to the finish.

Hood had gone 18 miles offshore and the veer in the wind affected him less than the boats inshore. He finished only 9 hours after *Scaramouche,* in twelfth place on elapsed time, and took the race on handicap. *Scaramouche*

242

intended to go to Britain for a crack at the One-Ton Cup, but when the boat was loaded onto a freighter at Boston she was trapped when the freighter lost her propeller, and it was impossible to get her to England. This was why Hood was available to defend the America's Cup that summer.

In the mid-1970s the organization of the SORC became slightly fragmented. There was feeling in the United States that the IOR was going the wrong way and that the new rule had begun to be exploited by designers. That was only natural, and it was also natural that owners would encourage this exploitation to keep in the winning berth. What was happening with the Bermuda Race was beginning to happen to the circuit – there were those who wanted to race their older boats yet did not want to face the latest designs. It resulted in a split of the types:

Division 1 being given to three classes of older boats and Division 2 to three classes of the latest boats.

By 1977 the split was total, with almost equal numbers of boats in each division. What was galling for the Division 1 owners was that the interest in Division 2, and the hot racing within it, completely overshadowed their division, with the possible exception of the bigger boats of Class A, where *Running Tide,* now owned by Al van Metre, and *Dora IV,* chartered for the circuit by Ted Turner to hone up his crew for the America's Cup, battled it out in fine style.

The cold winter of 1977 had caused problems for some of the northern yachtsmen. Huey Long's 79-foot *Ondine* had to have icebreakers to get her away from Derecktor's yard on Long Island Sound and the cold had spread sufficiently for frost to be troubling the orange groves of

Nassau landfall from the deck of Condor.

Kialoa, *the 80-foot Holland-designed maxi at the start of the 1982 Ocean Triangle.*

Florida. The opening Boca Grande Race was a cold one; it was also nearly the end of the Chance-designed *Bay Bea* of Pat Haggerty. She was the first wooden boat to be built for many years by Palmer Johnson, and on her first race the mast step, on the top of her centerboard trunk, began to let go. Haggerty pulled her out.

Three Frers 46s, almost identical, took the first three places in Class A in the racing division but the overall winner was the 40-foot Holland-

designed *Imp,* the latest state-of-the-art boat owned by Dave Allen. Her space-frame chassis, to take the rig and keel loadings away from the hull shell, allowed concentration of weight in the center of the boat. She won from the Farr-designed One-Tonner, *Sweet Okole* of Cy Gillette.

In the long race to Fort Lauderdale of 1977, the two maxis, *Ondine* and the 79-foot S&S *Kialoa* of Jim Kilroy, blasted their way around

the Keys to be a day ahead of the third boat and to save their time on handicap; *Kialoa* held all the aces to win. And while this was essentially a big boat race, *Imp* showed her hand in finishing fourth overall. In the Ocean Triangle, *Imp* lost her only race of the series in class to Berend Bielken's Peterson-designed *Champagne*.

Reversal of form saw *Ondine* beat *Kialoa* in the Lipton Cup. In that 1977 race *Sweet Okole* was overall winner; *Imp* won her class. It was not until the Miami–Nassau Race that Dennis Conner began to show with the 46-foot Peterson-designed *High Roler,* which he jointly owned with Bill Power. It was a race in which it paid to go well to the north of the course, and the wind veered throughout so that spinnakers remained in their bags below. Once again *Imp* and *Sweet Okole* won their respective classes, and any overall prize, had there been one, would have been virtually safe in the hands of Dave Allen.

Imp won the final race, the Nassau Cup, benefiting somewhat when her class suffered a general recall and started after the smaller boats in a freshening wind. With a port tack fetch to Booby Rocks and back on a starboard tack shy spinnaker, she beat the Kaufman-designed *Gem* of Bill Zeigler. It was *Imp's* SORC in all but name.

By 1978 the separation of old and new boats was breaking down. The two divisions still existed, but there were very few who wanted to race in Division 1; most now seemed to want to take their chance in the "real" racing — the modifications to the IOR rule had helped.

The Boca Grande Race saw six masts tumble, four of them in brand new boats. One was on Chris Dunning's *Marionette,* which had crossed the Atlantic with it to take part. Even so her results in the other five races were good enough for her to place second in Class C. In the first race, however, Class C went to the Peterson-designed *Love Machine.* Class D went to the Farr-designed One-Tonner *Mr. JumpA,* which had New Zealanders Murray Ross and Roscoe Guineven on board. The centerboarder went on to win her class in the series, as did *Love Machine.*

Glory: this is what ocean racing is all about.

Ninety-five boats took part, of which forty were new that year. Some were extreme, like the Cuthbertson & Cassian *Evergreen,* a centerboard Two-Tonner whose inward-opening deck hatches drew a disallowed protest on safety grounds.

It was good, therefore, that the outstanding boat of the series (still no official overall winner) was a conservative Frers 51-footer, Burt Keenan's *Acadia.* She failed to show well in the cold and windy opening Boca Grande Race, but then went on to record five wins in Class A and three best corrected times in fleet. Much of her racing had been almost boat-for-boat with Ted Turner's *Tenacious* (the 61-foot *Dora IV,* which he had chartered the previous year).

Dennis Conner was at the wheel of the 46-foot *Williwaw,* another Peterson design, which took five firsts and a second in Class B. Her only loss was to the similarly sized Frers-designed *Scaramouche* in the largely reaching Miami–Nassau Race, where the narrow-sterned sections of *Williwaw* were at a slight disadvantage.

The wind moderated for the other five races of the series, the final one of which brought some complaints from the bigger boats because it was held off the eastern end of New Providence Island, where the water *en route* to the course was too shallow to enable them to compete.

The 1979 SORC was marred by the loss of two lives, one in each of the second and third races. Tom Curtis was hit on the head by the boom of *Obsession,* an S&S 46-footer, when her helmsman overcorrected for a broach and gybed by mistake. The injury was too severe for the resources at hand, and Curtis died. In the very next race another highly experienced offshore sailor was to die; Tom Curnow went overboard from *Pirana,* and within 7 minutes, despite life-rings, lines, and the aid of *Pirana's* navigator in the water with him with a line, Curnow had slipped beneath the waves.

Conner, with a new Peterson 45-foot *Williwaw* won this Circuit – the divisions having been finally swept away, with six classes racing

Petersburg–Fort Lauderdale Race being all the more remarkable because she broke her mainboom. It was a race of mainly running, with a final beat north after the Keys in a rising breeze. The conditions were much the same for the Ocean Triangle, a spinnaker reach to Great Isaacs and then a beat northwest to a mark off Palm Beach and a run home. *Robin* won once more. *Obsession* took the Lipton Cup in light airs, while the fresh wind reaching of the Miami–Nassau Race seemed tailor-made for Ted Turner's *Tenacious.* The 27-mile Nassau Cup Race went to the smallest boat in the fleet, the Ragnar

on the same terms replacing them. The SORC organizers helped the older boats with an age allowance which started with boats built in 1977; such was the development race. *Williwaw* won because of the failure of *Aries,* a 46-foot Holland design in the St. Petersburg–Fort Lauderdale Race; she retired when her carbon-fiber rudder broke. Two other boats suffered the same failure, *Imp* and *Winsome Gold.* But *Williwaw* won the circuit because Conner outsailed his nearest rival, Burt Keenan in *Acadia,* in the final 27-mile Nassau Cup Race; *Williwaw* finished eighteenth in fleet and *Acadia* twenty-second.

Ted Hood's One-Tonner *Robin* won the two races in fleet, her first win in the St.

Hawkensen-designed Half-Tonner *Illusion,* with *Robin* second; a result that was to put Hood third behind *Williwaw* and *Acadia.*

Keenan had his revenge the following year. He forsook his clutch of Frers boats and went for a custom/production Serendipity 43 of Doug Peterson's design. He packed it with a strong group of New Orleans sailors whom he called "the boys." They strung together a consistent series in which they did not win a single race in fleet, but took the overall first place.

There was plenty of wind for the Boca Grande Race and the results were rather strange in that *Kialoa* and *Mistress Quickly* finished first and second and kept those places on handicap, while third place came from Class F, again that

Kialoa chases Condor – the two Holland 80-footers in a head-to-head battle in the 1983 Ocean Triangle.

old One-Tonner *Robin* of Ted Hood. Because a freighter had hit the Sunshine Skyway Bridge and brought down a span, the start of the long race was held out of Tampa Bay. Bob Hutton's *Tatoosh* won the race by 25 minutes from *Acadia,* and Classes B and C packed the top placings. The strong winds continued for the Ocean Triangle, and made this a big boat bonanza with eight out of the top ten coming from Class A. *Kialoa* won with the Kaufman-designed *Boomerang,* the 65-footer of George Coumantaros, second, and *Tenacious* third.

The Lipton Cup was another big boat race, but Pat Malloy's 50-foot Holland-designed *Intuition* from Class B was the overall winner. The reverse was true of the Miami–Nassau Race; the little boats of Classes E and F filled the top ten places; the overall first went to the 35-foot Cook design, *Thunderbird.* It left the Nassau Cup to provide the test of boat speed, and *Tatoosh* recorded another win from *Aries.*

The 1981 SORC will forever be remembered for the controversies that were to stagger ocean racing the world over. Boats with illegal ratings which topped the initial prize lists were subsequently disqualified. The battle raged on over *Louisiana Crude,* the Tom Dreyfus-owned and -built Serendipity 43, which was top scorer. Just where her rating certificate went to or came from no one seemed to know, and Dreyfus countered the USYRU with a $5 million suit for damages for humiliation and mental suffering, injury to reputation, loss of income, and lost value of advertising. His co-owner Dick Jennings also sued the USYRU.

But this was nothing compared to the scandal over the ratings of *Acadia* and *Williwaw,* both new boats for this circuit. After prolonged hearings, their owners, Burt Keenan and Seymour Sinette, were disqualified from racing for one and two years respectively.

The initial fleet standings put *Louisiana Crude* on top with *Acadia* second and *Williwaw* third. Their removal put the Peterson-designed *Intuition* at the front of the fleet.

If there was any justice it came the following

Boomerang, *the Frers 81-footer, preparing for a gybe set in the 1984 Nassau Cup.*

year for Dick Jennings, who navigated *Windward Passage*. The Ocean Triangle, with its two crossings of the Gulf Stream, is a navigator's race. It is recognized with a special prize for the navigator of the winning boat, and in 1982 the Ocean Triangle was won by the fourteen-year-old "*Passage*." There was considerable cheering in the Coral Reef Yacht Club when Jennings collected the trophy. *Windward Passage* went on to win her class that year, but the top award again went to Dennis Conner, who teamed up with Dave Fenix and Tom Whidden in the 51-foot *Retaliation*, a Frers design.

An Admiral's Cup year always heightens the competition of the SORC; the US selections are based on the results. The 1983 Circuit was a head-to-head between two of the Class-D boats, *Scarlett O'Hara* and *Locura*. The former, another of the Serendipity 43s, won overall, but *Locura*, a Soverel 42-footer, won the class and was second overall. They were choices for the Cup team.

It was the year of the new One-Tonners in 1984; their domination was total. It was just a case of which one was going to win the circuit; Class E was where it was at. Ted Irwin's *Razzle Dazzle* took the Boca Grande Race from the J 41 prototype *Dazzler* (with a masthead rig) and the Alan Andrews-designed *Allegiance*. *Dazzler* won the long race, with *Allegiance* and her fractionally rigged sister ship *Alethea* occupying third and fourth in fleet. The Farr-designed *Hot Tub* won the Lipton Cup, but Class E took the next three places with *Allegiance, Diva,* and *Razzle Dazzle. Diva,* the 39-foot Joubert–Nivelt design that was the top scorer in the Admiral's Cup, then began a late run with 1, 2, and 2 in class and 2, 6, and 14 in fleet to score a remarkable double – top scorer also in the SORC.

It was also a year of new maxis – six of the 70-foot raters raced, and the new 83-foot Mull-designed *Sorcery* showed that she would win a race or two, while the potential of the two Frers 81s, *Huaso* and *Boomerang,* was never realized. *Kialoa,* by consistency, came out best of the true maxis, but Richard Rogers' Soverel 55-footer *The Shadow* beat her on handicap in Class A.

Diva, *the Joubert and Nivett-designed One-Tonner, which in Berend Bielken's hands added the 1984 SORC fleet win to her top points score in the 1983 Admiral's Cup.*

Pure speed, while being the ultimate object of any racing sailor, has not meant much in statistical terms for one major reason. The weather affects times over various courses and has become the controlling factor rather than the skills of the men and the potentials of their craft. The great liners had their Blue Riband and it would not be far wrong to say that the sailors' is that from the Sandy Hook Light to the Lizard. It was a record that stood for many years to the 185-foot three-masted schooner *Atlantic,* which completed the 2,923.6 miles in 1905 in 12 days, 4 hours, 1 minute, 19 seconds, an average speed of 10.32 knots.

Skipper Charlie Barr was to hold that record for 75 years. During that time few came anywhere near the huge schooner's time until Eric Tabarly announced that he would try with the foil-borne trimaran *Paul Ricard.* On August 1, 1980, he had the Lizard lighthouse bearing due north just 10 days, 5 hours, 13 minutes after leading Sandy Hook, and the record was shattered. *Paul Ricard,* with her four-man crew, had averaged 11.92 knots for the crossing.

In the following year, when returning from the Observer/Europe 1 Two-Handed Race to Newport, Marc Pajot made a calculated, determined effort to wrest the record from his former mentor. With Patrick Toyon and François Boucher he drove the 59-foot catamaran *Elf Aquitaine* across the North Atlantic in 9 days, 10 hours, 6 minutes, 34 seconds. The Sylvestre Langevin design had averaged 12.935 knots for the passage.

That might have looked safe, but in the Transat en Double the following year, four boats did better times on the run from Bermuda to Lorient, a distance of 2,875 miles. While none was an official record, the performances are worthy of note. The 66-foot Joubert & Nivelt-designed catamaran *Charente Maritime,* with just Pierre Follenfant and Jean-François Fountaine on board, completed that leg in 9 days, 6 hours, 31 minutes, 56 seconds, at an average speed of 13.25 knots. *Jet Services* and *Brittany Ferries* averaged 13 knots, and *William Saurin* 12.96 knots. Early in 1984, *Jet Services,* skippered by Patrick Morvan, and *William Saurin,* skippered by Eugene Rigudel, were set to make another attempt on the record.

All the other major races in the book have record times for their courses and they continue

Record Attempts

to tumble. Bob Bell's *Condor,* a Holland 80-footer, took the record of her predecessor, *Condor of Bermuda,* a Sharp-designed 79-footer, at the end of the 1983 Fastnet Race. *Nirvana,* an 81-foot Frers design, broke the Bermuda Race record in 1982. The evergreen *Windward Passage* broke the former St. Petersburg – Fort Lauderdale record in 1984. The records are there, and add spice to the racing for the line-honors contenders. In one area particularly they are considerably germane to the issue – in racing around the world.

In this racing, records must be separated from those of the cruising circumnavigators. The best single-handed time was established when Robin Knox-Johnston in *Suhali,* the only finisher in the *Sunday Times* Golden Globe Race which ended on April 22, 1969, took 313 days, an average of 3.6 knots. Blyth bettered it, going the "wrong way" around in 291 days. Both those single-handed records have long since gone. The ultimate records belong to Philippe Jeantot for the single-handed circumnavigation and to Cornelis van Rietschoten and *Flyer* for the fully crewed best time.

Jeantot, sailing the 56-foot *Credit Agricole* in

the BOC Around Alone, took 159 days, 2 hours, 26 minutes for his solo circumnavigation. It beat the previous best time, that of Alain Colas in the 70-foot trimaran *Manureva* (ex *Pen Duick IV*) by 10 days.

Chay Blyth and his crew from the Parachute Regiment set the best time for a fully crewed circumnavigation when they clocked 144 days, 11 hours, with *Great Britain II,* the 77-foot Alan Gurney-designed ketch, in the first Whitbread Round-the-World Race which finished at Plymouth just before Easter 1974. The same boat, in the hands of a joint services crew, did almost 10 days faster in the one-stop *Financial Times* Clipper Race two years later. The time was reduced to 134 days, 3 hours, 50 minutes.

There came a quantum jump when the next Whitbread Race was held in 1981-82. Cornelis van Rietschoten and his crew were first home on each of the four legs of the course with the 77-foot Frers-designed *Flyer* for a total of 12 days, 6 hours, 34 minutes, 14 seconds. No one doubts that that record will go when the next race is held in 1985-86, and if ever there is a multihull race around the same course, the time will be much less.

Index

References in *italics* are to captions

252

Photographic Credits

Bibliography

Alone against the Atlantic by Frank Page, Observer.

America's Cup Fever by Bob Bavier, Nautical.

Asian Boating Monthly, various issues.

Atlantic Venture by John Grosser, Ward Lock.

Australian Sailing, October 1978, October 1980, October 1982.

Blake's Odyssey by Peter Blake and Alan Sefton, Hodder & Stoughton.

Cape Horn to Port by Errol Bruce, Nautical.

Flyer by Cornelis van Rietschoten and Barry Pickthall, Stamford Maritime.

Go Rainbow Go by Noel Holmes, Hodder & Stoughton.

Les Cahiers du Yachting, various issues.

Moxie by Philip S. Weld, Atlantic-Little, Brown.

Multihulls Offshore by Rob James, Macmillan.

Ocean Racing Around the World by Paul Antrobus, Bob Ross, and Geoffrey Hammond, Angus & Robertson.

Offshore by John Illingworth, Robert Ross.

Sailing – a Course of My Life by Edward Heath, Sidgwick & Jackson.

Seahorse, various issues.

The Admiral's Cup by Bob Fisher, Pelham.

The America's Cup by Ian Dear, Stanley Paul.

The Fastnet Disaster and After by Bob Fisher, Pelham.

The Lawson History of the America's Cup by Winfield M. Thompson and Thomas W. Lawson, published privately.

The Longest Race by Peter Cook and Bob Fisher, Stamford Maritime.

The New Yorker, July 18, 1983.

The Rudder, September 1908.

The Ultimate Challenge by Barry Pickthall, Orbis.

The World of Yachting Nos 1, 2, 3, 4, and 5, Editions de Messine.

To Beat the Clippers by Alec Beilby, Allen Lane.

Tom Diaper's Log by Tom Diaper, Robert Ross.

Two Tall Masts by John Young, Stanley Paul.

Voiles et Voiliers, various issues.

Yachting, various issues.

Yachting World, various issues.

Yachts & Yachting, various issues.

Abbreviations

Abbreviations are used in this book only after their meaning has been indicated, but for ease of reference those which occur often are given below.

CCA	Cruising Club of America
CYCA	Cruising Yacht Club of Australia
IOR	International Offshore Rule
MHS	Measurement Handicap System
MIT	Massachussetts Institute of Technology
NOAA	National Oceanic and Atmospheric Administration
NYYC	New York Yacht Club
ORC	Offshore Racing Council
OSTAR	*Observer* Single-handed Trans-Atlantic Race
RNSA	Royal Naval Sailing Association
RORC	Royal Ocean Racing Club
RWYC	Royal Western Yacht Club
RYS	Royal Yacht Squadron
S&S	Sparkman & Stephens
SORC	Southern Ocean Racing Conference
ULDB	Ultra-light displacement boat

Handicap Systems

In an ideal world, all boats would be created equal ... the development of yacht design, however, would then be stagnated. Originally, handicaps were awarded on a relatively arbitrary basis, to level the chances of all boats; but more equitable systems had to be found, ones that had more reference to the design characteristics of the boats than empirical estimates of what made them faster. The basic characteristics are those of waterline length, beam, displacement, and sail area.

For the huge racing boats of the late nineteenth and early twentieth centuries, there were rules which made use of the principal speed factors: the Seawanhaka Rule in the United States and the Linear Rating Rule in Britain. These were combined into the International Measurement Rule and then the Universal Rule. All have been absorbed into the International Yacht Racing Union Rule for the Meter-boat classes, where the Rating in Metres (R) is calculated according to the formula:

$$R = \frac{L + 2d - F + S}{2.37}$$

where L is the length 180 mm above the load waterline; d is the girth differences at 55 percent of the waterline length; F is the freeboard; and S is the sail area. There are other restrictions within each class to further equalize the boats.

Offshore boats were originally handicapped by either the Cruising Yacht Club of America Rule or that of the Royal Ocean Racing Club. These two rules were united in the 1960s with the formation of the Offshore Rating Council, which introduced the International Offshore Racing (IOR) Rule. This rule, by the use of many measurements of the hull of a yacht, attempts to "understand" its shape as well as its principal dimensions.

Yacht designers have always exploited rules – it is their duty to their clients to produce the fastest possible boat within those rules – and because of this rules are constantly revised. The older the rule, the fewer are the revisions.

Under the IYRU Rule, yachts race level. Offshore boats have to be handicapped according to their rating, and this can either be on a time-on-distance basis, allowing a number of seconds per mile for each boat against the scratch boat in the fleet (a method preferred in the United States), or on a function of the time taken by each boat (a method preferred in Europe and Australasia).